W9-AKW-712

Quest for Success

QUEST
for
SUCCESS

Legacies of Winning

Steven Ungerleider, PhD

WRS
PUBLISHING

A Division of WRS Group, Inc.
Waco, Texas

Copyright © 1995 by Steven Ungerleider

All rights reserved. No part of this book may be reproduced or transmitted in any form or by any means, electronic or mechanical, including photocopying or recording or by any information storage or retrieval system, without permission in writing from the publisher.

First published in the United States of America in 1995 by WRS Publishing, A Division of WRS Group, Inc., 701 N. New Road, Waco, Texas 76710
Book design by Colleen Robishaw
Jacket design by Joe James

10 9 8 7 6 5 4 3 2 1

Library of Congress Cataloging-in-Publication Data

Ungerleider, Steven.
        Quest for Success : legacies of winning / Steven Ungerleider.
                p.   cm.
        Includes bibliographical references.
        ISBN 1-56796-053-7 : $19.95
        1. Athletes--United States--Psychology. 2. Success--Psychological
aspects. 3. Athletes--United States--Conduct of life. 4. Athletes-
-United States--Biography. 5. Olympics. I. Title.
        GV706.4.U556   1995
796'.01--dc20   94-29723
                                                                     CIP

ISBN 1-56796-053-7

DEDICATION

*To my girls, Sharon, Shoshana, and Ariel,
and to our athleticism, academics, and
the wonderful blend of both.*

*and to the memory of my father,
who taught me a lot about the balance of both.*

TABLE OF CONTENTS

ACKNOWLEDGMENTS

As I interviewed these wonderfully creative and talented athlete achievers, a number of interesting things began to happen. For one, I began to appreciate the time, energy, and commitment that so many individuals dedicate to their sport as well as to worthy causes in their communities. My next revelation was that many participants in my research study had experienced a great deal of pain and trauma in their lives. Most chose to use this negative energy as a learning lab and shift the focus into a positive experience. I was struck by the openness and willingness to self-disclose by so many. I am deeply appreciative to all of the "high achievers" who took the time to think about my questions, reflect on them, and respond with insight and sensitivity.

This entire manuscript was a terrific learning experience for me. I learned a great deal as I interacted with fifty-one of the most talented and gifted achievers in this nation. Their training and competition stories were funny, sad, delightful and sometimes quite traumatic. I often came home after fourteen-hour days of intense interviews, feeling exhilarated by many of the insights and emotional experiences brought to our discussions.

On one occasion after interviewing a well-known Olympic coach, I had an intense experience that led to some understanding, insight, and healing for myself. By coincidence (if you believe in such things), I spent several hours interviewing a man who was presently coaching an athlete who turned out to be the son of a former coach of mine. As the interview progressed, I found myself becoming rather anxious and uncomfortable with our discussion of a particular athlete and his family. I suddenly realized that this was someone I knew from my past. The athlete was having a difficult time staying focused and competing, and his father (my former coach) seemed to be part of the problem. His father was not offering any support, emotional or otherwise, and was the cause of much distress for his son. I found it fascinating and rather revealing that, twenty-five years later, I could still recall those vivid images and visceral feelings of oppression, dominance, and insensitivity.

As I began to write this manuscript, several people provided encouraging words and were kind enough to review early drafts of the book. I wish to thank Cameron Stauth, an author of fine distinction, and freelance journalist David Higdon for their early review of portions of the manuscript. Dr. Bruce Ogilvie, often referred to as the "father of sport psychology," is a constant inspiration to me. My own mentors, Professors Milton Rosenbaum, M.D., and Martin Acker, Ph.D., also deserve a round of applause. I also express many thanks to my friend, colleague, and co-author on *Beyond Strength,* Professor Jacqueline Golding, who is always encouraging me to dig deeper into the research on elite athletes.

I also thank Brian Zevnik, Janet Schnol, and my colleagues from Integrated Research: Jack Dresser, Ph.D., Martin Molof, Ph.D., Colette Kimball, Stefan Kramer, and Deborah Fraley. Many thanks to advisors Michael Levin, Stu Perlmeter, and Bill Mason; and to attorney David Ulich, for his infinite wisdom and sound judgment. I extend an especially warm appreciation to my assistant Mary Ellen Gonzalez. My superb research assistant, Patrick Jennings, and transcriptionist, Julie O'Neal, both deserve major accolades.

Many thanks to Berny Wagner and the other chief administrators of national governing bodies for the United States Olympic Committee. I thank Olympians Nancy Hogshead of the Women's Sports Foundation of New York City, U.S. Senator Ben Nighthorse Campbell, and Professor Len Zaichkowsky of Boston University for their consideration in making time and referrals available for the project.

I thank my friend Kenny Moore for his wonderful guidance and feedback at different stages of the project. I also acknowledge another terrific athlete and dear friend, Kelly Jensen.

Finally, I say thanks and offer hugs to Sharon, Shoshana, and Ariel for putting up with dad's moods during various stages of the project. I thank my daughters (again) for encouraging me to write a book that even "kids" can enjoy!

FOREWORD
By Billie Jean King

Tennis is my thing and I love it.

Ever since I was a little girl I loved running, kicking, and throwing. Growing up, I played softball, touch football, and basketball. My dad recommended tennis when I was eleven years old, and from that time on I pursued it with a passion, like I do everything else in my life. I've always had a competitive instinct, and I knew right from the start that I would play to win.

But winning didn't come easily. I hit countless buckets of balls over endless afternoons. Practically from the first day I stepped onto a tennis court I preferred playing up at the net to standing around in the back court. I liked it up there because it was fun and I liked testing my reflexes. My coach was right, of course, in insisting that I learn a good forehand and backhand, but I suppose it was a matter of personality.

Then, too, I enjoy winning matches. I don't like it one bit if I spend three hours under the hot sun and come off the court a loser. It just isn't quite as much fun. And this may be an obvious point, but you need hours of learning your craft and you've got to be prepared to have discipline in your life. Know that it's not immediate gratification, but delayed gratification.

I made up my mind after my first tennis lesson with Clyde Walker that I was going to be the best and do whatever it took to get there. I had to. Before going to Australia to train with a top coach, I boldly announced publicly, "I'm leaving to become the Number One player in the world." As soon as I said it I was terrified. It's bad enough when you tell yourself, but when you tell other people—Wow! You suddenly feel that maybe you just don't have it.

But I did, and it was a lot more than just a good serve-and-volley game.

Wimbledon is the Olympics of tennis, and the internal drive to reach the pinnacle is the same as for the athletes in this book. Through his in-depth and often personal interviews with these high achievers, psychologist Dr. Steven Ungerleider is able to peel away the outward layers of success to reveal the inner workings that motivate them to push their personal boundaries. In this book you will find the ingredients for success for any endeavor: desire, passion, goals, perseverance, mentors, mental conditioning, and believing.

We're all in the same game. Life *is* competition.

What really counts is for us to be able to fulfill our potential in whatever way we choose. And the awareness of that possibility—that right—is only the beginning; the achievement is the end.

Go for it.

PREFACE

Quest for Success: Legacies of Winning is about fifty-one prominent individuals and how they achieved success in sport and in life after athletics. This book profiles the personalities of success and the drive for great achievement. The personalities examined here are of unique individuals and their athletic pursuits, and how they went beyond their physical and psychological constraints to develop a legacy of winning. This manuscript probes the discipline, perseverance, and resiliency that assisted these great achievers with rising to the very pinnacle of their sports and their life's goals.

This book emerged as a natural extension and follow-up to an exhaustive study in 1987 of 1,200 Olympic athletes. These elite athletes and their unique strategies for success were documented in a book, *Beyond Strength: Psychological Profiles of Olympic Athletes* by myself and Jacqueline M. Golding, Ph.D. (Brown and Benchmark; Madison, Wisconsin). *Beyond Strength* was released in October of 1991 and dealt with how Olympians use mental practice, visualization, dreams, and a matrix of coping strategies to deal with the intense pressure of competitive sports. Our findings suggested that athletes use an unusual set of coping and resiliency skills to promote high achievement attributes in the pursuit of their goals.

Quest for Success examines that dimension of "high achievement" for the mainstream reader. The manuscript was developed from in-depth interviews with some of the world's most prominent and talented athletes. It is fast-paced and documents the fundamentals of training and the pursuits of excellence for the lay reader and those who are just fascinated by sports heroes. It covers aspects of sport from the perspective of the individual and the cultural institution in America that supports and endorses our fascination with winners and losers. *Quest for Success* looks carefully at the interface of athletes' wills with their dreams for high achievement and athletic success. It covers all aspects of the athletic and achievement spectrum: from early childhood to the victory stand, to life after the glory of winning a gold medal. This book looks at the role of sport in our culture and, more importantly, how those who play the game influence our daily lives and the images that rebound in our communities.

Quest for Success examines these athletes' lives from early childhood to the present. I spent many hours with each achiever to acquire an in-depth profile of who they were as athletes and to understand what choices they made as they underwent the transition from sport to the real world. The book begins with hard-core issues that deal with: the development of the achiever; training and the pursuit of goals; and life after the competitive experience. In the first section, I discuss childhood, parental influence, coping strategies, and family distress within the home. In Section Two, I discuss role models, coaches and mentors, mental practice and dream strategies, and the politics of sport. The third and final section of the book covers the transition from the thrill of victory, the agony of defeat, achievers giving something back to the community, and an overview of the achievement personality.

Each of these three sections includes several chapters that profile well-known high achievers in sport whose personas are reinforced daily with film credits, television commercials, breakfast cereal marketing, and expert sports commentary. Examples of these high achievers include Bob Mathias, a 1948 and 1952 gold medalist in the decathlon who went on to public service as a four-term U.S. congressman from California. I spoke with Peter Westbrook, a five-time Olympian and America's first black fencing champion ever. Willie Davenport, a four-time track and field Olympian and one-time bobsledder in the Winter Olympics had much to say about longevity in sport. Harvey Glance made three Olympic teams but actually competed for nearly thirty years including his World Championships, Pan American competitions, and Goodwill Games events. Kathy Johnson, a CBS, NBC, and ESPN sports commentator, defied all age and gender constraints and won two Olympic medals in gymnastics at the age of twenty-four. By the same token, public relations executive Anne Warner Cribbs set an American record at fourteen, won Olympic gold in swimming at fifteen, went back to high school, and retired from the sport shortly thereafter. Congressman Tom McMillen, a 1972 Olympian and Rhodes Scholar, and U.S. Senator Ben Nighthorse Campbell, captain of the 1964 Olympic judo team and the only Native American in the United States Congress, both offer keen insights into the role of politics in sport.

In addition to getting perspectives from prominent high achievers, several chapters discuss the role of mentors and teachers who had an impact on the lives of these individuals. I interviewed many coaches who also served as "mentors" for these achievers both in and out of the athletic arena. The implications for understanding this precious—yet sometimes delicate—relationship are discussed in detail throughout the book. Along the journey of understanding the discipline, motivation, and personal struggles of each achiever, I interviewed Bill Bowerman, the famed 1972 Olympic coach and co-founder of the Nike Corporation. He shares insights on how a coach is first a teacher and demands excellence on the field, in the classroom, and in the community arena. Brooks Johnson, the long-time Stanford University coach, offers tips on how he gets the most from his already "talented and gifted" kids. Ken Matsuda, coach of U.S. Open and Wimbledon players, and NFL stars, has a lot to say about compassion and support for his high achievers while at the same time offering caution about self-indulgence.

The profiles of these gifted men and women represent more than three-hundred hours of taped interviews, more than three years of research with résumés, biographical data, and magazine articles. The individuals discussed here represent a broad spectrum of talent over six decades, with a cross section of athletic disciplines including swimming, wrestling, shooting, track and field, ice hockey, gymnastics, basketball, bobsled, water polo, figure skating, and downhill skiing. All of the individuals interviewed are unique in that they not only excelled as elite athletes, but have made the transition into diverse and productive careers in banking, commerce, teaching, public health, social work, sports medicine, psychology, engineering, law practice, broadcast journalism, and law enforcement.

These high achievers made the transition from sport into productive lives in the community and now share models of success with a younger generation struggling with the challenges of peer pressure, drugs, and communities in decay. Some, like Magic Johnson, Scott Hamilton, and Bruce Jenner, have established programs and nonprofit foundations to give something back to their families, communities, and institutions. Some have written books, and others are providing financial and moral support as mentors and positive role models to youth.

Some of the people you are about to encounter share deeply emotional and extremely personal dramas. When approval and informed consent was given, I share names, places, events, and traumas as they relate to the whole picture of an individual's rise to stardom. When people requested confidentiality, I turned the tape machine off and honored the anonymity of the person while discussing the situation as it related to the goals of this book. The process of interviewing and writing about these talented and gifted individuals was inspiring, educational, and oftentimes enlightening for me. I was struck by the number of lives that were touched by family tragedy and emotional trauma in early childhood. High achievers spoke candidly about physical, psychological, and emotional abuse, as well as incest. I was touched by how achievers and their mentors coped with some of these traumatic events and how some channeled this "energy" into demanding and self-disciplined workouts. High achievers who had experienced personal crises noted in our interviews that "it wasn't until years later that I realized that I was running or swimming away from the pain and not confronting it. Workouts were a way to bury the hurt, repress those deep dark secrets, things that I couldn't even tell my coach or family about."

I acknowledge and appreciate the courage that went with so many personal disclosures during the interviews for this book. Most everyone felt that it was not only educational, but perhaps even therapeutic, to "tell the real story" of their lives. Most felt the need to share insights with future achievers so that they might better understand some of the more complex motivations and emotions that accompany elite level training and the pursuit of excellence.

Quest for Success is a book that goes beyond strength, beyond the psychological and emotional dimensions of sport and achievement, and offers a unique view of the whole individual and his quest for success.

SECTION
1

DEVELOPMENT OF
THE HIGH ACHIEVER

CHAPTER 1

THE INFLUENCE OF FAMILY: CHILDHOOD ROOTS

"My mother was not too available, although it wasn't her fault; she was in the hospital with tuberculosis for twenty-two years and my dad suffered from alcoholism. I think that's the thing that kind of drove me on as a kid. I had to fend for myself, it wasn't so easy. I think minority kids with a dysfunctional home life tend to like combative sports like boxing, wrestling, and judo. They might not have any more physical ability than anybody else, but they've got the drive from being on the streets, and they don't have that support and safe family life to fall back on."

U.S. Senator Ben Nighthorse Campbell
1964 Olympian
Gold Medalist, Judo

Childhood seemed like a good place to start when we peek into the lives of high achievers. After all, we constantly hear touching stories of bravery and sacrifice by brothers and sisters offered by the champion from the victory podium. In examining the influence of parents and siblings on high achievers, I wanted to understand peer pressure and sibling rivalry. I wanted to get to know the parents who wake up every morning at 4:15 to take their kid to the gymnastics academy or the YMCA pool for five-hour workouts. Is it a myth or do we live vicariously through the successful achievements of our children? This chapter looks at the lives of five unique achievers, representatives of different sports, yet individuals who share a common bond of struggle and perseverance in their quest for high achievement status. All five have unique backgrounds and offer insight into the role of family influence on their athletic and professional careers. Ben Campbell starts us off, followed by Milt Campbell, Russ Hellickson, and finally, the Mahre twins, Steven and Phil.

Ben Nighthorse Campbell is a Native American, a judo Olympian, and a United States Senator. I asked Senator Campbell to reflect on his beginnings. I wanted to hear about life before politics, before Olympic competitions, and before his successful jewelry-making business. I wanted to know his parents and live momentarily within his family.

"My mother was not too available," he said. "She was in the hospital with tuberculosis for twenty-two years and my dad suffered from alcoholism. I think that's the thing that kind of drove me on as a kid. I had to fend for myself, it wasn't so easy. I think minority kids with a dysfunctional home life tend to like combative sports like boxing, wrestling, and judo. I think that is why some Puerto Rican kids and some African-Americans do well in boxing. They might not have any more physical ability than anybody else, but they've got the drive from being on the streets and not having that support and safe family life."

Campbell speaks fluidly and without hesitation when he discusses his background. He believes that there is an emotional or psychological void with kids that have had a tough upbringing. They want to lash out at somebody, they want to hit something. Campbell naturally gravitated toward sports with physical contact. It was part of his emotional spirit to want to participate in a combative sport rather than tennis or skiing or something more docile. "I think that is what kind of drove me into competitive sports. I liked to hit people hard."

His absence of a parental guide or role model contributed to a lot of rage and rebellious behavior. His grades were down, he wasn't plugged into school, and he felt inferior to most of his peers in the classroom. "When you sit next to your friends in class and you have holes in your pants and your shoes are all worn down, it makes you feel pretty awful. So you tend to overcompensate through sports so that you can prove to everybody that you're as good or better than they are. There's got to be some force there that drives you on."

Campbell has vivid memories of his childhood. It is a childhood without a home, a childhood with no one meeting you after school, and certainly a childhood where you didn't shoot hoops with dad in the backyard. There were lots of missing pieces in his early youth. "Dad just wasn't there, physically or emotionally. He was either in jail or drinking. My dad never beat me, so I can't really say it was physical child abuse. He drank an awful lot and he was gone, in jail and out of jail and back in. He wasn't physically tough with us kids; I wasn't sexually abused. I think it was an emotional abuse with dad, because he wasn't there when I needed him and I was on my own working at twelve years old. I was on the streets, in juvenile hall and getting my taste of the criminal justice system. Mom just couldn't provide for me, she was so very sick, all the time."

Campbell's voice is strong and political, yet trails off a bit when he re-visits his family. He lets me know that there is this special place that we all go when we have to face these ugly situations growing up. All of us have that special desire that drives us on to try to prove we're as good as the next guy or better. But we have it in different degrees based on our childhood and family support system. "I've seen this phenomenon in other minority athletes. In the seven years I coached after the Olympics, I found that young kids from affluent families had a hell of a time getting focused and motivated. I couldn't get them to commit to the sport, unlike those little Hispanic kids who were right off the streets. I coached a lot of different youth. The minority youngsters, you could put them in a judo outfit and make a champion out of them in about three months. That's all they ever knew—scraping and fighting and scrambling and competition, whether it was in the streets or with the gang kids in the barrios."

He relates well to the rough and tumble world of judo athletes, to the kids from disadvantaged backgrounds. He doesn't relate well to the children of easy affluence. "Those kids from good homes had never been hit and didn't have a clue how to react. I don't mean intentionally, but they had never been hit by accident or intention. So if they got kicked in the knee or hit in the nose three-fourths of the time, they would break out crying. First, you had to teach them to take a licking, take a blow. The little Hispanic kids—you hit them in the nose and, boy, you've got a fight on your hands."

Ben Campbell's mom and dad were absent, or more appropriately, nonfactors for nearly all of his life. He, indeed, had a lot of growing up to do—by himself. His brother, father figure, and emotional support system, was found in the person of Yosh Uchida. Yosh was not only a college coach, but a significant influence in Ben's life. Uchida, a man steeped in the tradition of Oriental philosophy, believed in denying oneself for the betterment of a goal. He filled the void left by absentee parents. "As my coach, he was absolutely insistent that I maintain a minimum B average in my studies. No grades; no play and no competing on *his* team. Yosh didn't want to train just jocks, he wanted to train kids in self-discipline, self-motivation, and perseverance."

Part of Campbell's political ego lets go, his guard is down, and the real, core essence of Ben Campbell emerges when he reflects on Yosh. "You're training through a physical mechanism that is supposed to allow transcendence so that you might improve in all aspects of your daily life. I think Yosh lived and believed that ethic because he was very firm with us about our personal behavior, our dress, our hair. When you trained with this man you had to be groomed, you had to be presentable, you had to be composed. That was all part of the deal. Just knocking someone down and winning wasn't the only goal of our training. And coming from my family, or lack of one, this was an important reality check for me, a real eye opener in discipline."

Ben Nighthorse Campbell clicks into a new gear. He seems aloof, perhaps even apologetic, when he begins to talk about the other people that influenced his childhood. He had four uncles, two of whom were outstanding boxers and one who fought on the same card as Jack Dempsey in the early 1920s. Somehow, the child is gone, the hurt has disappeared, the political armor returns. After all, Ben Campbell had to do it on his own. He didn't have connections in Washington. He has been an outsider most of his life. He had to pull himself up by the boot straps and kick some butt.

Milt Campbell (no relation to Ben) won a silver medal in the decathlon at the 1952 Olympics, and then one-upped himself by winning the ever-coveted gold in 1956. He was just a kid then, a high school jock from a poor New Jersey family. Campbell was the first African American to ever win the decathlon and the first African-American to earn the title of world's greatest athlete. Milt Campbell speaks with a voice filled with pride and emotion when he reflects on that accomplishment, even though it happened some forty years ago. His mother was a strong influence in his life then and continues to badger him today about unfinished business.

"The most important person in my life, perhaps even my mentor, is my mother. She is still a great influence in my life today. I talked to her a few days ago on her birthday. I told her about my writing project and my motivational tapes and she reminded me that I had been dragging my feet on this goal for a long time. She let me know that it was time to get my butt in gear and get cracking. She never lets up! She is a constant reminder that when you feel committed to a goal, whether it's the Olympics or writing a book, the one thing that you never do is give up. She taught me never to quit! If you want something, you just gotta keep going after it. You'll find a way to make it happen."

Campbell seems almost childish when he conjures up that voice of mom instilling a strong work ethic and never-quit mentality. He insists that it's the little things that he took to heart that helped him become the world champion. "Mother is a woman with a sixth-grade education, and she kept reminding me every night at the dinner table that I had the potential to be the greatest athlete in the world. We speak on the phone every week and she is still reminding me about my potential for a new career path."

Mrs. Campbell had a powerful voice and influenced a strong work ethic since day one. Even after competing in the 1956 Olympics in Melbourne, his second tenure at the games, Milt was not willing to hang up his sweats. His mother was right there prodding and gently supporting a new athletic career. He came home from Australia and won a spot on the NFL Cleveland Browns roster, behind famed running back Jim Brown. His first year playing for Cleveland was 1957. He came to the Browns during the exhibition season and made the transition into his new sport with agility and grace. "It was easy to move out of the Olympics because I was good enough to go into another sport. You have to realize that most of the decathletes that came along during my time did not show the athletic ability that I had. I was an excellent football player and at the same time I was able to come out of the decathlon and go into the hurdles. I loved the hurdles, and I subsequently set an indoor and outdoor world record in that event in 1957, and then turned around and got discharged from the Navy so that I could play professional football."

Family values and extended networks are key phrases with this man. His mother always let him know that there was support to be an achiever, but there was also strong support to be just a good person. Campbell maintains that proper acknowledgment is not happening among young African-Americans today. "Our young people are not getting that pat on the back. They're not being told how great they are, how great they can be. They're not being told the important lessons of motivation. We have a tendency to identify kids from economically depressed areas and then label them based on their social status."

When Milt Campbell goes on the road to speak to inner city youth, his message, which he attributes to his family values and maternal upbringing, is that you are totally responsible for what you do. The softness drains from his voice and he turns professorial. "If you intend to go out and take drugs or hang out in the streets and destroy yourself, you can't look back and blame anyone. You can't blame the system or anybody else. You're responsible." He tells kids to take responsibility for their own behavior, and not to point fingers anywhere. He borrows lines from his mother and lets kids know that they're capable of achieving anything that they put their minds and hearts to.

Campbell's athletic prowess and achievements did not end with a little Olympic history and a stint in the NFL. To his list of credits along the way was a title as an All-American swimmer in high school. "Even though it was unusual to see an African-American on a swim team, I loved the sport and I excelled in it. I guess I didn't believe everything I was told as a kid about stereotypes." Indeed, Campbell stretched his boundaries so that he believed in himself as an achiever and could excel in nearly any sport he dared to dabble in.

Milt mellows and his voice returns to that child-like quality. He declares that the best lessons he ever learned were at home. "I didn't have to go far to find the root of all motivation and goal setting. Mom was right there at the dinner table, she kept reminding me that I could be the best athlete in world. She never let up."

Campbell explained and put into perspective the meaning

of the words: the world's greatest athlete. After having a career like his, one of the greatest rewards that you can receive is to be accepted by your peers. "To be placed in the position of your peers calling you the best among the greatest athletes is quite special." Campbell was feeling rather cheerful that afternoon that we spoke, in the fall of 1992, since two nights earlier he had been inducted into the Olympic Hall of Fame.

When Russ Hellickson, the talented Olympian and present-day wrestling coach, talks, people listen. He has a commanding presence and speaks with authority about his sport. He knows the art and craft of wrestling; he is a scientist in the nuances of the sport. When he speaks about his family, he is not self-assured, but rather stumbles along, groping for the right words to describe his feelings.

"I had three brothers and they were all athletes. My sister was a very good athlete, but they didn't have women's sports at the time. My older brother Howard was an exceptional football player, played basketball and baseball in high school, went to college and actually ended up being a great collegiate wrestler. All of my life I have respected my brother and I always felt that he was a better athlete than me. I felt he had a better quickness and agility than myself. It wasn't an envy or anything like that. I just wanted to be like Howard and losing him was one of the toughest things in my life. He died in the early 1970s in a farm accident at age twenty-seven."

Losing a brother devastated Russ Hellickson. The tragedy changed his life, shaped his athletic career and future achievements, and had a major impact on his parents. "I think it changed my dad quite a bit. My father was not an outwardly, emotional person. My father had a great sense of humor, was a great teacher, was a very caring man, but he wasn't openly involved in our lives. I think he became more involved with his kids after my brother died in the accident. Growing up, he was a stern disciplinarian, but I think he lightened up a bit after the accident. The accident shocked him into the reality of our lives and he got more personally involved with family life after that."

I sensed that Hellickson was talking about himself when he described his father's shift in behavior. Hellickson believes that we are all shaped by the family influence of both parents as well as the coping strategies employed in a family tragedy. "My mother was the type that if she played cards with you, she hoped you would win. Sometimes I think she would let you win. My dad would never have done that. I think they made a very good pair. One was sympathetic and came in there with the right kind of concern at the right time. My father was just very, very stern and demanding and said that if you get into something, you stay and finish it the right way. You never take shortcuts." Hellickson learned those lessons well!

An eleven-time national freestyle champion, Hellickson won a silver medal in the 1976 Olympics and was named captain of the 1980 U.S. Olympic wrestling team. He took his father's advice to heart and never quit. He is an authority on wrestling style and was recently honored for his contribution to the sport by being inducted into the National Wrestling Hall of Fame.

Speaking in emotional, yet controlled sentences, Hellickson still reflects on the tragic loss of his brother. It's been twenty years since he lost his brother, but his physical strength and emotional character are still very present with Russ. In the back of his mind, there's an ongoing obligation to do something the right way, because Russ knows that's the way his brother would have done it. He still feels that he owes him something. "It probably isn't true, I don't necessarily owe my brother anything, but he would have wanted me to try as hard as I could or a little bit harder, when I wanted to give up. There have been many, many times when I have thought about my brother, especially when I've been involved in athletic quests. I'm thinking about him even now with my team this year. Can we win the Big Ten and the national tournament? And the thought goes through my mind, it would be great if it happened and then wouldn't it be nice if my brother could have been here to see it."

Hellickson is blessed with a strong ability to use imagery. He has taught his athletes that in sport and in life, one must use positive images to visualize success. Hellickson invoked the powerful images of his inspirational brother just prior to his Olympic quest. He gathered the emotional, physical, and spiritual strength from those images and moved to a higher plane, one that led to the winner's podium.

There is a subtle, yet powerful feeling, that Russ Hellickson doesn't believe he belonged at the Olympics, or at the victory stand. That honor really belonged to his brother. "I have this pride in what I am doing each day and a loyalty to people who have been a part of my life. I feel that Howard was responsible for my getting to where I am today. I owe him a great debt."

Steven Mahre is in a unique position to talk about brotherly love and sibling rivalry. He is one half of the most famous Olympic skiing twin team that ever lived. His family had obvious influences over his skiing career: they raised him in a ski resort. Beyond the obvious presence of mountains and snow and wholesome outdoors is a unique relationship, one that may not ever be explained or completely understood.

Steven Mahre made the U.S. ski team in 1974 with little formal coaching. He and his twin brother Phil came from a family of nine kids and there wasn't a lot of money saved for luxuries such as coaching or special training camps. Both brothers worked at the local ski area in central Washington during the summer in exchange for a season lift ticket. Their parents were supportive of ski careers, but the boys had to do it on their own.

The Mahres' parents had a positive and healthy outlook on child rearing. They knew that both boys were gifted athletes and they wanted to give them every opportunity to pursue their dreams. Being a twin was also a factor in the athletic equation. "People talk about twins, the bonding issue, and that when twins are miles and miles apart and when one gets hurt, the other one feels it. I don't think we've ever really had that cosmic experience, but we do empathize with each other on a very deep level. We are also best friends as well as twins. My parents didn't raise us any differently than our other brothers or sisters, even though our accomplishments might have been more public. Everybody in the family skied, but my brother Paul even made the national team. I think he skied on the team for seven years, but was injured five of those seven. It just seemed like every time he started to make a comeback, he got injured again and so it really hurt, cutting into his abilities. I think his best finish at the world level was ninth place in a Canadian race. We always said that if it wasn't for bad luck, Paul wouldn't have had any. And my older sister and older brother, Chris and Davie, they showed a lot of talent and had the ability to ski well but chose to further their academics instead."

The Mahre family moved to White Pass, a ski area in the remote Cascade mountain range some fifty miles from their home today in Yakima, Washington. "You had to get along with your brothers and sisters when you lived that far from any city. There was only one other family in the area that had kids. They had four kids, one our age and the rest were all older, and if you didn't get along with one another or do things together, it would have been a boring and lonely existence."

Steven Mahre speaks of his twin Phil with an intimacy that is hard to articulate. He and Phil became best friends along the way to developing their brotherhood. One could say it was survival, or just circumstance of being in the serenity of snow-packed mountains and great ski conditions every day of their lives, that led to their unusual relationship. I don't think so; another force of nature was present here.

Steven Mahre attributes the level of closeness to always having a buddy to talk to, to ask questions of, or to get support from. "If one of us was having a tough time, the other could lend an emotional hand. If you look at our careers through the years, you see a pattern of one being up in the ski rankings, the other being down. We swapped consistencies and inconsistencies on the race circuit. When one brother was losing, the other would pick up the slack and win the big one. We were the ideal team; mirror images of success and achievement. Phil was often the stronger athlete and the more consistent finisher. He is always a great support system and a terrific inspiration to me."

The Mahre twins coached each other. They had their own in-house Olympic training center, their backyard. Typically, a good coach can recognize what you're doing wrong or give you a pointer on what you might try. The ideal coach can see the mistakes before they happen, and in skiing, those mistakes can be fatal. The Mahre brothers became each other's coach and feedback loop. They were a mutual support system in looking for and correcting their errors. They used two-way radios all the time with one another on the ski team. "I would call up the mountain (from below) and offer some advice to Phil after inspecting the race course. I would tell him if there was a tough section; a lot less snow here, slicker and icier there, just making sure that we both were safe and had the best possible ski runs under all sorts of adverse conditions."

Even in the Olympic games, brotherly love, support and mutual respect took priority over winning the gold medal. Although years of training, competition, and prestige were on the line, the Mahre brothers put their family relationship first. "In the Olympics, I ran the course before Phil. I called him on the walkie-talkie after my run to tell him that the course was a mess, chunking up with some bad snow. Sure enough, he visualized all my feedback, nailed each of those spots, and had a magnificent run. And then he did the same for me. We were each other's eyes and ears and sixth sense on the course. That year we ended up number one and two, gold and silver, and we were real happy. It was quite a family affair!"

The other half of the twin team, Phil Mahre, lives just down the road from his brother in eastern Washington. I located the other pieces of that special kinship when I spoke with Phil. Mahre believes that the key factor in their relationship (both at home and in the Olympic arena) was that they never really competed against one another. "We competed *with* one another, and there's a big difference there. When you compete against someone, you basically do whatever it takes to beat that person. That includes playing mind games on that person. You'll do anything. I mean, you'll just basically be destructive or do whatever it takes to take that person out as a game player. When I competed with someone like my brother, I would do anything I could to help him versus destroying him. We had a little saying called 'keep it in the family,' and we would invoke it as a bond when we needed it. Basically, if he couldn't win, then I'd better, and vice-versa. Throughout our careers we worked very, very well with one another, both in training and in competition. I think that a lot of my success has to be credited to my brother. Had he not been there, I don't think I would have been pushed as hard."

Phil relates strange ironies about growing up with a competitive twin. He would look to his brother for motivation and peer support. He would watch his brother ski and feel real lousy. "If you had a clock on us, I might have been beating him. On that same day, he might be watching me ski thinking, you ski so well and I feel pretty shitty. So I always had somebody to compare myself to, always that mirror image on both good and bad days. I always had somebody to push myself against or I could turn around and motivate him."

High achievers emerge out of different family experiences, each molded and shaped by events from the past. Some childhood events are small, seemingly insignificant; others are earth-shattering, perhaps, not too unlike yours and mine. Is there a magic formula that carries one from childhood to the paths of glory? Can we predict those passages? The brother/sister family support system comes in different packages and in varied dosages and stems from tragedy to the wonders of emotional and spiritual healing. Each athlete achiever has a moving story to tell about his childhood. Individuals here opened their hearts for a brief glimpse of their sadness, joy, exuberance, deep respect, and in the case of the Mahre brothers, a powerful and unique bond created at birth and forged by a wonderful blend of friendship and sports camaraderie.

CHAPTER 2

IS THERE A PERSONALITY FOR SUCCESS?

"I think there was a lot of competitiveness in my family and not much jealousy. I would contribute to my brother's eagerness to be better than I was, and he would contribute to my eagerness to be better than the other siblings. I think my family was a major contributor to my need to succeed and my being an Olympic gold medalist. When you come from a family that's pretty fast and some of your most competitive races are with your brothers, then you know you are training hard and growing up quick. My family really fueled the fire and shaped my personality for high achievement more than anything else. We were all very competitive; we all believed we were better than one another."

Harvey Glance
1976, 1980, 1984 Olympian
Gold Medalist, Track and Field

This chapter begins with a look at one individual who had a great need for achievement and indeed a personality that was success driven. This Olympian was not someone I was able to interview—he died in 1961—but his legacy is well-known to children, young and old, around the world. I begin with Olympian and toy creator A.C. Gilbert, then move to three-time Olympian Harvey Glance, followed by gold medal decathlete and U.S. Congressman Bob Mathias, followed by five-time Olympic fencer Peter Westbrook, and end with another great athlete achiever, swimmer Stephen Clark. All of these athletes had different styles of motivation, but all shared a competitive spirit driven by a common bond in their personality for success.

Probably the best-known Olympian ever is not a person familiar to the public for his athletic prowess, but a person known for what he accomplished after he left sports. Dr. A.C. Gilbert, a gold medalist in the 1908 London Olympics with a jump of twelve feet, two inches in the pole vault, was a superstar on the track and in life, as well. Gilbert, who received an M.D. degree, never practiced medicine, but went on to prominence in the business world for inventing the Erector Set, American Flyer trains, and a host of other toys. Before he left sports, however, he made some scientific calculations of the physics of vaulting that are used in coaches' guides worldwide to train elite athletes. Alfred Carlton Gilbert, known as A.C., was born in Salem, Oregon, in 1884 and joined the circus for a short stint at the age of thirteen. He went on to Pacific University and set records in nearly every sport before settling into track and field. At eighteen he had a world record of fifteen feet, nine inches in the long jump. He went on to Yale to get his medical degree, made time to get serious about his pole vaulting, and invented the "bamboo pole," which was used by many athletes worldwide before fiberglass was introduced.

After the 1908 Olympics and with a gold medal in his pocket, Gilbert started the A.C. Gilbert Company that made toys, including the Erector Set and a host of home appliances. His sets are used by millions of children today as well as by engineers who need to simulate structural design projects. Gilbert was not only someone who used the discipline and imagery of sport to transition to the workplace, but a real pioneer in several spheres. His company showed deep concern for employees and an unusual sensitivity to their families for that period of history. Gilbert's company had fringe benefits such as health and life insurance, maternity leave, legal service, pension funds, and of course, a sports and wellness program. At his death he left his memorabilia, including a gold medal, and a legacy of innovation and creativity to the Gilbert Children's Museum in Salem, Oregon.

Harvey Glance broke all the rules, all the conventional wisdom. He was on the 1976, 1980, and 1984 Olympic teams and then became an administrator for the 1988 Olympic Team in Seoul. As a sprinter, it is rare to return to elite competition for twelve consecutive years. I wanted to know his magic formula, what kept the dream and the drive alive for this achiever.

Perhaps the dream began at home, with a tight-knit family. Glance reflected at once on his upbringing. "If there was any jealousy in my family, it wasn't shown. I mean, it was a well-kept secret and I don't think my mom and dad would allow it. I think there was a lot of competitiveness in the family and not much jealousy. I would contribute to my brother's eagerness to be better than I was and he would contribute to my eagerness to be better than the other siblings. I think that my family was a major contributor to my need to succeed and my being an Olympic gold medalist. When you come from a family that's pretty fast—we had many races in the street—and some of your fastest races and competitive races are with your brothers, then you know you are training hard and growing up quick. My family really fueled the fire more than anything else. It wasn't a jealousy thing as much as it was a competitive thing. We all did believe we were better than one another."

Harvey Glance was always looking for an edge, a fair advantage, and one that would give him success. He decided early on to research the art and technique of running. He became more knowledgeable about "how" to run than the other guys. "I started reading books and looking at the biomechanical equations and got some early education about the science of the sport. After that, I became pretty difficult to beat."

Glance had lots of love at home. Often it was tough love and even competitive love! His sibling support was great. "When I came back from the Olympics after winning the gold medal, my entire family was there at the airport greeting me with flowers and cards and hugs and kisses, and it really made me feel great. With all the folks at the airport from the natural community, I was looking forward most to seeing my family. I knew that they shared in the winning of that gold medal, just as much as I did."

Glance's need for achievement was not met merely by winning a gold medal and making Olympic teams. His personality and upbringing demanded more of himself. "The real success came for me in making the third Olympic team, because it was something that very few people would ever experience—especially as a sprinter. It was much talked about, judging back over the years, how a sprinter's longevity would be three to four years. And all of a sudden here is a guy who started training for the Olympics in 1972 and now it's 1984. That's twelve years of consistent training and competitiveness in the sprints. It felt good to know I could beat the odds. It was definitely a peak memory of success when I made the third Olympic team. I knew it was something that, if not the first person to ever do it, I would be one of the first."

Aside from drive, sheer determination and sibling support, Glance talks about the other ingredients that go into the high achievement recipe. "A combination of things account for my longevity and personality for success. One is that I had a God-given talent—that's number one. Number two, my ability to focus for that many years was an advantage I had over a lot of people. Not altering my lifestyle after twelve years, staying completely focused, and knowing my goals is definitely a plus with any athlete. Number three is mental discipline, and that's part of being tough. When I say tough, I also mean keeping yourself completely focused. That is all focus is, knowing where you want to go, then your ability as an athlete or as a person follows. If you have the mental capacity to do that, then the job is so much easier. The same strategies I used for myself, I now pass on to the kids I coach at Auburn. These factors are truly a part of my personality for success model."

Coach Glance has a format and a set of motivational success models he employs today. "I start off with a goal session. I sit with all my athletes and I ask them what they want to accomplish academically as well as athletically. This lets me know where their minds are. It also lets me know whether they are here in reality, focused, or whether they're out there in left field. If I have a kid walk in here and tell me that he wants to be in the 1996 Olympics and he has never run track at the college level, then I have to sit down and talk to this youngster. It becomes reality check time! I need to get him oriented to what goals really are and the steps you need to take. I really work with their minds a great deal, because I think that is the key ingredient to anybody ever being successful. I am not just referring to track and field, but in life, period! You have to be realistic about your goals. You have to know what it takes to reach that goal to be successful."

Glance uses a special test every year to assess motivation and drive among his athletes. He runs a 3.5-mile time trial in the beginning of the season. He once had forty-two runners tested, and forty of them had personal bests from the last race they ran. Glance feels that this is his way of testing their focus, their determination, their mind set, and their personality for success. After the time trial, Glance puts his special mark on their experience by building positive imagery and self-esteem. Glance writes his athletes a personal note, a motivational note: "This was indeed a great time trial. I could not have been more proud of the effort everyone put forward. To have the strength and the desire to push yourself, when fatigued, will only make you tougher mentally. Everyone did a fine job mentally, please continue to think positive and stay focused. You're well on your way to reaching your goals and I'm very proud of you. Keep studying! Warm up and warm down, get treatment as needed and, for goodness sakes, keep on stretching. Again, a great job." Signed, Coach Harvey Glance.

Bob Mathias has been viewed by many as the champion of champions in many arenas for the past forty-five years. He is someone who has a personality for success and is driven to public service by strong bonds to a work ethic. His commitment to excellence began in August 1948 when he won the gold medal for the Olympic decathlon. Shortly thereafter, he went off to study pre-med and play ball at Stanford. His father was a doctor and Bob entertained the idea of a career in medicine—for a while, at least. Since he had already achieved a major career objective prior to entering college, he needed to get refocused about his future goals and the next phase of his life. This was 1948, and Olympic medals were just Olympic medals and not an initiation into sainthood.

Before college, the demands on Mathias' time were great. He found himself traveling, doing speeches, a lot of promotional tours. He found this lifestyle exciting and a creative distraction from academics. So much for pre-med and medical school. His academic major soon changed to education, with a minor in radio and TV. He still, however, did not know exactly what he would be doing once he got out of school and into the real world.

Mathias had family support to be whatever he wanted to be, including not being a doctor. "Dad was a G.P. and practiced some surgery. He didn't really express his disappointment about me not following in medicine. He told me to follow my opportunity as an Olympian. Be a coach, a teacher, something that will give you fulfillment."

The next few years were a blur, a flurry of activity including television commercials and a seduction into the glitz of Hollywood life. This new endeavor led to a series of movies including feature roles in *China Doll* starring Victor Mature, and *The Troubleshooters* with Keenan Wynn. "And then there was the best box office hit ever, the *Bob Mathias Story*, with Ward Bond and yours truly."

Mathias and Hollywood were not a match made in heaven. He got tired of sitting around waiting for agents to call with new film offers. He accepted a diplomatic mission and went to the Melbourne Olympic Games in '56 as President Eisenhower's personal representative. In 1960, he made two films in Europe which were followed by color commentary work for one of the networks covering the 1960 Rome Games. During a lull in his acting career, he opened a summer camp for kids in northern California. It was there, by chance, that a parent of one of his campers invited him to a meeting of Republican politicians, thus launching his political career.

"Politics happened almost the same way as sports did, a bit of chance and good timing. A good friend of mine from my hometown of Tulare had his kids at my camp—and he was the Republican chairman of Tulare County. We were talking politics one night and he recommended I get involved and run for office. He told me about the incumbent in Tulare County, the 18th Congressional District, and said the registration was terrible. I thought about it and I decided to run for Congress. The main reason I chose to jump in the political ring was that I had toured the world as an athlete and had been a special emissary, and I liked foreign lands and different cultures. I had been to three continents for months each time. I knew and understood the people and cared about their problems. I knew the athletes, the coaches, the teachers, and their educational policies, so it was an easy transition for me to get into the political arena."

Mathias got into Congress and first served on the agriculture committee because his district was in a rural California district. Two years later he got his wish and was appointed to the foreign affairs committee. He served eight years in Congress and felt that the experience was very educational. Mathias learned a good deal about government and, of course, about politics. Perhaps too much. His frustration with the system is no big secret. "You certainly need seniority to have any power back in Washington. The guys with twenty to thirty years of experience, chairmen of the committees, that's where all the power is. It's very rewarding to help your constituents with their personal problems with Social Security conflicts or cutting through the red tape to solve some dilemmas. That part was fun. The frustrating part was having your ideas go to a subcommittee, and by the time they got out of the subcommittee, the full committee, the full House—your ideas weren't really yours. By then, someone else had their name on your ideas and your public policy concept was ripped off. I felt helpless and got the feeling that one guy couldn't really accomplish much back in D.C. He could affect change in his own tiny, tiny way with his own district, his own constituents, but with 435 folks in the House of Representatives, it was pretty hard without seniority to do much." Mathias is not a whiner, but one who makes the best of a lousy situation.

Mathias has a theory about perseverance, and the personality for drive and success. He makes sense of the metaphor that athletics is just a part of our training for the real world. "One issue that we all deal with is perseverance— all those long days of practice make you realize that you have to practice and dig in on other things, too. Not only in how to high jump or throw the shot, but in following through on the work you are doing at the time. I really think the experience I had in athletics paid off in all kinds of community service arenas. Athletics is a training ground for the rest of your life!"

Stephen Clark was not the usual run-of-the-mill overachieving Olympic-caliber athlete. Along the way to three gold medals in two Olympiads, Clark picked up an undergraduate education at Yale and a law degree from Harvard. Are we talking underachiever here?

Clark swam at Yale for each of his four years. Athletics was a big part of his life and identity then. "People think of Yale and Harvard as not having athletes who are committed, but that really wasn't true with me. I think that was probably the ground, the anchor around which I revolved when I was at Yale. It was part of my drive for success, a large part of my self-esteem and personality." Clark is not your average run-of-the-mill competitor; winning was very important to him and the threat of losing had dire consequences.

Clark described his state of mind and how he would win and cope with the possibility of losing a swim race. He used to mentally prepare himself by imagining finishing first and standing on the victory podium. But first, he would use a type of autohypnosis and work into a state of anger at his competitors. "I think there are lessons that I learned about competition. It seems that I have a certain kind of principle that gets me through a competitive situation. My mental preparation for competition, as far as I can remember, did not stem from a teacher or coach. It was self-taught. I would put myself off in a corner and isolate myself from the rest of the team. When I was young and first started to compete, I used to get very nervous and have an upset stomach before each race. When I was in my early teens, I would throw up before most competitions."

Clark explained that he needed some mechanism to deal with this unpleasant stress response. He said he finally happened upon a unique way of coping with his anxiety, perhaps tied to his fear of losing or even his fear of winning. When he began to get extremely nervous prior to a race, he found that gradually he could cope better when he focused on the race and the competition. "If I could channel my emotion into anger or an aggressive mood a day before a major competition, that would get me pretty focused and I'd be ready for my competitors. I didn't really want to talk to my competitors and generally I stayed at arms length from them. A couple of hours before competition, I would go into a cocoon-like state, withdraw from everyone, and just try to channel all of that aggression into positive images. The images would usually be pleasant ones of me swimming with ease, not breathless, and doing what I wanted to do most in the pool, which was WIN!"

Clark was born in 1943 in Oakland and presently lives in Lakeport, California, with his wife and their three daughters. He is currently an attorney with the law firm of Bronson, Bronson, & McKinnon specializing in general business, real estate, and corporate practice. He visited with an old friend from his swimming days, a person who used to be a tough competitor as well. Reflecting on this win/loss battle and his personality for success, Clark told his friend, "You were the only competitor I couldn't hate. You were such a nice guy that even when you beat me, I couldn't hate you. Even before a big race when I knew that you were my main competition, I couldn't hate you, because you were a good guy."

Clark says that hate is a strong word with a bad connotation, but he believes that the process of trying to hate his competitors was important to his win/loss coping struggles. "All I knew was that I was better when I was aggressive. Actually, the imagery and sense of hate was so strong in my body that at one point I would have a physiological reaction. There was a tingling in my fingers and the higher it went into my arms, the faster I was going to be. I knew the feeling, it was something that kind of crept into my body because of this emotion of hate and aggressiveness. I got so good at this technique that by the Rome Olympics in 1960, through my competitions in Tokyo in '64, and my final nationals at Yale in '65, if I could somehow create that tingling feeling, I knew that I would compete and compete well. This technique numbed my anxiety, allowed me to focus the tension into aggression, and gave me the strength to be a tough competitor."

Clark swam for the U.S. at the 1960 and 1964 Olympics, winning three relay gold medals at the 1964 games in Tokyo. From 1965 to 1966 he served as the Peruvian national swimming coach, and in 1966 he was inducted into the International Swimming Hall of Fame. Clark often remembers quite vividly his coping strategies from his days as an Olympian. He recalls that the feelings would begin before the Olympics, perhaps even a month before the Olympic Trials. It was a gradual buildup, somewhat unconscious and nothing that he did deliberately. In fact, he told me rather apologetically that this state of mind was "not what you would call a nice social characteristic."

"I was two people when I swam. I created this strange dichotomy and occasional distress in my life. I have always prided myself on being an honest person and being a good supportive friend to my peers. I don't think those ethics ever interfered, but the aggressive part of my personality would gradually emerge when I got into my swimming persona." Today, in his law practice, Clark does not use this same strategy, at least not on a conscious level. His personality for success does not carry over into a competitive work style or legal strategy that he might deploy in a big case. He took a deep, long breath and said that he has mellowed considerably since his swimming days. "Law practice is a challenge, but not anything like what I was up against in the pool. Those days are long gone, thank goodness!"

Peter Westbrook was the subject of a feature article in *The New York Times* in the Fall of 1992. It was reported that Westbrook was now focusing his athletic energies and personality for success toward recruiting high-risk kids to his sport of fencing. Peter Westbrook, the founder of the Westbrook Foundation, feels that it is time to get inner city youth off the streets and into the gymnasiums. He doesn't even want to see kids hanging out shooting hoops on the streets! If that is *all* they are doing, then "we are missing the boat for constructive learning while playing."

When Peter was young, his mother felt that the only way to impose discipline on youngsters was to get them into a sport that demanded absolute attention to detail, absolute focus and concentration. "My mom didn't want me hanging out on the basketball court. She felt that the guys who played hoops were the same guys who did drugs and got into big trouble. She wanted me to learn about stress, how to win, how to lose, and the ups and downs of life. She felt that the best place to do that was in the sport of fencing."

Mrs. Westbrook must have known something about drive, discipline, and the personality for success and achievement. Peter is not only America's preeminent fencer, but a five-time Olympian, the third American to ever medal in the sport, and the first African-American champion. He was also honored in Barcelona as an official flag-bearer for the 1992 games. Peter knows that fencing is not a glamour sport. Shooting hoops and having a Shaquille O'Neil guy come over and do a slam-jam, rip-the-backboard-off dunk, is more thrilling. But he loves fencing and he wants to expose youngsters to the beauty and grace of his sport.

He now has more than one-hundred kids from Brooklyn, Queens, and the Bronx that come to his gym every Saturday from nine to twelve. "They are the neophytes, the beginners. We are just introducing the sport to these kids. Then on Tuesday and Thursday I work with the more advanced athletes, the ones who show talent and are naturally gifted. We are letting these kids know that fencing is a positive and healthy outlet for their anger, their hostility toward society, their rage toward a family member. It is a safe environment to act out internal conflicts."

Westbrook knows about internal conflict. He grew up wanting to make a name for himself, yet he could not find the right channel for all of his high energy and spirit. He was not part of the privileged class that had access to coaches and private clubs. He was not part of the elite Ivy League fencing community. He struggled to find the right teacher and role model. Dr. Samuel Dambola, a physician and friend of the family, guided Westbrook into the fundamentals of the sport. "He saw that I was not only a good tactician, but I had that burning desire to compete, that I would fight anyone to the very end. He absolutely believed in me."

The Westbrook Foundation is Peter's dream. He wants to return the favor and the gift he received from Dr. Dambola and his mother. He has an ambitious project underway. He has a five-year plan. "I want to build our fencing base here in New York City first. The next phase will be to have fencing institutes in Harlem, Washington, D.C., and Newark. The third phase is to set up fencing programs at African-American colleges throughout the country. Finally, I want to have our own building in New York City where young athletes can come and train but also get study and academics as part of the program. I want to train our staff in New York and then have them branch out around the country. My dream is to introduce the art, grace, and agility of fencing to minority athletes who have no sense about the sport. I want them to get turned on to the ethic of discipline in sport so that they can believe that fencing is as cool as dunking and shooting hoops."

Peter Westbrook's dream has some great dreamers attached to its vision. Former N.Y.U. president and U.S. Congressman John Brademas, Harvey Schiller from the Olympic Committee, Steve Sobol of the national governing body, the Lilly Endowment, and the Carnegie Foundation are all believers and have signed on. The late Arthur Ashe was also a major player in Peter's dream. "He was a great inspiration to me. I saw and felt all the incredible work he did for sports, for blacks, and for the ethics of competition. He worked so hard for our foundation, even traveling and fundraising just days before his untimely death. He was such a great human being, I hope to follow in those great footsteps."

Peter Westbrook was the feature story in the fall of 1992. *The New York Times* could have written the same piece twenty years ago, the day he earned passage to his first Olympiad.

There is a tragic footnote to Peter's story. Just days before going to press with this manuscript, Peter sent me another *New York Times* clipping. This one was not from the sports section, but was the lead story in the *Metro*. It was dated March 22, 1994. The headline read: "Kindness, Then Rage: The Death of a Woman." Beside the headline was a picture of Peter Westbrook and his beautiful sixty-five-year-old mother, Mariko Westbrook. Mrs. Westbrook was beaten to death on Bus No. 24 in downtown Newark on her way home from shopping at Woolworth's. As of this writing, there was no indication of any rescue attempt by the bus driver, and the murderer had not been caught. According to *The Times* article, "Mariko Westbrook's favorite thing was going to Newark's Penn Station to feed the homeless people. People who knew her, even the drug addicts, used to watch over her."

From A.C. Gilbert to Olympian Harvey Glance; from gold medal decathlete Bob Mathias to swimmer superstar, academic Stephen Clark, and then on to five-time Olympic fencer Peter Westbrook, there seems to be a common thread throughout the quest for achievement and success. This winning and success-oriented personality trait, at this elite level of accomplishment, is one that comes along rarely. This personality for success is a unique blend of athlete and public persona, driven by peers and adult mentors to a level of accomplishment that most of us only dream about.

CHAPTER 3
WHEN TRAGEDY STRIKES

*"I never told the psychologist that I got raped or anything
about my trauma. One of his techniques was to ask all
athletes if they have a source of anger that you can call
upon to use to enhance your swimming. I would always
tell him, yes, in fact, I do have some anger in there! I used
to cry in the water and it was just a very safe place for me
to really let loose. I buried myself in the pool. Swimming
was a safe retreat. It was cleansing, and I didn't have to
face anyone. I could spend hours in a sensory void with
no sound, no feelings, except for the warmth of the water
and security of knowing that I was with my female cohorts and a supportive coach."*

Norma Hilgard
1964 Olympian
Gold Medalist, Swimming

Brooks Johnson, the Ivy League track and field coach
and former world record holder, offers an intriguing overview
of the role of trauma and dysfunction in the lives of gifted
athletes and achievers. Johnson's theory of "greatness"
extends beyond the sweat and toil of rigorous workouts to a
belief that all gifted athletes are created out of distress,
trauma, and major family dysfunction. Brooks Johnson is
convinced that the common denominator among many gold
medal Olympians and other high achievers is that some
"heavy shit" happened to them early in their life. Athletics
is a way for them to cope, refocus, and channel that negative
energy into high-level performances. This chapter looks at
his insights and diagnostic perspective, and then turns to
four extraordinary individuals who shed some light on the
dysfunction theory. These achievers include Bobby Douglas,
Theresa Andrews, Norma Hilgard, and Tonya Harding, all of
whom confronted demons from their past. Their lives were

intense; they dealt with tough issues and then moved on to tackle challenging careers.

Brooks Johnson is a no-nonsense type of guy. He feels that in order to understand the role of trauma and dysfunction in the lives of elite athletes, we must go back to square one and examine the dynamics of the athletic personality. He suggests that all great athletes have a deep desire to be competitors. An outstanding athlete is a person who is wired in an extraordinary fashion. A competitor is one that has a compulsion or desire to win. The compulsion to win is really a need to overcompensate for a sense of inferiority. "Athletes feel that this awful thing happened to them because they have done something wrong, that they are to blame for the child abuse. The old man kicked the shit out of them because they deserved it. If he's molested them, it's because they are somehow leading him on. The idea comes across that they are somehow dirty, tainted, inferior, less than. Now how are these athlete achievers going to purge themselves of this?"

Brooks Johnson puts it on the line and asks tough questions when he is getting to know his young collegiate stars. He explains that often the treatment plan for an individual is to purge oneself the same way a bulimic does. He notes that his athletes are searching for something that they can get "control of" and they absolutely get "obsessive" about their athletic training. The more obsessive they are about it, the more they can exercise control over their lives. Sport offers a certain aspect of control over your life and this is what his kids are looking for, this is their therapy.

Johnson looks at the dysfunction in one's home and knows that all the red flags are there. "You may not be able to control the fact that your father is dysfunctional and comes in as drunk as a skunk and beats the shit out of you or molests you. But you can control what you do in that damn pool looking at those tiles for five hours each day. It's all about trying to get control, and all great achievers need that control because they have a sense of inferiority. The inferiority is that you are somehow less than other people and you have to constantly prove that you're superior. Now, when things like status, prestige and love are thrown in, it's an addictive, and necessary, elixir for these people... for these very sick people. It's a heavy chemistry. And that's what I think you have to understand as a coach. The better the competitor, the more serious trouble they're in and the more you have to prepare them to deal with this trouble when the crowd is no longer cheering. That's why everybody stays in the game one year too long."

Johnson operates on the premise that there's always some dysfunction somewhere. It may be in the family or it may not be in the family. He extends his theory to the intact family as well. There are some kids who come into his program who are boy scouts and girl scouts (from well-balanced families), and they're not going to go anywhere competitively.

Although well-versed in clinical psychology and diagnostic jargon, Johnson says his role is not to be therapist. "There are professional people who can handle that. My function is not to bullshit people. It's up to me to find the mechanism to allow my athletes to empower themselves." Coach Johnson also extends his model to the workplace and beyond, to the real world. He tells his athletes that if you are a woman, you need to deal with the fact that you can only expect to make up to 65 percent of the salary of what your male counterpart is going to make regardless of your SAT scores or your GPA. If you are black, you can expect to make even fewer dollars than that, but you need to deal with that.

The high achievers that work with Brooks Johnson know what the score is, early on. He lets them look at their family, their background, and their dysfunction with a giant mirror. He lets them take a long, hard look.

Bobby Douglas' grandfather was an important person in his life. "I did not have a male role model other than my grandfather. He was the first male in my life. From the age of three until I was eight, I spent most of that time with my grandpa, Anthony Davis. He was six-feet, five-inches, 240 pounds, and quite the wrestler. The positive memories that I do have are with my grandfather. But then he left, too. He died when I was eight."

Olympic wrestler Douglas was born in Bellaire, Ohio, in 1942 and presently lives with his wife and their son in Ames, Iowa. His childhood was sprinkled with emotional turmoil and severe trauma from the time he was born. His father was in prison for theft the day Bobby arrived in the world. His mother suffered a life-threatening car accident at twenty-seven, which left her with a crushed pelvis and an invalid. Her pain, both emotional and physical, led her to alcohol abuse and she became chemically dependent.

What happened next in Douglas' life still causes recurring nightmares. At age three, Douglas and his mother, Belove, were home alone one night when a man broke into their home and assaulted them. Belove was raped and suffered sixteen stab wounds in her chest and abdomen. Young Bobby suffered head wounds but managed to get help from the police. His mother survived but never fully recovered from the assault. Bobby's approach to life and, in particular, his love of his athletes stems from an early hurt in his soul.

Douglas, who was guided and mentored by his grandfather, learned the sport of wrestling both as a technique for self-defense and as an art form. Bobby reflects on his wrestling career as an anchor for the only real secure feeling he knows. Everything else in his life seemed to come and go, without any sense of longevity or security. Douglas recalls the images of his childhood as if it were yesterday. "My grandfather was a coal miner and he was a gardener. He also ran numbers and was a bootlegger. I spent a lot of time with a variety of different people that he came in contact with, from the church people to the gamblers to the bootleggers to the numbers runners and coal miners. I spent time with those people from age three to eight. There is not a whole lot I can remember or recall about some of the conversations that took place other than that a lot of the people we dealt with were miners. Everybody was very poor and incredibly hard working. They were church-going people. There was a dark side and then there was the other side."

In dealing with his childhood trauma and the severe dysfunction in his home, Douglas also reflects on the positive images that emerged as a result of his work with a college coach. "George Kovalick was from an old Polish family of coal miners. He was a fine man, a no-nonsense person. He was an excellent educator, a fantastic coach, and a master of the fundamentals. George had an important impact on my life. Other than my grandpa, I didn't get a lot of emotional support or guidance from home. I got most of my values and hard work ethic from my coach." Douglas learned his lessons well.

Douglas went on to great achievement in both the academic and athletic arena. He uses both his undergraduate and advanced degrees in physical education as a backdrop to his approach to the science of wrestling. Recognized as an expert technician with a scholarly approach to the sport, Douglas served as head wrestling coach at Arizona State University for eighteen years before accepting the same position at Iowa State University. He became a two-time Olympian in 1964 and 1968, served as a member of the U.S. coaching staff for the last four Olympics, and guided three American wrestlers to gold medals.

Bobby Douglas looks back at his past, his family, his personal tragedies, and appreciates each day that he is alive and in good shape. There is a deep sense of understanding with this man, a feeling that he has truly met his destiny and loves his role in life. His mission is one that integrates loss and one that understands gain. His Olympic athletes are not just wrestlers, but young men who must look deep into their souls to find their reality as they strive for excellence.

"I think a lot of my real needs were met through swimming. It was a way to get out of my home and get away from some unwanted and undesirable behaviors." Theresa Andrews, a social worker and a double Olympic gold medalist in backstroke and the medley relay, shares powerful insights about her dysfunctional childhood. Her swimming career was briefly interrupted when she left school to help her brother who was almost killed in a tragic bicycle accident. That episode in her life was painful, but paled by comparison with the shame and humiliation she felt with the abuse she encountered during her adolescence.

Theresa sought therapy for emotional support on more than one occasion in her life. Things were not going well. She came from a close family, but one that did not escape the ugliness of dysfunctional behavior. There were certain things that she never spoke to her family about, little secrets that got tucked away deep down, for many years. "I don't know how to explain this problem. This is something I never discuss—I was sexually abused as a child... and it was very painful! It took forever for me to get in touch with those feelings, to even say those dirty words. It was such an ugly experience.

"I think part of my sensitivity and my caring toward other people comes from feeling alone as a child. I hid most of my life. I couldn't let people know my dirty secret, it was too awful. Swimming was my escape valve. I desperately wanted to get out of my home and away from what was causing so much pain."

Theresa was emotional, yet steady, when she talked about her incest experience. It wasn't until three years after the 1984 Los Angeles Olympic Games that she went into therapy to try and sort out the unfinished business from her childhood. It was a tough time for her. "I was hard to reach emotionally during that period because I was retreating from people and didn't know how to handle various relationships." The pool was her place of retreat, her solace, and a safe, survival haven. She would use the pool as her physical and emotional therapy. "I would go swim for six hours a day and get it all out of my system. However, when I stopped swimming it got hard because I no longer had that coping mechanism. Then everything started hitting me hard. All the things I never dealt with were flooding into my mind, and I wasn't able to process this past abuse. I wasn't training anymore and I couldn't suppress and push it down anymore."

Andrews only recently dealt with her sexual abuse by writing and disclosing some of the pain that she has felt over the years. She participated with other athletes in frank and open discussions of incest and emotional trauma as part of her personal recovery process. "This was the first time I revealed to anyone (other than my therapist) the real pain and trauma of being violated. I'm a gold medalist, an incest survivor, a social worker, and many other things. These are all parts of my identity, and I take responsibility for each and every part. It's important for me to tell other folks, athletes and nonathletes, that we are survivors and we can lead productive healthy lives!"

In becoming a social worker, Andrews learned to integrate her own experience with the empathy she feels for her own patients. Often there is a startled response from audiences when she lectures. "'How could you be so successful as an Olympian when you were molested as a child?' There is the belief and mystique that incest survivors must continue the cycle of dysfunction in their own lives. This is not true, and I know through my therapy that I can break this traumatic cycle in my family, and healing can take place."

Andrews works in the pediatric hematology/oncology section of the University of Virginia Medical Center. She knows about pain, and she can relate to her patients' experiences. After more than five years of therapy, a lot of Theresa's issues have been dealt with, but the pain is still there. She used to be oblivious to her family background. She had no idea that this was any of her history. Her greatest strength and that which contributed to her success as a swimmer was her ability to disassociate. "My first therapist said, 'My, God, Theresa, no wonder you were an Olympic champion. You're ability to disassociate is so powerful and then you went into a sport that reinforced that skill.' I can tune out pain so much so that it took me two years of therapy just to get me back in touch with my body."

Andrews' cycle of pain and denial is quite intriguing but, unfortunately, it is a story that we hear all too often. She originally dealt with so much pain in her life from the incest that, out of survival needs, she found solace and protection in the pool. Yet, she gravitated to a sport that demanded her to push past pain. She needed to reinforce in the pool the pain she was experiencing at home. Yet, paradoxically, the pool was also a soothing environment, providing nourishing contact with other teammates and a feeling of acceptance and belonging. "I would just keep dealing with the pain in the pool and ache and ache and ache, because in my own little world of massive denial, it didn't really hurt yet. I was so good at tuning out, dissociating from everybody, that during the 1984 Olympic Games I only remember swimming my 100 meters and seeing only the lane markers and nothing else. There were ten thousand people in the swimming venue cheering and screaming and I had a camera man following right behind me, and all I saw were the two lanes. And it's taken me years and years to learn how to undo that skill and recognize that that is how I survived in my home. I would just click off, space out, and go into that denial zone. Today as a clinical social worker, I watch this behavior with my own clients and see immediately what they're doing. They're surviving through some trauma and dysfunction, and its too uncomfortable for them to bring it to the surface. My background really has provided me with some great diagnostic tools."

Theresa goes to another place when she thinks about the second most traumatic event in her life. This, too, was painful and made her look again at the dynamics of sibling relationships. "I think my brother's accident really taught me about life and pushed me hard toward my career goals, both in swimming and now in my profession of social work. When I work with spinal cord accident victims, I know from whence they come, I know about their pain!" Theresa went back to the beginning and slowly, methodically, relived the tragic episode.

"Danny got hurt on August 3, 1983. I was at the Pan-American trials at the time. They wanted me to finish swimming and my folks wouldn't tell me the details of his accident. I called home and demanded answers, but all they told me was, 'We want you to go on and swim, make the team, and then hurry home.' I knew immediately something serious had happened to my little brother, Danny. If my mother wasn't getting on the phone, I just knew that something was seriously wrong. I remember vividly swimming the first fifty meters and doing everything that you're supposed to be doing. And then into my turn I lost it mentally and, the whole second half of my race, I just kept thinking what's wrong with Danny? Is he dead? I was a million miles from that pool. I flew home immediately after the race and got the bad news."

Theresa revisits the accident as if she were learning about it for the first time. Her images are clear and haunting. "He was hit by a car while riding his bike. It was four o'clock in the afternoon, lots of daylight. A lady was making a left hand turn, spaced out, wasn't paying attention, and hit Danny about forty miles an hour. No alcohol, no drugs, she was just out to lunch. The first two weeks he was in shock and traumatized, and he was pretty much touch and go. They didn't think he was going to make it. He developed infections and secondary medical problems. He was a lacrosse player down at the University of North Carolina, a defensive player and a good athlete. He couldn't talk so he kept writing one question over and over; will I ever play lacrosse again?

So, in terms of me swimming for a medal, it was so much easier to swim when it was for Danny!"

The next few months were emotional roller coaster rides for Andrews. "It was a time when our family was feeling a huge loss and I was being pushed into a year of intense training for the Olympics. There was a special person, a social worker, who came into our lives who helped us when my brother was hurt. I've always remembered her and her special sensitivity and talent. More and more, as I dealt with my issues and my own sadness, I decided to train in social work so I could reach out on a deeper level."

It was crunch time for Andrews. Her swimming career was peaking. She actually considered quitting her sport. Her brother told her he had always done his best. And when Theresa tried to deny her commitment to swimming and those five-hour workouts, her brother, now paralyzed and confined to a wheelchair, told her, "I just try to do my best and I don't focus on what I don't have. I'm focusing on what I do have. If my best is learning to maneuver in this damn wheelchair today, then that's my best. I'm not going to focus on not having my legs. I'm focusing on the skills I do have."

Andrews felt the strength of her brother that year. He was able to give her something special. Even though she had lived through the uncertainty of her brother's accident and recovery, she felt some incredible force coming from Danny. She found acceptance in her swimming that year, acceptance of her training and perseverance toward the ultimate goal: making the Olympic team. She found strength and commitment in her brother's understanding of his paralysis. It gave her a new sense of self, an inner strength and focus about the important things in life.

"Danny is so positively focused that he's gotten into wheelchair running and wheelchair tennis. He's just graduated with his law degree from the University of Baltimore and is about to begin practicing law. Along the way he fell in love and recently got married. He's incredibly mobile, independent, and extremely active. He's become an activist for wheelchair and disability legislation. He clerks for a judge in Annapolis and has a busy life."

Theresa is moved to tears when she recalls the next segment, the next visual in her life. She brings back to life and into focus her gift of acknowledgment to Danny that millions of viewers experienced for a brief moment in 1984. Moments after winning the gold at the Olympics for her sensational backstroke race, she turned from the podium and presented the medal to her brother Danny, wheelchair-bound on the pool deck in Los Angeles. Danny gave her a hug, an embrace, and told her he would hold the gold for her until she got dressed. Theresa grabbed Danny lovingly and told him, "No, Danny, this medal is for you!"

At the age of twenty-one, Norma Hilgard was the number-one ranked swimmer in the world going into the 1964 Tokyo Olympics. During her senior year of college, she quit swimming, just dropped out, disappeared from the athletic arena! "The reason I quit was not because I just got tired of swimming—I had an awful experience. I was out running at 4:30 in the afternoon on campus and a large guy came out of the bushes and beat me up. Then he raped me! The ordeal lasted for two and a half hours, and the trauma has been with me forever. I was hospitalized with a fractured skull and broken ribs, so physically I couldn't compete and emotionally I could not get it together to practice. My life was a living nightmare. The bad dreams continued, and I just wanted to wake up and believe that the whole thing never happened."

In a clear, steady voice, Norma explained how she dealt with this terrible violation and trauma. She denied the real hurt and went to that inner sanctum of defense, a place where no one could get to. A place that didn't allow hurt to enter. She ran to the pool, and to a focus and discipline that eventually led to three Olympic gold medals. The expression of anger seemed to play a supporting role in her movie of run and hide. Hilgard explained that the police never caught him. The whole episode was unresolved in so many ways.

"He was a very big man. He had been drinking and wasn't particularly clean and the whole event was so ugly and violent. I don't wish to relive the imagery, the flashbacks, the pain. It's too much to go through again. He was black, and acted as though I was an uppity white bitch and needed to be knocked down a few pegs. I started to cry after two and a half hours and then he finally let me go. He just left me there, perhaps to die. I got the feeling that if I had started to cry earlier he would stopped sooner. His final words were, 'You know, I really respect you.'"

Today, Hilgard still tries to put the traumatic event into perspective. "This man needed to degrade me and get pleasure by inflating himself and simultaneously deflating me. I felt something about him and his perspective after the rape. I felt something for this powerless man... there was a lot in his eyes. I feel that desperate people like him should have more opportunities, power, whatever. I felt his lack of power in being a black male, and his struggle with not being recognized in this world. I really felt for him. He's not real powerful in lots of other areas, and this was one way that he could feel powerful."

Norma Hilgard still lives with the ugly trauma. The pain is forever branded in her psyche. She feels that such an event will never change. "Our society will continue to have rape and violence perpetrated toward women, even on campus, until people allow one another to achieve their own identity, their own sense of strength and power."

Norma chose not to seek psychotherapy at her time of crisis, but turned to her coach and best friend for emotional support. "I didn't get professional help right then; it was too tough, I was in denial, I wasn't ready. I have sought professional help since. As I got older I realized the importance of working through this stuff, but I didn't recognize it then and I definitely, definitely wish I had. I went into the college counseling center and the therapist said, 'Why aren't you feeling X, Y, and Z?' I just wasn't there yet. I couldn't get to those feelings. It was easier for me to bury this shit in the pool, just swimming a zillion laps a day."

Her physical scars healed quickly. Because she was in top athletic shape, her body was resilient and the black and blue disappeared rapidly. The emotional injuries, however, didn't recede as fast. "The hard part was not being able to sleep at night. I became addicted to sleeping pills and was anxious all the time and worried—never feeling safe—that was the hard part. The physical stuff was pretty easy. When you are a competitive athlete, you can deal with the injuries."

Hilgard made the best of a tough situation. She decided

to get back to her swimming and the rigors of five-hour workouts, both morning and afternoon doubles. There was some healing and even strange ironies throughout her recovery period. "Getting back into swimming was great for me. I started working with a sport psychologist, just to swim faster, but I never told him that I got raped or anything about my trauma. One of his techniques was to ask all athletes if they have a source of anger that you can call upon to use to enhance your swimming. I would always tell him, yes, in fact I do have some anger in there! I really did release a lot of my anger and other emotions while I was swimming. I used to cry in the water and it was just a very safe place for me to really let loose and be me."

The pool was also a place where she got a lot of validation. Norma trained hard and she swam very fast in practice. She enjoyed getting a lot of strokes from her coaches. She buried her feelings, her emotions, and herself in her swimming; the pool was a safe retreat. The water was cleansing, and she didn't have to face anyone. She could spend hours in a "sensory void" with no sound, no feelings, except for the warmth of the water and the security of knowing that she was with her female cohorts and a supportive coach.

Things did not always go well for Hilgard. Repressing the emotions and the acts of denial only went so far. "Toward the end of swimming I was having a hard time. It was like I had to find another angry experience. I just couldn't be angry about that any more. To this day it is difficult to sort out. It used to be easy for me to be mad almost all the time. I was just mad at everyone and I was a feminist and I wanted to be effective as a feminist. I wanted to make a difference in the world and I was unable to do so, because all I ever heard was how angry I was."

For Hilgard, the anger is over and she is now able to step back from the trauma and realize the strength she has gotten from her sport. "I give a lot of credit to swimming. I'm glad to have been able to work out the anger because I've been able to make a difference as a feminist and help empower women in my work. God works in mysterious ways, and I am grateful to have work that means so much to me."

The next Olympian was *not* able to step back from the trauma of her past and, indeed, the passion for the sport itself may have created the elements of her downfall. I first had contact with Tonya Harding on November 12, 1992, the day marking her 22nd birthday. At that point in her career she had made the 1988 Olympic team as an alternate, finished fourth at the Albertville Games of 1992, and was one year and three months away from her third Olympiad. We spoke for some time about her relationship to her coach, Diana Rawlinson, who had been her mentor for eighteen years. According to Tonya, "some say it is more of a mother/ daughter relationship." We spoke about her asthma (and not her smoking), her mental and physical preparation for her competitions, and finally her game plan for Lillehammer. Then the interview came to a screeching halt. Tonya did not want to talk about her family, her marriage, her challenges for the coming months; the interview was over. As we wrapped up our conversation and I asked for my standard release to write about her, she told me that she wanted to be referred to as Tonya Harding Gillooly; "All three names, and that is spelled G-i-l-l-o-o-l-y, Tonya Harding *Gillooly!*"

Fourteen months later, nearly to the day, Tonya was known to most of the world, not for what she accomplished on the ice, but what happened to her around the edges of the rink. Fourteen months later, Tonya wanted to be known merely as Tonya Harding. Tonya Harding became known to most of the world in January 1994, just a few days after the national figure skating championships in Detroit, Michigan. She is not an Olympic hero (although she made the U.S. team three times), but a victim of circumstance; a victim of many years of family dysfunction and abuse.

When our women's figure skating champ stepped off the plane in January 1994, just weeks before the start of the Lillehammer Winter games, a crowd of reporters and fans wanted to know how Tonya felt about her win over rival Nancy Kerrigan. Her first words into a reporter's microphone were: "All I can think about now are dollar signs!" Little did we know the irony of those words, sounds that would ring and reverberate in the international spotlight for eight nonstop weeks.

Forty-eight hours before the Olympic trials in Detroit, a deranged man assaulted and brutally attacked Nancy Kerrigan, another Olympic ice queen. A week later, the trail led to Portland, Oregon, home of national champ Harding, her estranged husband, and a group of unsavory characters. A few days later, the twice divorced husband, the skater's bodyguard and two "hit men" were arrested and charged with conspiracy to commit assault on Nancy Kerrigan, a class B felony. Three of the four men implicated skater Harding and, subsequently, she came under investigation by a grand jury. It all seemed quite bizarre and rather surreal, perhaps a good story line for a novel.

As the sordid details of the assault on Kerrigan unfolded in the press, a psychological case history profile of Harding began to emerge that gave us a composite picture of a deeply disturbed individual. Harding's mother married six times, often to emotionally and physically abusive men. Young Tonya moved each year of her adolescence to a new city, barely spending more than eight months in any one school and never having secure and bonding relationships with peers. She dropped out of school at sixteen, completing a GED to fulfill her high school requirements. She married an abusive man, who she divorced twice, and with whom she had to sign a restraining order to protect her from physical harm. Her husband had, in fact, threatened to "break her legs" and end *her* athletic career not long ago.

The drama that unfolded with the Kerrigan-Harding affair is deeply tragic. Unfortunately, it is not a completely isolated situation, even among superstar athletes. According to psychologist Dr. Gregory Briehl, many preadolescent tennis stars have been plucked from the throes of childhood and launched into stardom, subjected to lawyers, agents, corporate seductions, and coaches who have many conflicts of interest. "Many young female tennis players have been physically and emotionally abused by their fathers. They often become sexually involved with their coaches, escaping one abusive situation at home and then finding themselves repeating this scenario on the tour. Kids are highly vulnerable, they are out of the home, with no *loco-parentis* and given diplomatic immunity from the real world. When you give a thirteen-year-old a check for a million dollars for hitting a few tennis balls well, there are bound to be abuses and a lack of boundaries imposed."

With skater Tonya Harding, one does not have to study clinical psychology to understand the dimensions of despair and her lack of coping resources. According to psychologist Briehl, who has worked with a number of top-ranked athletes; "Most people learn the language of intimacy, conflict resolution behavior, and social norms. Tonya grew up with a language of dysfunction with a different set of norms that supported a survival mentality and street-smart behavior." As we learned from police blotters and district attorney disclosures, Tonya Harding spent nearly all of her waking hours on the ice throwing triple axles and never learned another language. She surrounded herself with dysfunctional people and those that never had adapted to societal norms and social resources that would allow them to understand consequences of their own behavior.

With Tonya, we have learned that elite athletes may be more at-risk for academic failure, lack of adequate coping mechanisms, and poor job skills because of the perks and years of special treatment. Most psychologists I spoke with regarding the Tonya Harding case spoke candidly about other situations where abuses of the system had taken place. Many were angry that most of the time, unless there is a criminal investigation, many situations get glossed over or covered up by sports authorities. All agreed that it is time for the United States Olympic Committee to step up to the plate and take decisive action. After all, in the 1980s we had rampant abuse of steroids, HGH, and blood doping. The Olympic Committee stepped in and declared an assault on these abuses and pledged a return to a level playing field in all sports. Now we have reached new heights in achieving Olympic glory, one that has witnessed physical violence in order to preempt the competition.

Experts agree that governing bodies must take action to prevent and intervene before more tragic events like the Harding affair occur. Olympic officials should insist on minimum educational requirements before competition is allowed. Counselors or therapists should be made available and recommended for all athletes who are at-risk. Academic tutors need to be available to all athletes when traveling or training away from home.

On March 17, 1994 (some three weeks after the 1994

Winter Olympics), Tonya Harding pleaded guilty to a felony charge of hindering prosecution in the conspiracy to harm her rival Nancy Kerrigan. More important than the plea bargain, however, was that the judge mandated a stiff fine. In addition to paying court costs and fines (totaling $165,000), Harding was required to make a $50,000 donation to the Special Olympics. Additionally, she was mandated to five-hundred hours of community service and required to undergo psychological assessment and treatment as needed.

The gold medal, in that turbulent year of bizarre Olympic events, should have gone to Judge Donald Londer of the Multnomah County District Court in Oregon. He asked Tonya at her court appearance whether she understood the consequences of her guilty plea and whether she was suffering emotional or mental instability. Harding responded, "I don't know."

An important message is being sent from the courtroom at which Tonya (and other athletes) will need to take a serious look. Her life typifies goals and dreams that were driven by escapism, denial, and rage. Her life was encumbered with a family dysfunction that impaired her judgment for more than two decades. None of the criminal justice recommendations can undo a life devoid of parental role models and perpetual dysfunction in and about the home. No overhaul of our Olympic ideals and ethical standards will ever make up for Harding's twenty-three years of hard-scrabble, acting out of impulse, street-smart lifestyle. However, most experts agree that a small dose of education, prevention, mentoring, and appropriate goal setting could lead to more fulfilling outcomes for our national heroes.

As Brooks Johnson set the stage for the athlete-dysfunction-success theory, one must pay close attention to the *powerful* actions and emotional words of Bobby Douglas, Theresa Andrews, and Norma Hilgard. These athletes and high achievers, transitioning from the Olympic podium to the real world, have pain and some gain, and real images to share with those struggling with the quest for success. These images involve discipline, training, perseverance and, most of all, coping and resiliency skills. Resiliency that allowed them to overcome severe odds, and coping skills that allowed them to get through life and survive a big dose of trauma.

Bobby Douglas, Norma Hilgard, and Theresa Andrews were able to use the power of a traumatic event and channel raw energy into finding themselves, their identity, their sense of self. Tonya Harding had a series of traumas in her life, and perhaps never a respite from the rollercoaster of dysfunction. Her only solace, her timeout from the school of hardknocks, was on the ice. There, she was a queen, on top of the world, and safe from her own cruel circumstances. Off the ice, she was out of her element, a player in a rough-and-tumble world with no rules, no boundaries, and no limits. In many ways this chapter (and much of this book) is about the Tonya Hardings of the world. There are many. There are many talented and gifted athletes who go through life, virtually unknown outside of their small communities, who struggle with their identity, their self-esteem, their sense of value and purpose in life. Many come from homes that are severely dysfunctional, riddled with substance abuse, verbal and physical assault, and other events that leave deep emotional scars. Many young athletes are able to find support from coaches, teachers, mentors; those guiding lights outside of their immediate family structure. Many never find it.

CHAPTER 4
GETTING BEYOND THE STRUGGLE

> *"The main thing I learned as a competitor, both in the battle of cancer and the battle on the mats, is that you can look into your opponents' eyes and get a good idea of what they're thinking. And after a lifetime of looking into people's faces, you can tell the ones that are about to get beat."*
>
> *Jeff Blatnick*
> *1984 Olympian*
> *Gold Medalist, Wrestling*

This chapter looks at the role of adversity among two high profile achievers. Jeff Blatnick battled cancer for many years, and Bruce Jenner had to overcome the stigma of dyslexia. Both individuals still struggle with their afflictions today. Each copes with the stress of his problem in different ways. Both are people who take pleasure in sharing their messages about coping with and overcoming adversity. Both are in touch with their role of giving something back to others who are less fortunate. This chapter looks at the role of adversity in one's life and tries to shed light on how we overcome, or perhaps compensate for, a deficiency. I begin with Jeff Blatnick.

Jeff Blatnick is a story of human struggle and a study in mind over matter. Struggling with a life-threatening illness, this wrestling gold medalist is the epitomé of tough guy. Or perhaps I should say *tough mind!* Probably one of the more sharply etched emotional memories in Olympic history is the picture of this courageous athlete crying tears of joy and achievement after winning the Olympic gold medal in wrestling at the 1984 games.

Jeff was diagnosed with Hodgkin's disease in 1982, the day before his 25th birthday. He had already made the 1980 team two years earlier, but didn't compete as a wrestler because of the U.S. imposed Olympic boycott. He began his second Olympic quest for the 1984 team with cancer working through his system. He knew it might pose a problem to his health, but he kept training as he felt the twinges in his neck that lead to the biopsy and correct diagnosis of this life-threatening disease. By then, he was already in the early stages of his cancer.

A member of the 1980 and 1984 U.S. Olympic teams, Jeff won a gold medal in the Greco Roman wrestling competition and served as the U.S. flagbearer in the closing ceremonies of the 1984 games in Los Angeles. When he found out about his diagnosis of cancer in 1982, he immediately felt the need to compete and entered the Empire State Games in New York. He had to prepare himself for the possibility that he might never wrestle again. Blatnick followed doctors' orders and began the radiation treatments. He battled the side effects of fatigue as the radiation sapped his strength over a period of many months. "I often felt fine right after I received it, but after weeks and weeks of it, even after you've stopped getting the treatment, you haven't really bottomed out physically yet from the side effects. They were trying to prep me for the side effects that I wasn't experiencing, so I didn't see any reason to anticipate a problem. The main reaction I had was that my salivary glands in my mouth went crazy, so I lost my sense of taste. Garlic and a lot of wonderful spices no longer tasted wonderful anymore. Worst of all was that Captain Crunch was an old friend of mine. I liked the cereal and because my throat was very, very sore (from the radiation treatments) anything crisp—even toast—was pretty tough to handle."

Although Blatnick was determined to train for the 1984 games, he had interruptions along the way. "There were always blisters and cracks from the radiation. I had over twenty places on my neck where that would happen. There's an ointment they prepared for me and it literally melts when you put it on your skin, because your skin is hot like a sunburn. It would help in soothing the skin and healing the cuts, so you didn't have that dry feeling every time you moved."

Probably the toughest thing for Blatnick in overcoming Hodgkin's disease was learning about his body and how much it could endure. He had to learn a new training regimen and a strategy to cope with fatigue during the recovery period. Few who watched him receive his medal in 1984, as tears poured down his face, will ever forget such an intense moment of personal glory.

Blatnick's struggle was physical for sure, but the emotional and psychological components were a big part of it. He explained that he did a lot of walking to help flush the body out. He wanted to rid his body of the dead cells in his system due to radiation and the surgery. "One time I did not have the white blood cell count to receive the chemotherapy. You had to have a minimum amount, otherwise you were at risk of internal infection. So, the doctors refused to give me chemo on a Friday. I said, 'Hey, I'll come back on Monday.' The doctor told me, 'No you'll need at least a week. See me Thursday.' And I said, 'I'll be here on Monday!' And I showed up on Monday and I had the white blood cell count I needed. So again, there's a situation where there was a mind-body connection. I would sit and I would just concentrate, visualize myself healing. I would see clean cells coming in and my body getting stronger. I'd think of times when I was working out and I felt great. You know, you have that feeling where you get up and your heart's just pounding and you look at your arms and you just know—nobody can do this like me. That kind of imagery really helped and it got my white cell count up."

Blatnick's psychological strength seemed to be a great asset during some of his tougher days. "The chemo is powerful shit and I was lucky enough that I never vomited or lost my hair. I played basketball and I ate pizza even before my chemo shots. I broke all the rules and I had success without getting sick. I was able to play tennis with my doctor the very next day after my shots. I seemed to have a strong will and a good physical conditioning. Even when my fingers and hands went numb, I could still hold a basketball and play hoops. But put a cold glass of water in my hand and, unless I focused on holding it, it would fall out of my hand. It was just the weirdest thing."

Mind over matter is one thing, but sometimes things did get rough. "At one point I had to quit doing the combative wrestling. I would pass out sometimes during a workout and my buddies would say, 'You're stupid. If health is really your priority, what the hell are you doing?' So, at that point, I had to resign myself to the fact that I may never wrestle again."

The mental toughness game took its toll with Olympic champion and high achiever Blatnick. He realized at one point that it was diminishing returns to try and emotionally push through the beating his body was taking from the chemo and radiation and rigorous workouts. He was not improving his wrestling at all. "I was just throwing my body out there, at all costs, to do well. If you're trying to literally help your body help itself, then you have to set the priority to help your body heal. You don't do that by going out and tearing the living hell out of it in a practice with a bunch of guys who are all dreaming about the Olympic games. I had to back off, and I eventually stopped training altogether."

Blatnick learned important lessons from his sport. Looking at opponents, sizing them up, and assessing their abilities and strengths gave him the same tools to beat his medical nemesis. "I gained a lot of confidence through the sport of wrestling. A lot of things I do in my life are directly related to the physics of wrestling. You learn about energy and how to not get totally expended—all of these simple little rules I now apply to my everyday life."

Ultimately, Blatnick had to confront some important lessons about his cancer and a shift in lifestyle. "It sucks, getting beat up by this weird disease with its toxic cells. The important lesson I tried to key in on is that something good is going to happen at the end of this therapy. Those kinds of lessons from sport carry over very well. Don't get expended, don't burn yourself out, keep your game plan, don't quit training. I highlighted all the days I was supposed to get treatments and focused on the fact that when those days came, be on time, none of this putting it off and whining—get it done.

"The other thing you learn as a competitor—and I'm sure it doesn't matter if it's even a physical sport or not—is that you can look at your opponents' eyes and get a good idea of what they're thinking. And after a lifetime of looking into people's faces, you can tell the ones that are about to get beat. Walking into a doctor's office and taking a look at an individual, you can see some that have pretty much set their sights on the fact that they're losing. I didn't want to be like that! So that was another psychological game plan for me. That's why I said that I'd eat pizza before going and getting chemo. I'd play basketball after my injections. I even wrestled once—at a sport clinic right after I got my treatments. I went right to the school and did a clinic for these kids."

Blatnick was born in Schenectady, New York, and

uce Jenner – *Decathlon; 1976.*

Ben Nighthorse Campbell – *Judo; 1964.*

Milt Campbell – *Decathlon; 1952, 1956.*

ıil and Steve Mahre (upper and lower photo) – *Skiing; 1976; 1980; 1984.*

Stephen Clark – *Swimming;*
1960, 1964.

Peter Westbrook – *Fencing;*
1972, 1976, 1980, 1984, 1988.

Harvey Glance – *Track;*
1976, 1980, 1984.

ob Mathias – *Decathlon; 1948, 1952.*

Holly Flanders – *Skiing; 1980, 1984.*

Theresa Andrews – *Swimming; 1984.*

Bobby Douglas – *Wrestling; 1964, 1968.*

Mamie Rallins – *Hurdles; 1968, 1972.*

ff Blatnick – *Wrestling; 1980, 1984.*

Russ Hellickson (left) – *Wrestling;
1976, 1980. Pictured here with
Olympic wrestler Jeff Blatnick.*

Brooks Johnson – *Coach.*

Berny Wagner – *Coach.*

Ed Burch – *Coach.*

Bill Bowerman – *Coach.*

Photo by Jerry Wachter

om McMillen – *Basketball; 1972.*

Bill Toomey – *Decathlon; 1968.*

Photo by Tony Duffy, USA Gymnastics

Tim Daggett – *Gymnastics; 1984.*

Willie Davenport – *Hurdles; 1964, 1968, 1972, 1976. Bobsled; 1980.*

Tim Daggett – Gymnastics, 1984.

Photo by Tony Duffy, USA Gymnastics

Willie Davenport – *Hurdles;* 1964, 1968, 1972, 1976. *Bobsled;* 1980.

Photo by Jerry Wachter

om McMillen – *Basketball; 1972.*

Bill Toomey – *Decathlon; 1968.*

Mitch Gaylord – *Gymnastics; 1984.*

Kathy Johnson – *Gymnastics; 1980, 1984.*

Marilyn King – *Pentathlon, 1972, 1976, 1980.*

presently lives with his wife not far his home town. He earned a bachelor's degree in physical education from Springfield College and was later awarded an honorary doctorate in humanities from the same school. He is a highly sought-after motivational speaker for corporate America and often discusses some of his struggles on and off the mats. His perseverance and discipline as an athlete is legendary. "I was back at work two weeks after surgery for my spleen removal and then began the radiation treatments. They didn't slow me down in any real way, other than the time allotted to do it. The hole in the middle of my body—this fourteen-inch gap from the spleen removal and just the side effects of my skin cracking due to radiation—tends to slow you down, but my focus and discipline was still strong."

Blatnick, who has just passed his eight-year "cancer birthday" with a clean bill of health, is a great role model for overcoming adversity. His lessons learned in the gym and in the real-world arena are powerful ones that can be taught over and over, without redundancy.

Bruce Jenner had a rude awakening! "It wasn't until I was in fifth grade and started getting involved in sports, where for the first time, I could lift my head up high and have some confidence in myself. For so long it was just a big ugly secret. I could eventually go out on the school athletic field and compete against these guys who were good students and strong readers. I could go out there and clean their clock and, let me tell you, that was important to me. That was when I first began to experience self-confidence."

Bruce Jenner does not battle the uncertainties of cancer or a life-threatening disease. He does battle a learning disability known as dyslexia, a disability that has plagued him through childhood and continues to be a struggle for him today. He has had to overcome the stigma of not being able to read, an adversity that deeply affected him for many years. Jenner, the 1976 decathlon champion, today spends a good deal of his time reaching out to children with disabilities. For one thing, he loves kids. He and his wife Kris have eight children and, as Bruce told me during our interview, "I'm just part of the hired help here. I do quite a bit of chauffeuring around Los Angeles every day."

Bruce also feels linked to his work with disabled children since he continues to struggle with the problems associated with dyslexia himself. Dyslexia is part of a family of disorders known as learning disabilities. According to one expert, "LDs are intrinsic to the individual and presumed to be due to central nervous system dysfunction. These disabilities manifest by difficulty in reading, writing, listening, and mathematical reasoning." Jenner's disability went beyond the confines of the classroom. It was an affliction that went undiagnosed and had a major affect on his career, including his athletic life. "The biggest fear of my life was to have to read before the class, in front of all the kids. It was not an issue for me to go up against the world competing in the Olympic games. But growing up being dyslexic and having a difficult time learning a very simple process called reading—now that is scary!"

Jenner said that he lost interest in school as he became insecure and felt inferior to everybody else. "I had this painful fear of going to school and having to read in front of the class and everybody knowing that I couldn't read and feeling incredibly stupid."

Jenner gives time and personal resources to the LAB School for Learning Disabilities which assists children with dyslexia. He tells kids about winning the gold medal in the decathlon at the 1976 Olympics and earning the title of World's Greatest Athlete.

"I never thought that sports would mean that much to me and have such a big impact on me. And getting started, I never thought I would go as far as I did, but I think athletics builds a type of character and a good mind. As time went on, I found out my greatest attribute was not my physical talent, because I wasn't as physically talented as a lot of the other guys. I found out my greatest talent was my mental and emotional strength. I realized over time that I could get the performance out of me that I needed. Growing up, my greatest weakness, I always thought, was my brain. Then I found out later on in life that it was my greatest asset. Mentally, emotionally, and cognitively, being able to get my body to do what I have to do, that has been my stronghold."

Jenner, in describing his method for overcoming

adversity and achieving success, notes that when the pressure was on and he needed a performance, he got the plus, it was there. "I just knew how to handle the pressure and fear and all those terrible things that created failure for so many other great athletes. With tension and pressure, I would thrive, that was my arena. Give me a lot of pressure and I will come through." To Jenner, that pressure and the stress of competition had nothing to do with physical shape, because everybody is physically talented. This is part of your mental capacity. His philosophy is that there are two athletes in the universe. There is the athletic body and the athletic mind and, in most cases—a lot of cases—they don't mix. You find great athletes with great potential. They often have terrific talent, and yet they don't have the head for it. The second type is the guy with a great head and he doesn't have the physical ability. Jenner says that one of the few people that represents the integration of mind and body is Carl Lewis.

A Sullivan Award winner and Associated Press Male Athlete of the Year in 1976, Bruce Jenner was inducted into the Olympic Hall of Fame in 1986. His greatest achievement, however, was coping with and working through his dyslexia. "I had to build my confidence with my learning disability. There is nothing you can do right off the bat when you are LD. You can't just take two aspirin and get plenty of sleep and be over this dyslexic thing. You are stuck with it for life. And, of course, it was hard to diagnose, especially when I went to school in the '50s."

Jenner has an interesting metaphor for describing his learning disability and how he copes with it. When he speaks to young people on campuses across America, he tells them this story. "God sort of took away something of me in one area... but he gave something special back in another area, and your job is to find that niche. I found it in athletics. Now you may find it in art. You may find it in music. You may find it anywhere, but your job is to find it."

Today Jenner still has a problem reading, but has found creative ways to get around it. "If you had ever told me, when I was in grade school, that some day you will stand in front of a camera on Good Morning America with forty-two million households watching and read a teleprompter, I would have said you were crazy. I could never do that in a zillion years. It just won't work. I can't read in front of a class, let alone read a teleprompter in front of the television audience watching the Olympic games in Barcelona!" His trick is that he never reads anything cold. Jenner never reads anything that he hasn't thoroughly prepared. He uses cue cards and never reads every word, just the main words. He prepares his television appearances by reading the cards a couple of times and then committing everything to memory.

Jenner implements the same focus and inner discipline in confronting dyslexia that he used for sport. "I found out that my greatest fear in life (reading), and being dyslexic, wound up being my greatest asset. The reason I say that is because I was special. I wasn't like all the other kids who go through life and they're average and they can read and there really are no disabilities. Because I was dyslexic, I was special. So, when I found my thing in life, I worked harder at it. It became more important to me, it became an obsession, I needed that in my life. Deep inside my soul, there was always a feeling that I was inferior to other people and that meant that I had to work harder. So I developed a great work ethic. I never felt that I was better than anybody else. I always felt I was a little behind, so it made me work harder. It made me concentrate more on what I was trying to accomplish in life and it made me more focused. I needed this for my soul to feel good and to feel proud of me as a human being."

Jenner was born on the east coast and moved to Iowa for college where he graduated from Graceland College. Although he spends much of his time acting, directing, working as a television sportscaster, writing books, and running a number of diverse business ventures, he still finds a large chunk of time for kids.

Jenner and Blatnick are two athletes who represent different styles, different sports, and are worlds apart in lifestyle and public persona. They shared the limelight in Olympic victory, yet have chosen different paths as they came off the podium. They have shared an ethic of hard work and discipline, not only in the athletic arena, but in the arena of life and in overcoming personal crisis and adversity.

SECTION
2

TRAINING OF
THE HIGH ACHIEVER

CHAPTER 5

SEND ME IN, COACH

"The thing you have to understand is that successful coaches, as well as successful athletes, all have a screw loose. In other words, they are desperately trying to compensate for a sense—a real or an imagined sense—of inferiority."

Brooks Johnson
1976 and 1984 Olympic Coach
Track and Field

Among the handful of coaches I interviewed for this book, all were in agreement about the fundamentals of discipline, time management, and a rigorous work ethic. Each coach, however, had his own unique philosophy about what made an average athlete great, how the Olympic competitor emerged, and what created a high achiever. I chose eight coaches for this chapter, each from different schools of thought, each offering a special blend of psychology/physical attribute style of motivation. I interviewed Brooks Johnson, Bill Bowerman, Bobby Douglas, Ken Matsuda, Russ Hellickson, Mamie Rallins, Berny Wagner, and Ed Burch here. We begin this chapter with the philosophy of Brooks Johnson.

Brooks Johnson was the first African-American head coach in the history of Stanford University. He was named coach of the year by *Runner's World* magazine in 1982, served as the 1976 Olympic sprint coach, and was the U.S. women's track coach for the 1984 Olympic Games in Los Angeles. He has impeccable credentials. He demands self-discipline from all of his athletes and pays absolute attention to the details of training an individual including their time management strategies. In fact, he is a fanatic about the importance of time management among elite athletes. "The biggest difference between Stanford athletes and athletes at places that I've been before wasn't that the Stanford athletes were any brighter; it's what they do with their spare time, how they handle unstructured time. The people at Stanford use their time more efficiently and are much more effective at time management."

Johnson is considered a well-rounded coach in that he promotes a well-balanced diet of athletics and academics for his student athletes. "There are some downsides to managing academics and athletics and setting lofty goals. There is tremendous stress, and the kids at Stanford are not immune from it. I think there is an inordinate amount of pressure put on those kids in an environment that is already a pressure-packed situation. You have to coach these student athletes, who are also training for the Olympics, to realize that stress is stress. There is no real difference between mental stress and physical stress. It's stress. If a day calls for one hundred units of stress and you have fifty units of stress dedicated to the track workout and fifty units is coming from the library and study demands, then you have a full compliment of stress. But if that kid has already been stressed up to seventy units before he gets to his or her workout, then you can only plug in thirty units without overloading the system. So I always have to be mindful of midterms, of when papers are due, and you have to coach more with an eye toward what's happening on the other side of campus as opposed to your side of campus."

Johnson knows about the limits of stress and when his athletes reach saturation points. "You just know it after a while because you understand one's body language. Body language does not lie. When kids are in trouble, their bodies will express that, and the distress will manifest itself in other areas that we monitor. We are constantly asking our kids how things are going academically. We constantly check in with our athletes."

His philosophy of coaching as it relates to competition and winning is simple. "There is no way you can do the things necessary to be a PAC-10 athlete or even an Olympic trials qualifier and not be clinically neurotic and, in some instances, clinically psychotic. You may mask that in ways that society and the college will accept, but in point of fact, if you were to take a clinical inventory of your athletes' characteristics, you would find them neurotic and, in some instances, actually psychotic. It is the same thing with coaches. The extremes to which athletes and coaches will go to be successful and/or win are well beyond the norm. So, by definition, athletes and coaches are in it together and they are very abnormal people."

Johnson's clinical diagnosis seems to penetrate a winning philosophy. "What you try to do is put the athletes in a situation where they have a stronger sense of themselves and so, as a result, they don't need to overcompensate. However, that is diametrically opposed to them being successful as an athlete; as a competitive athlete. It allows them to become a better human being, but it does not do a damn thing about them becoming a better competitive athlete—and that's the fine line, that's the Catch-22."

Brooks Johnson is not a shrink, but he does have a treatment plan for creating a well-balanced individual. He notes that the trick to a balanced program is to make athletes nonobsessive about what they are doing. He feels that much talent is wasted in this country because coaches think more is better. "The Puritan work ethic is so pervasive in athletics, that it is counterproductive. If you look at the amount of yardage that swimmers swim, at a certain point about 80 percent of it has nothing to do with the physiology. It has to do with the psychology of the coach and the athlete. So, the overtraining phenomenon is for real. And the rationale for overtraining is that coaches have their own set of anxieties. Remember that coaches have the same kinds of ghosts and anxieties as the athlete. They don't have innate confidence and arrogance in their ability. Coaches think that if you work hard and make a kid work hard, then the responsibility for failure is not theirs. The responsibility for failure falls back on the bad romance or the pot hole in the track."

Brooks Johnson explains that coaching is a dysfunctional phenomenon. He notes that we have an obsessive-compulsive society and we want results yesterday. Everything is fast food and instant gratification, the future is now. "I think that athletics are basically a springboard and a transition period into real life. When I talk to these kids, I don't talk to them about athletics per se. I talk to them about political, social, and economic issues. I talk to them about gender and Title IX problems, about inequities as they relate to minorities, and I coach in those terms."

Johnson is always willing to offer his global perspective

on the role of coaches and their influence on the athlete. The major point that he stresses with the kids at Stanford is that they are no more deserving than the people on the other side of Highway 101, that they got to Stanford because of some chance of where they were born. He tells his kids not to get the impression that because they are at Stanford that it is their birthright. He tells them not to get the impression that they got there because they are more deserving than other people. "There are people on the other side of Highway 101 who have worked just as hard, who have the exact same high moral and ethical standards that you have. So now that you're here, you need to rededicate yourself to earning this superior position that you now occupy. Because it's not yours as a matter of birth. You have to deserve this over and over and over again, because there are people who are being excluded and, therefore, being suppressed because they are not here at this privileged institution. The reason you're here and the reason your parents made the sacrifice to get you here is so that you will have a running head start on everybody else."

Johnson reminds his kids that Stanford University is not about getting an education. He tells them it's about opportunity. "You can go to any junior college in the country and, if you digest every damn thing they have in their library, you will come out very educated. So you could have gotten a good education anywhere. What you get at Stanford is an excellent opportunity."

He lets his kids know that there is no such thing as a free lunch. He believes that the fact that his athletes are competing at Stanford, "in the ivory tower existence with all its wondrous loopholes," does not offer diplomatic immunity from the real world. Johnson is fond of saying that you cannot get an extension in life. You cannot get a postponement in life. "If you are a surgeon and a patient needs a heart transplant, you can't call up and say look, I am going to need an extra day or so because I don't feel quite right today. And if you argue a case before the Supreme Court, you are not going to be able to get a postponement at your convenience because you have a hangnail."

Bill Bowerman is an individual who, probably, has done more for the sport of track and field than anyone else in the world. His name is known throughout the world, including on street signs entering the international headquarters of Nike Inc. The sign reads very simply "One Bowerman Way," and is placed there out of respect and adulation for the cofounder of this giant international shoe and sportswear company in Portland, Oregon. In truth, there is only one Bowerman Way.

Born in 1911, Bowerman served as head coach of the University of Oregon from 1949 through 1972. He won four NCAA Team Titles, coached twenty-four individual NCAA champions, and produced twenty-eight Olympians on the way to becoming a legend. One of his student athletes was Phil Knight, the CEO of Nike Inc.

Bowerman is an educator/motivator and not your typical coach; in fact, he abhors that term. Bowerman has a philosophy of sport that once you engage a kid in athletics, you are setting the foundation for great motivation. "Sport is not for everyone, but it keeps the high energy people occupied. For a lot of high energy kids, there isn't enough opportunity for them."

Bowerman loves animals, including his prize bulls. He says that they have a way of enhancing motivation. Bill Bowerman is a student of motivation and has had a great impact on a number of athletes over six decades. The essence of his coaching strategies and the influence that he exerts over high achievers is reflected in a delicate and meaningful relationship between athlete and coach.

Kenny Moore is one of Bowerman's prize students. He epitomizes the role of an athlete who grew up under the watchful eye of a demanding coach and flourished under his tutelage. He not only learned his lessons well on the track, but became a superstar in his profession as well. Bowerman takes all the credit. He notes that Kenny was an average marathoner physically, but psychologically "he was as tough as they come." Moore was a two-time Olympic marathoner (in 1968 and 1972), but has a great deal more to show on his résumé than long-distance running.

Bowerman reminds one that a good coach is first and

foremost a great teacher. "After all, I look back at my own educational career and I had some good coaches, but they weren't all great teachers. I know who the great teachers were because they inspired me. Jim Gilbert was one of them; he was so inspirational that they named a building at a major university after the guy. There are major differences between most of the so-called teachers/coaches and the real teacher. My track coach at Oregon, Bill Hayward, was a great teacher. He was a great educator and a constant inspiration to me."

Kenny Moore says that even today he reflects daily on the wisdom of his coach, a man who truly was a great educator. "Bill was always full of surprises, he was absolutely the most diabolical coach I ever knew. Just when you thought you knew his system, he would pull out a new trick. He loved to yank us out of races at the last minute so that we wouldn't get too cocky and over-race. Most of all, he wanted to keep us hungry for the next battle. He also wanted us to learn how to set our own limits in training, in racing, and in life as well."

Bowerman explained that there are specific differences between those who play the role of coach and those who really care about their athletes. He offers some dramatic examples. He had polio as a youngster and couldn't run very well. In fact, he was rather "slow of foot." He explained that his run was kind of a gallop, but he could catch the ball, so they made him a receiver and he averaged two touchdowns a game. He didn't really want to play football in college at Oregon except that Bill Hayward, the coach, offered to work with him on his running and sprinting.

"Between my freshman year and my sophomore year, I spent time with coach Hayward and learned how to run. He taught me how to use my legs the way they are supposed to operate as if I hadn't been crippled. So, I was able to overcome my disability and the crippling effects of the disease based on his strategy and the mechanics of movement." This turned out to be a powerful lesson for Bowerman, one that stayed with him throughout his long career.

Bowerman reviewed his philosophy of coaching and how his training methods carried over into an attitude about discipline. He declared that we have real problems in this country because budgets are failing and the general consensus is a nine-to-three school day mentality; get the reading, writing, and arithmetic out of the way and send the kids home. Bowerman seems terribly distressed by this national dilemma. "If you lock up the schools every day at 3:00 p.m., and close the playing fields and don't allow the kids to play out there, then the opportunity of education is too limited. Education needs to involve physical education for everyone including the kids that have a lot of energy. These youngsters ought to have an opportunity to burn off those calories rather than exploit somebody in the neighborhood. Let's give them exercise so they can avoid the gangs, the drugs, and the hellraising."

As a coach for twenty-five years at Oregon, Bowerman applied his training rules to everyday life for both athletics and academics. Kenny Moore noted that his strategies were complex, he always was one step ahead of the kids. "He was a coach, a role model, and a father figure to all of us. He would go out of his way to know all his athletes personally, know their families, and understand their personal dynamics. Occasionally he would move roommates around, getting certain kids who had greater motivation to bunk with those less-focused athletes. He would interrupt the status quo, be disruptive if necessary. He never wanted an athlete to sit back and get too comfortable. He expected us to grow, to mature on and off the field, and he did whatever it took to achieve this goal."

Bowerman is grounded in the school of common sense; he is definitely allergic to bullshit! He used to tell his athletes that if you have to stay up all night to study for an exam, you better get your butt in gear the following day. "It's dumb that you didn't study earlier during the term, but if you have to stay up, *just do it.*" Sound familiar? I think so. Bowerman believed that you come to a university to be a student first, be an athlete second, and learn to take responsibility for your behavior along the way. "And if you decide to stay up all night and chase girls, and then come to track and field practice bleary eyed and wiped out, I'll give you one warning, and the second time around, you are gone." That was Bowerman's only training rule. If one of his athletes was off base and raising hell somewhere, they were history. Bowerman said it didn't matter who the person was—the collegiate record holder, the American, NCAA, or even Olympic caliber athlete. If they didn't play by the rules, they were gone!

Bill Bowerman feels strongly about the issue of motivation. He was a dedicated coach and motivator to his athletes when he was appointed head track and field coach of the 1972 U.S. Olympic Team. He brought the same motivational ethic to business when he retired from coaching and started designing the now-famous waffle shoe for Nike. "I don't think I've ever changed my feelings about getting kids involved in sports. But if you're going be involved in something, involve yourself. And if you don't want to get involved, stay home. But if you jump into the ring, step up to the plate and give it your best shot. You must always remember one thing, and I've said this to a hell of a lot of teams and individuals: know ye not, but in a race run all, but only one obtains the prize. So... if you're going to bleed to death in a competition, give it your best shot."

Today, athlete and preeminent journalist Kenny Moore validates the notion that he and his cohorts did a lot of bleeding. "He worked our asses off, but he also knew balance and would caution us against overtraining and possible injury. He also knew us emotionally. When I told him I was going to drop out of Stanford Law School, he didn't bat an eyelash. He knew it was the wrong place, the wrong time, and that practicing law was not my passion."

Bowerman paid one of his top athletes the ultimate compliment last year. When he was approached by several people preparing to write his biography, Bowerman told them there was only one person who could do the job. And do the job with grace and style and professional expertise. Olympian and *Sports Illustrated* journalist Kenny Moore was chosen to work on the authorized biography of William Bowerman.

Bobby Douglas, a two-time Olympian and the U.S. head wrestling coach for the 1992 games in Barcelona, has a distinct message about the role and influence of coaches. He looks at sport from a cultural/anthropological perspective and expects his athletes to have a sense of history before they hit the mats.

"Wrestling is man's oldest sport, and modern wrestling

stems from the ancient struggle for leadership; the fight to the death, the battle that took place to select the chief. In primitive times, primitive man was selected as the chief and that happened through battle, hand-to-hand combat. This fight became part of selecting the leaders of different armies and their generals. The top wrestlers were then selected as the leaders."

Douglas should know about leadership. Under his guidance, three American wrestlers captured gold medals, including his own assistant coach at Iowa State in the 1992 Olympics. For Douglas, the influence of the coach upon his sport goes way beyond the individual and may be considered a cultural event. Douglas believes that modern wrestling is derived from hand-to-hand combat of earlier days. Those fights were serious and involved weapons, which ultimately led to many fatalities. According to Bobby Douglas, the art of wrestling was developed so that you could trip your opponent, throw your opponent, and hold your opponent. "It even goes back further than that when man was at the cannibal stage collecting food. His major food was other people and, to protect himself, he had to fight—he had to fight animals, so developing the wrestling techniques became natural to man. As man started to develop, you couldn't have all your warriors fighting each other and killing off the cream-of-the-crop. So they had to insert some rules. Henceforth, wrestling holds emerged so that you didn't kill everyone and terminate the species. Along with the rules came an awareness and strength of the body and an appreciation for beauty, agility, and movement."

Douglas believes man's survival mechanism is the essence of sport and the ethic of wrestling. "Therein lies man's ability to look outside of himself at his God-given talents. And there begins the spiritual process." Bobby Douglas believes that the influence of a coach goes well beyond the confines of a university gymnasium. He exposed his student athletes to the spiritual world of sport and competition. "We went to Turkey and trained with the Turkish team and we saw this ceremony where they slaughter two goats. After the slaughter, they dip the hand of the wrestler in blood and they put a mark on his forehead. Then the wrestlers dance and they are praised by their peers, and finally, there is community prayer for their success."

Bobby explained this ritual. Historically, prior to all wrestling competitions, athletes prepared themselves in a spiritual manner. "They would get by themselves and start visualizing and rehearsing, and maybe even praying; I used to pray a lot before my competitions. When you are going to compete, you are asking for help, not only through your preparation, but you're asking for help outside of yourself. That's the spiritual relationship between a wrestler and his sport."

Douglas tries to instill a deeper meaning into sport when he coaches his wrestlers. His techniques may be unorthodox but he gets the most out of his athletes. "As a coach, I pray an awful lot. I don't pray for a victory. I pray for wisdom to lead these men in the right way. I'm not asking for the victory over this guy or that guy, but I just pray for the wisdom that I'm training them properly. I am wanting to instill in them the right type of attitudes and arousing them to an action that is going to be positive. I'm instilling in them a faith and a confidence that's necessary to be the best. I think that is the important thing here, to be the very best all-around person and have faith in yourself."

Douglas says that the social environment is just as important as the athletic arena when you are building strength of character. "You have to associate with the right people. You hang around bums, you become a bum. You hang around people that are working their butts off, you'll work your butt off because it is catching. Desire is something that can't be taught—it has to be caught. The will to win is worthless without the will to prepare. A man of faith can't be beat, as long as he believes in himself."

Douglas is a true believer. He is a man who instills a sense of culture and history which strengthens the bonds between athlete and coach. He puts certain words and concepts in front of his athletes; he talks to them about their role in history. He feels that every day he awakes and can go out and run is a privilege for him. "I don't feel that I work to live, I live to work. Those are things that I want to instill in my athletes because there is no certainty that I am going to be here tomorrow. I know that ten years from now I'm not going to be able to run like I run now, so I'm going to enjoy every minute of that because I want to make sure that I live life to the fullest. That's the key to preparing yourself. Every day is a masterpiece. You're living a life, you're living a dream."

Bobby Douglas is excited about waking up in the morning. He tells his athletes that they have to set goals every day, and they have to be willing to work hard to achieve those goals. Bobby Douglas is a true believer, he practices what he preaches.

Ken Matsuda, a well-known and highly respected coach in many disciplines, gives each of his athletes a major, first-time only speech. His speech deals with one issue and one issue only: accountability. Matsuda believes that athletes have two frames of mind. First, they're hoping that the other competitors mess up, and second, they're hoping they have a great competition day. He says that if you examine your sport carefully, break down all of the components of the athletic movements, write them down, and systematically study them, then the process of training becomes a science. Ken takes the scientific approach. "You have to know what muscles are involved with your event and how they fire and interact with every other part of your body." Matsuda should know something about muscle groups and the talents of the men and women who developed under his tutelage. During his career he has worked with a number of well-known athlete achievers, including O.J. Simpson, Charles White, Ronnie Lott, Tracy Austin, Michael Chang, and Jim Grabb.

Ken Matsuda has a simple coaching philosophy. He doesn't admonish his athletes for staying up late; he is not a strong believer in the do's and don'ts strategy. What he simply lays out is a question for each of his athletes. "Is it a plus or minus? That's got to be determined before you do anything. If it's a plus you come out ahead. If it's a minus, and you go ahead and do drugs all night, you're going to be accountable the next day or at the next performance. If you don't work out today, that's fine, but you now have a minus and you can never make that minus up. You can work out twice tomorrow, but you'll never make it up."

Matsuda is also big on time management. His athletes are required to set aside a schedule of twenty-four hours and then delegate specific tasks to each time slot. He asks his athletes to challenge themselves by writing down what they hope to achieve in their waking-hour time periods. He requests that each day his athletes look at available hours and budget their time wisely. He is a big proponent of "prime time"; that is, building in structure, time management, accountability, discipline, and of course, motivation. "Once you have those ingredients, everything else falls into place."

In his thirty-seven years of coaching world-record holders, Matsuda believes there are three areas that reflect goals for successful performances. A goal is defined as "a dream with a deadline," and so he sets up a triangle principle that breaks out the goal. On one side of the triangle there is the physical and mechanical part; the second part of the triangle is nutrition and rest; and the third part is the psychological and spiritual components which reinforce all of the physical stuff. This includes the visualization and imagery work.

Ken's prescription for disciplined athletics is to stay away from the four "Fs." "I tell my athletes that you get in trouble with the four Fs: the female, family, finances, and just plain farting around. If you get into trouble, it's for sure one of those four Fs."

Another individual well known for his hands-on, personal-involvement style of coaching is Russ Hellickson. Hellickson, currently in his seventh season as the Ohio State University head wrestling coach, is respected for his practice of discipline and structure. And, similar to Ken Matsuda, Hellickson is a strong proponent of looking at his sport scientifically. "You've got a physiological component, a technical component, and a psychological component. I've always felt that success is not so much an occurrence as it is an attitude. If you have the right kind of mental attitude, you will overcome all of the discouraging confrontations throughout your preparation to excel. If you don't have the right attitude, as soon as you meet up with something negative, you drop out."

Russ should know. Along with his coaching responsibilities, Hellickson is widely recognized as an authority on wrestling and he also works as a television sportscaster, covering wrestling at the 1992 Barcelona Olympic Games. Hellickson is absolutely sure about issues of motivation and growth and how one gets beyond the defeatist attitude. "I've seen it happen where an athlete is constantly beaten by a situation, and he doesn't improve or get better. The individual who, in defeat, learns something or continues to struggle, is the guy who improves and gets better. There are many ways to teach the art of wrestling. Some guys get in great shape, some guys become so strong with their weightlifting, and some guys just have that heart and that grit and that determination. Some athletes become so technically superior in executing and reacting to their opponent that they can dominate. A number of people improve in all of those areas. What I've found as a coach, from both watching other people and from my days as an athlete, is that there are lots of ways to grow and enhance the quality of your athleticism."

Hellickson feels that the emotional components of training are a big part of his methods when exerting a coaching influence. He notes that there's a false assumption in the athletic world that the only way a coach can improve an athlete is in the physical nature. Hellickson disagrees with that notion. "I think you can have greater success by working in the psychological area—getting the young man to understand that pressure is something that he will always be subjected to, no matter how good he gets. Pressure is something that the athlete achiever must always face if he is going to ever improve."

Hellickson explains his coaching philosophy using the metaphors of behavioral psychology. He says that most people try to create a situation where they can learn and practice some form of relaxation to eliminate the pressure. "In sport you don't ever eliminate the pressure, you just plain deal with it." He believes that the athletes who learn to deal with it and understand the anxiety that comes with it are the ones who just keep stepping up to that next level of success.

Russ Hellickson is scientific about certain things, but not all. He balks when he is asked if he scientifically approaches his sport using textbook adaptations of mental imagery and visualization. "No, I guess I don't. I'm much more scientific about setting goals and establishing a plan to accomplish the goals. I want all my athletes to write them down. They have to talk about them. They have to see them and believe in them. I think that athletes have to understand that what separates an individual from being the best and some other guy who doesn't even give it a shot is determination and attitude."

Hellickson explains that many young athletes don't want to realize or take responsibility for their success. They think it's a gift. "You cannot control the ability you are inherently born with, that skill level that you might have, that muscular strength, that speed, that quickness. And you can't control opportunity, because you may be the greatest or second greatest athlete of all time in your sport, but you may be in the sport at the time the greatest athlete of all time is there and he's in your same weight class. So, you're never going to be number one, but you have to aim for that goal."

Coach Hellickson tells his kids to remember that athletic competition is about the quest. He reminds them that it isn't about the failure to attain a goal, it's the failure to ever set one. Russ is a believer in imagery and behavioral cues as well. He had team sweatshirts made that said, "Big Ten and NCAA Champions—Keep On Believing." He has a big NCAA sign that he hangs on the wall and every kid on his team touches that sign when they walk in and again when they exit his office. He tells them that when they touch that sign, they will have to think about something positive—standing on top of the awards stand, receiving that first place medal, getting that take-down that wins it, or putting that man on his back and pinning him. "The guy who plays that little visual fantasy with himself often enough will achieve such a drive to reality that you almost can't stop him."

Part of Hellickson's training regimen is to create a scenario using imagery and visualization strategies that focus an athletes' desires. "I tell my kids the famous fish story. A Spanish barracuda is put into a large aquarium. In that aquarium, on the opposite side, is a Spanish mackerel. Then a glass partition is inserted in the middle of the aquarium. The barracuda cannot swim over and get the Spanish mackerel because of the partition. He will try. He will see it, but he keeps running into it and running into it, and running into it. Now, after a period of time, he accepts the fact that there's something in the way and he can't get to the most cherished thing in his life, and that's the food he wants to eat. The glass partition is removed, and what happens—nothing, because, in the barracuda's mind, that glass partition is still there and will forever be there.

"And people are like that. My athletes are like that." When he needs to, Hellickson invokes the great fish story. It's a great motivator!

Hellickson is compassionate about the personal lives of his athletes and about the academic responsibilities that go with training demands. Academics is most critical to him. He feels personally responsible for seeing that his athletes are prepared academically to do the job in the real world. Hellickson is passionate when he speaks of the deficiencies on campus today. "We have a problem in America which presidents of universities think they have addressed. But they have not! Just because someone has athletic ability does not mean he has a right to go to college. If you're not a student, you don't deserve to be in college. But for some reason you get a preponderance of those guys who are on the borderline. There is a myth in America that we have to do everything we can to keep this kid eligible. This notion that, because he's such a great athletic talent we must keep him eligible, is way out of proportion. We as coaches at every level need to deal with that issue."

Hellickson, the coach and caring professional, completes each workout reminding his athletes about the definition of discipline. "Discipline is doing what you don't want to do when you don't want to do it. That is what I try and instill in my athletes every day."

Not far from Russ Hellickson's gym is the office of track and field and Mamie Rallins' domain at Ohio State. Her philosophy of discipline and commitment to excellence goes one layer deeper than that of her colleague, Russ Hellickson. When she applies the ethics of sport to her coaching principles, her female track and field athletes stand up straight and usually listen carefully. Rallins notes that some of her male colleagues don't really understand the role of the coach. "You see, I'm not coaching the women just to be athletes. When I coach and recruit for this university, I always try to tell my athletes that I will coach you as if you were coming to a finishing school. When I get through with you, you will know how to dress, eat, do anything else in the world that you want to do. In my job, you get people from all walks of life—from the inner cities to the wealthiest—and if no one is teaching them how to be young ladies and mature adults along the way, then they won't learn it. These young women are looking to you as a role model, because they have problems with their social, academic, and personal lives."

Mamie Rallin's philosophy of coaching stems from growing up fast, and becoming self-reliant at an early age. "I lost my mother at age thirteen, so I had to learn things from the streets and sometimes the hard way. I have always felt that my responsibility to youngsters, whether they're rich, poor, or whatever, is to teach them something so that, when they leave this place, they will know something about life. They will learn how to dress, how to put clothes together, how to eat with the Queen or the president of the United States. They will know how to read an airline ticket (an issue that has caused problems in the past) or find out which way they need to go, how to be organized, and on time. So as a coach those are part of the things I stress."

Rallins believes in the ethic of training, but her conviction toward social and psychological preparation is even greater. She always talks to her kids on the track. They talk on the bus, on the airplane, or whenever there is quality time. She tells her girls about the game plan, from the simplest planning of a meal to the more complex strategies of winning a race. Mamie feels that the role of coaching is to provide a perpetual flow of information while enhancing the educational process. "I constantly emphasize the fact that being an athlete is just one component, being a young woman in school is just one component, that every day you are preparing for the real world and the rest of your life."

Rallins, who has had great success in her coaching tenure, sees her role in the universe from a global perspective. "My goal is to prepare these young female student athletes for any situation. It is my goal that someday in my lifetime the women will run the country and all you men will have to come to us for jobs and assistance. I want them to believe that they have the skills and the ability to go out there and be the president of a major company or, for that matter, of this country!"

Mamie Rallins harps on the academics because she didn't go to college until she was thirty. A lot of doors did not open for her until she had her credential. "The credential is the only way that most people will look at women of color. If you don't have your education and your credential, then your chances of getting something done in this world is next to zero." Rallins is proud of her graduation rate; after sixteen years of coaching at Ohio State she retained a 99 percent matriculation rate. Her philosophy is that, regardless of a woman's color or status or whether she is the biggest superstar on campus, you are left at home if you miss study table and don't get your work done.

Rallins is a proud, bright, and elegant woman. She is a four-time world record holder in the hurdles and a two-time U.S. Olympian in 1968 and 1972. Mamie went back to finish her college degree at age thirty. She would much rather talk to you about academics than any of her other great achievements!

Berny Wagner, formerly of the Athletics Congress in Indianapolis, is an individual who is committed to understanding the mechanism of athletic competition and training styles. With Berny's assistance and blessings, Professor Jacqueline Golding and I were able to complete a four-year psychological study of elite athletes, later published in our book *Beyond Strength: Psychological Profiles of Olympic Athletes*.

Wagner, now retired and living back in his home state of Oregon, believes strongly in learning how to diagnose an athlete. He notes that there are many types of athletes, and there are some who just break coaches' hearts. "There are some kids who have that competitiveness. They have the desire, and they'll run through a brick wall if you tell them to. But they just aren't hooked up right biomechanically. Then there are those athletes who are gifted but don't have the desire or the competitiveness of an Olympian."

Wagner is big on the integration of both physicality and emotional components. "There are some that just have talent, which is how you're put together physically. When you take the talent and add the psychology and the mental aspect, you have the winners. Back in 1896, at the first modern Olympics, you just had to have the physical talent. But now in modern times you have to have both. You have to be willing to accept all the problems, to give up social commitments in order to go ahead and achieve, because the competition is so tough. Where the coach comes in is helping the athlete find the best way to continue that competitive drive and how to put forth the effort."

Wagner says there are frustrating experiences in the coaching profession. "The heartbreaker for me is that you occasionally see that one-in-a-thousand athlete who comes along, and you just think, 'Oh my gosh, there are loads of people who would like to have that talent and this guy has it and is throwing it away.' There are a lot of those kids out there with the gift."

Wagner's belief is that only a few exceptionally talented individuals have all the pieces. Not many are at the very upper end of the normal curve. "It gets pretty thin at that point." Wagner says some kids really disappoint a coach, and it takes a long time to try to rationalize this within yourself. Often he finds a person who is a great jumper and could be a greater jumper if he would get everything together, but that person happens to think jumping is not that important. "Maybe that person thinks that going to the disco is more important or drinking beer is more important. I lost two excellent athletes because their religion did not allow them to explore their full potential. It was too self-aggrandizing to achieve in sport. It was more important for them to follow the precepts of their religion than to compete. There are people who would rather go hiking than run on a track. They liked cross country but they didn't want to run on a track."

Wagner is no stranger to intervention when he believes his athletes are in trouble. "It's a delicate process and you don't try to restructure a family when there is a crisis. You try to lend the support and fill in the void for that particular athlete." He notes that often a kid needs a coach, but he also needs a father. And when the coach becomes a father figure, you try within your own limits to spend quality time with the individual athlete. "You try to offer them help, both on and off the field, through sports, academics and in resolving their personal crisis."

Wagner shared some rather unusual incidents where he, as coach, had to wear many hats. "Once, I had to get the police involved in a domestic dispute. One of my athletes had been thrown out of the house by an angry wife, so the cops were called to intervene so he could get his books and get back to studying. Sometimes you find yourself in the middle of a serious and hostile marital issue. You try to work on solutions and it usually boils down to crisis intervention and management. I found later in my coaching career that the best way to assist an athlete in crisis is to not solve a problem for them, but allow them to wade through the distress for themselves."

Berny Wagner is a strong proponent of letting each person be responsible for his own actions and behavior. He supports the notion that the emotional event must be owned by the athlete. He says that if you let this personal responsibility take place, it carries over into sport itself. "When the athlete feels better about the emotion he was dealing with, he invariably does better on the field."

Berny Wagner as coach, and then later as chief administrator for the national governing body of track and field, has become a strong proponent of sports psychology. He wants more teams to participate in the psychological preparation and evaluation process. "We should always have at least one sports psychologist around each of our national teams so that we can do the testing and education of the athlete as well as the biomechanics. If each high school team could have a sports psychologist, if each collegiate team could have a sports psychologist, we would see a lot more people not only excel in sport, but also stay in sport. You hear too many people say, it's 90 percent mental and then they spend 100 percent of their time on the physical."

Wagner has great stories, some of them belonging in the hall of fame. One in particular is an anecdote about gold medal jumper Dick Fosbury. "I started working with imagery many years ago when Fosbury was at Oregon State. He did the visualization work so well. When he was rocking back and forth out there before his high jump, he would drive everybody crazy. I wasn't sure all the time what he was doing, but it turns out he was visualizing his hips over the bar. That's what he told me, anyway. But he visualized and he blocked out any distraction, and he had probably as much competitiveness as anybody I've ever known. He couldn't jump very high and he really wasn't our most talented athlete, even though he won the gold medal in Mexico City. Tim Vollmer, our discus thrower, had a better vertical jump reach than Dick."

Fosbury's mental conditioning, including his visualization strategies, significantly shaped the future of high jumping. Berny was a part of this process and is very proud. Wagner speaks fondly of his athletes including Dick Fosbury, who in addition to everything else, had a good sense of humor.

"Dick told me lots of stories. In fact, he told me that the reason he took a curve run on his approach to the high jump was because he practiced in a pit in his backyard where there was a tree he had to run around. I told it to five-hundred people in Detroit at a symposium. Later he told me he made up the story."

Wagner has an entire wall filled with pictures in his office. They are pictures of unheralded athletes, great high-profile athletes, and just terrific human beings. He smiles as he points to his athletes on the wall. He has had a terrific coaching career and is proud of these kids. Wagner's collage of athletes is a tribute to his long commitment to athletic excellence and high achievement of his students on and off the field.

Ed Burch, head coach of Gold Cup Gymnastics Academy in Albuquerque, New Mexico, is a rebel. He has been called the Ross Perot of the coaching world. He likes to blow the whistle when things get out of control. He has been called "an irreverent iconoclast who likes nothing better than turning the sports establishment purple with anger." Burch is proud of the labels.

He loves the sport of gymnastics but hates the politics that surround team selection, including the bias shown toward cute little girls with the right bodies. He gets enraged when he talks about the 1992 Olympics in Barcelona. "During the 1992 trials there was a great pool of talent among our women's team. But the U.S. coaching staff is very biased when it comes to the correct look—the right body type—for our women athletes. They are not necessarily searching for the best athletes, the best talent, but the best all-around precious look." According to Burch, international gymnastics is very subjective and you have to look the part when you get before the judges.

Burch is notorious for his outspokenness, including the correct body type issue. He claims that this sort of whistleblowing has kept him off the international roster for Olympic coaching jobs even though he has produced some of the best gymnasts in the U.S. Trent Dimas, the 1992 gold medalist, and Lance Ringnald, the two-time Olympian, are part of his stable. Burch went to Barcelona as a private club coach but not with the clout of an Olympic decision maker. He had to jostle for position and carefully maneuver his way into the good graces of the international gymnastics leadership. After all, gymnastics is all about image, who you know, and how you look.

Burch was incensed when he found out about the rotation of events and when his premier athlete was selected to compete. "I had to fight with the coaching staff to get Dimas into the last rotation on the high bar. I knew that the U.S. would have a chance for a gold in Trent's performance if they would let him compete last. I know the way scores go and, if he could get in last, we would have a shot at the gold. Scores seem to creep up about two-tenths of a point every rotation."

Coach Burch loves his athletes. He is a father, teacher, and friend to all of them. He has trained Trent Dimas since childhood; he knows him intimately. He knows what it takes to get the best possible performance out of him. "The day before the finals, Trent comes up to me and says, 'Burch, there is a big party tonight. All the guys are going, everyone has been invited.' I said, that's fine, but you're not going. He was really upset. He said, 'Burch, the games are over.' I said, you have finals. You are still here. He kept trying to tell me that all these other jocks had finals, too. No dice, he was not going to the party, it wasn't time to celebrate—yet! We're here to represent the United States and let's do our very best."

Dimas next asked his coach if he thought he had a chance to win a medal. Burch responded in his typical, positive, self-actualization way; declaring "maybe you don't, but I'm going to get you to win a medal." Every one of Dimas' buddies went to the party and he stayed home. The rest is Olympic history! Trent stayed in his dormitory room that night. He went into his head space and mentally rehearsed his high bar routine two-hundred times. Ed Burch didn't go to the party either. He, too, went to his room that night and went into his own head, over two-hundred times. "I did the same thing in my room that Trent did in his. All the coaches went to the party, but I stayed, concentrating on Trent's routine. We put ourselves into a perfect sync. I think it paid off."

This type of synergy sounds extraordinary to the neophyte, but is a standard game plan for Ed Burch and his athletes. He typically stays right with his athletes, physically and emotionally, until competition time. Five hours prior to getting on the Olympic podium, even during warmups, Burch has every step, every movement, every image, planned. He is a master of detail and expecting the unexpected to happen.

"When we walked into the gymnastics arena in Barcelona, Trent turns and says, 'thanks for not letting me go to the party. I feel very comfortable. I'm very relaxed and I'm ready to compete.'" Burch talked about the high bar, the routines. He likes to get his athletes prepared but not over psyched. "We talked about our warmups that we were going to do and how long it would take for each warmup. We did about seven warmups in another gym so he wouldn't be watching the other competitors and getting distracted. He screwed up his warmup. He almost hit the bar on his release move. He came down hard, and was a bit shaken." Burch told his premier athlete to relax and to get in touch with the bar, stay in contact. "Now that you know you almost screwed up, get up there and do what you're supposed to do. So, he got back up the second time, and he did the most beautiful release move. He came down and asked if there was anything else I wanted him to do. I told him no, you are now ready to compete."

For many of us in Barcelona and for those who watched the slow motion television replay of Trent Dimas' flawless gold medal performance, it was poetry in motion. His work on the high bar was the culmination of sixteen years of physical, emotional, and spiritual preparation under the tutelage of Ed Burch. As he hit the perfect dismount after the perfect routine, Burch and Dimas both knew it was party time!

Bill Bowerman, Bobby Douglas, Ken Matsuda, Russ Hellickson, Mamie Rallins, Berny Wagner, and Ed Burch all have something in common. They know their sport! They also know a great deal about their individual athlete achievers who play their sport. The coach is the conductor, the therapist, the parent, the role model, and ultimately the teacher. In some cases they set the stage and build the foundations for life-long achievement. Whether coaches have a few loose screws, as Brooks Johnson suggests, remains to be seen. The delicate and often intimate relationship between coach and athlete is one that is cherished and respected. It is a relationship that cannot be duplicated in any other arena.

CHAPTER 6

THE MENTAL PRACTICE GAME

> *"Unless you are really strong psychologically and committed to staying healthy, you can get injured so easily in ski racing. Your reaction time in an injury-causing situation is not something that you can think about and react to. It is something that is already trained inside of you. It is already a part of your muscle memory. In racing, it's very important to visualize everything! We use visualization every moment of our training and, if you incorporate the wrong mental pictures, SPLAT... you hit the wall, you are toast, and blood flies everywhere. You have to practice your ski runs physically as well as in your mind visually. Often when you have a bad run, you just back up the tape (in your mind's eye) and do it again, so that you don't splat all over the slopes!"*

> *Holly Flanders*
> *1980 and 1984 Olympian*
> *Downhill Ski Racing*

We begin this chapter with the voices, or perhaps the images, of athlete achievers who have that uncanny ability to see themselves create the perfect move, and then implement it. Holly Flanders, the downhill ski racer, was so proficient with her visualization practice that she actually saw herself doing some very bizarre things with her imagery. Olympic champion Steve Mahre and superstar Marilyn King both had access to their own private visual screens. Willie Davenport, a five-time Olympian and achiever had a unique approach to imagery and healing as he came back from a career-ending injury.

I knew from previous work and research on track and field athletes that nearly everyone practiced imagery and visualization, but I didn't know about individual styles. Dr. Jackie Golding and I, in our first book *Beyond Strength*, attempted to define and quantify this mental practice strategy. And in so doing we found that many athletes do a certain amount of imagery in preparation for the day of their workouts. In fact, one gold medalist noted: "The night before competition, I also do imagery and visualization practice so that I can get into the rhythm previously established during my workouts." The following athlete achievers in this chapter offered even deeper insights about their unique practice and implementation of imagery and visualization skills, both on and off the playing field. We begin with Holly Flanders.

Holly Flanders took skiing seriously. She trained hard, was diligent about her workouts, both on and off the snow, and she practiced mentally. She said one of her coaches, Warren Witherell, was influential in focusing her on imagery as well as other training strategies in downhill ski racing. In studying her techniques, the core lesson she learned was that the journey of training was just as important as the competition and the end results. "What is important is not where you end up, but in the journey to arrive there." Holly often speaks to youngsters about the process of training, and she reminds them that it is a process, on and off the course. "You need to enjoy every day of your training, even though you are striving to get up to a higher level. Part of that training (and enjoyment) is seeing yourself in the best possible position and form, using mental practice to get you tuned up before you hit the slopes." Holly is self-assured, she had great coaches, and she attributes much of her success to her ability to rehearse mentally.

Flanders is a student of sport and achievement. Mental preparation is not something she picked up listening to a coach's pep talk or by flipping pages in a health magazine. She is a student and one who takes her lessons seriously. Holly has read the journals, the technical material, and she knows the jargon. She once read that mental practice is the repetition of a task without observable movement. Imagery is considered a very deep, focused, type of mental practice, often using all of the senses in order to create an experience in the mind. Some athletes are able to imitate the actions of others because their minds "take a picture" of the activity that they use as a model for their performance. Essentially, imagery is the process of receiving information through all senses from the external environment. However, we can also generate information from our own memory, such that we are creating our own internal environment or images.

Thus the interface of these two environments—both the imagined and the real-life ones—have a powerful effect on our nervous system. When Holly Flanders talks, this author pays attention!

In the case of skiers, gymnasts, and other very visual athletes, the imagery process may be conceptualized by thinking about our home video players. Our brain acts as its own unique VCR unit, scanning for images and sensory input before they are collected and shuttled onto the picture screen. Unlike the VCR hardware from the discount store, our internal equipment, when trained and used properly, will recall visual, auditory, kinesthetic, and an assortment of other images with ease.

Flanders says that these images and this type of training carry over to everyday stressors in life. "The discipline of racing gave me certain skills that I can now implement into other arenas of my life. I can handle a lot more stress than had I not been in competitive experiences. For example, when I was racing in my early and late twenties, I was a downhiller, and that's the event where you reach eighty to ninety miles an hour, so there is a lot of fear involved. If you're really committed, you're willing to risk a lot for your goals. Fear and the statements one makes to counter fear is very important. You must know that everyone who races (downhill) is afraid and often scared out of their wits. We all know the risks: you can buy the farm at any point; you are constantly risking your body and your life. But in order to survive in this sport you have to maintain your mental focus."

Imagery and visualization training is not optional in this business, it is mandatory training for skiers like Holly Flanders. She has to control all of the thoughts and mental pictures cruising around in her mind, so that she can have a safe, successful run, not to mention the best time in the world. Flanders feels that every skier can have an effect on whether they are going to get hurt or not, based on the amount of mental rehearsal they perform—daily!

One of the great things about building confidence in the sport of ski racing is that one can improve their mental abilities as they improve their racing strengths. "I can ski eighty miles an hour and run into a difficult situation, be off-balance and heading for the trees. And I can call up the proper imagery along with the correct muscles, and literally pull myself back up so that I don't get hurt. This power is inspiring for me, to know that I am able to perfect my skills to such a high level. Likewise, injuries are often brought on if I allow myself to get down psychologically. When something is off-balance emotionally, my skiing is shitty and I am in big trouble."

Holly explained a bit more of her theory about the relationship of imbalance and unfocused training to injury proneness. "Unless you are really strong psychologically and really committed to staying healthy, you can get injured so easily in ski racing, because your reaction time in an injury-causing situation is not something that you can think about and react to. It is something that is already trained inside of you. It is already a part of your muscle memory. You have to work on it psychologically and emotionally. In ski racing, it's very important to visualize everything! We use visualization every moment of our training and, if you incorporate the wrong mental pictures, SPLAT... you hit the wall, you are toast, and blood flies everywhere. You have to practice your ski runs physically and practice those same runs just as hard visually. Often when you have a bad run, you just back up the tape (in your mind's eye) and do it again, so that you don't crash all over the slopes! Your mind can play tricks on you, and it is important that you rewind and run that section through again, so you make it perfectly."

Holly Flanders knows fear and anxiety. She has spent most of her youth dealing with it, trying to make peace with it. "You must deal with real fear in this sport or you get into some hot water. And big trouble means big-time injury and pain. Skiers often get caught up in the negative replays; many racers, in fact, imagine themselves in a million broken pieces." Flanders says that part of her imagery and visualization process is to not glorify oneself in a bad fall. She says that often when we take a bad fall we conjure up images from our childhood when we were sick or injured, where we were getting lots of attention and secondary gains. "Often I get stuck on that unconsciously, where I fall and want lots of sympathy."

After the 1980 Olympics, Flanders had severe psychological problems. She wasn't ready for the notoriety that she received. She did not imagine the attention and the limelight and often she thought that people were watching her and other downhill racers so that they could see them crash and burn. "I was at a real psychological impasse there. I went to see a shrink and worked on these negative images using audiotapes. I eventually identified the problem and reframed the thoughts and then removed the negative pictures from my mental rehearsal screen. I had this one image of myself falling, getting injured or even killed, and people really enjoying it. It affected me in a serious way."

Holly has seen and confronted her demons! She knows that this is part of her death wish, a scenario that many athletes in risk-taking sports have to come to terms with. Her crowd-pleaser crash-and-burn scene was part of her own projection. At one point in her life she didn't want a crazy life of zipping down a mountain at two-hundred miles per hour. Fantasies of death and destruction are an easy way out. Flanders has always been shy, and her life script did not include events that might get her to the Olympic games. "I didn't realize the power of my own achievement, that if I excelled at this sport, I would achieve notoriety. I just couldn't handle the fame, especially inside this very private person. It interested me to excel and deep down I wanted to be the best I could, but my internal conflict was that I didn't really think I could succeed as an athlete."

Her internal paradigm was twisted. She didn't expect much from her skiing, it was more fun and games, thrills and occasional spills. Suddenly, her stature as an Olympic-achieving athlete began to take shape. Part of her acceptance of this fame and fortune was to take responsibility for the potential for serious injuries. "Some skiers actually thrive on the thrill of being close to injury and possible death. I was trying to cope with that notion and learn to thrive on the ability to have self-confidence in my skiing and stay free of injuries. I had one ski season where I didn't fall once. Not while racing, not while free skiing, not while training—not ever. The reason I didn't fall that season was because I had heard that the great German skier, Klaus Vllamer, didn't fall once during his best season. He was one of my mentors, so I decided to build my confidence and my imagery around him, being injury free and staying healthy. It was the best ski season of my life; I won everything."

Holly Flanders has seen and confronted her demons. Today, she is feeling very good about herself!

Steven Mahre is another great winter athlete. His credentials are impeccable on and off the slopes. His most vivid images of successful ski racing took him to a place in Germany, to a tough downhill course he had to conquer. "I remember I was in the German Alps at the starting gate, and there was one spot on the ski course I was unfamiliar with. I didn't feel confident about it and it wasn't feeling right. I went down the course and fell right in the place I had been thinking about. It's as if I had locked into a negative image on that one turn. I just couldn't seem to undo that program in my mind. And once I fell I was fine. It was now out of my system, off the picture screen. Now I was ready to race again. I just had to remove and erase that bad visual image."

Mahre says that the trick to good skiing, as a racer or a weekend recreational athlete, is to not talk yourself into a fall or a crash. Often you see a spot that might look bad from the chairlift and you start visualizing catastrophic events. Mahre reminds us that you can't have any negative thoughts right from the start. "Negative thoughts often lead to apprehension, which leads to a muscle and tendon tightening. And then boom! Chances are likely that you're going to screw up and get yourself hurt." Mahre says that the trick is to conduct self-talk and say such things as, "No, I'm not going to fall and I'm going to be solid on that turn or on that icy patch. You have to maintain that positive attitude. As soon as you start backing off of any turn, any slope, you are inevitably going to screw up."

As a champion Olympic racer, Mahre notes that aggressiveness is important or you tend to lose your focus. "You've got to take those chances, which is all about being on the edge, if not over the edge. You find that line for yourself and then that's where you push yourself to. You're right on the threshold and, as time goes by, that threshold gets higher and higher and higher with better training."

Mahre does an enormous amount of imagery work and visualization training. He constantly trains his mind to pick up on visual cues so that he can do effective imagery when it is race time. He inspects all his courses before any race and then runs through it in his mind fifteen to twenty times before he even gets to the starting gates. In a slalom race he goes from the bottom to the top of the mountain, often stopping at specific gates to get a good mental picture of the slope and the individual turns. "I hike up five gates and then run through those five gates in my mind. Then I hike another eight, and then run through those gates mentally, and then hike seven more and so on. I always memorize where it gets steeper, where it's flatter, where the combinations are, and what the snow conditions are. I always look at whether the gates are on a roll or are back from that roll so I can anticipate where I might lose some pressure with the ski. With skiing it's a visual recall phenomenon. And that recall of images triggers the feeling part so that you can put weight and pressure on your skis at the gate, at just the right moment."

Steve Mahre watches other athletes. He typically watches the first five or six guys and then he doesn't watch anybody until the guy right before him. He does make a point of always watching his brother Phil. "I ski enough like Phil that if he had a good run, by God, I was going to have one too. He is always a positive influence for me—to see him go and nail his ski runs right on target. If he did that, then I would always have this positive image that I would nail my stuff as well!"

And what if your twin brother had a lousy run? I wasn't sure the word lousy was in his vocabulary, since the Mahre brothers have more medals and trophies than any family on the planet. In classic Mahre, he explained that if his brother screwed up, then it was up to him to keep it in the family. "I had to keep it together for him, for me, for all of us. It's a case of the family honor being on the line."

The Mahre brothers have a unique way of working, competing, and achieving success off of each other in a positive, mentally rehearsed, and supportive way. They did it in their childhood, they did it in the Olympics, and they continue to visualize new horizons when teaching youngsters at their ski school.

Marilyn King grew up in New York but moved to California to find her fame and fortune as an elite athlete achiever. She has a huge repertoire of skills, from her days as an Olympic pentathlete, that she carries regularly into the Oakland schools.

Marilyn King spent years perfecting her high level of mental practice expertise. She knew she would need it to make the 1972, 1976, and 1980 Olympic teams, but deep in her heart she knew there was a more profound reason to learn those skills. King works with troubled youth from dysfunctional families in the Oakland, California, public schools. From the moment she walks in the door of each classroom, she challenges her students and dares them to imagine that they can perform better. Her program is called precisely that, "Dare To Imagine!" She invites youngsters from tough, disadvantaged, and often abusive families to go beyond their dreams and actualize their goals through daily imagery process. Marilyn uses her experience as a former track and field star to enhance the quality of life for some of her future stars, those who haven't seen the light yet.

In order for her students to visualize their success in life, King shares with them some of her history, struggles, and traumas. Her story of how she got to where she is today is quite remarkable and she uses it as a springboard to guide less fortunate youngsters in the inner city. Marilyn King's saga was chronicled in the book *Dare to Imagine*, by J.S. Whisler and R.J. Marzano. It had all the makings of a Hollywood made-for-T.V. miniseries. That, however, is the farthest thing from King's mind!

King was always clear about her future. She always had a sense that there was something important for her to do, but she wasn't quite sure what that was. "I was considered only slightly above average as an athlete, but I decided to go out for track anyway. I met older girls who traveled to national championships, and I thought they were amazing and wished that someday I could be like them—but I really didn't think that was possible.

"I enjoyed track and field and working out with a team. As I got deeper into the sport I realized that I was not a star, but I dreamed about someday traveling to a national championship and, perhaps, running on a relay team. That year the Eastern States Pentathlon Championships were held at the same time as one of our regular competitions. The pentathlon has five events—hurdles, shot-put, high jump, long jump and the 200-meter sprint. Only two athletes showed up; three are needed to have an official competition. So I volunteered to compete even though I had never even tried two of the five events. I came in third." As her story unwinds, some of Marilyn's kids show interest. After all, most of them have never won anything.

King's story continues and becomes more intriguing. "I decided to get serious and train for the championship the following year. I trained hard that year and it paid off—I won! Next I went to the nationals. There I placed in the top ten for the entire United States! Then something happened that changed the rest of my life. I went to a meeting where they were going to announce which athletes were invited to the Olympic training camp for the 1968 Olympic Games in Mexico City. I knew I was not being considered. That was okay until they invited two girls I had beaten in competition. Not only had I beaten them, but I knew that I was a better athlete." Marilyn was pissed!

At her next workout Marilyn King thought seriously of becoming an Olympian. All of a sudden it didn't seem so unbelievable. "It actually seemed like there was a slight possibility that I could go to the Olympics. I kept saying this to myself. As I jogged around the track I would repeat, I could go to the Olympics." Marilyn now has her students' full attention. This is when she lights the fire and lets her kids know that anyone can build self-confidence by using positive thoughts and statements. This is where she takes the chalk out and starts scratching the board with funny pictures about voices and restructuring our inner thoughts with the desire to compete and win. It sounds a bit unusual and the kids giggle. But they are listening.

King has this "deep into her soul" belief that by aligning passion, vision, and action, all kids can reach their potential. This impact is everywhere from the educational arena, to the athletic venue, and even into the big, confused, challenging world of inner-city Oakland, California.

She tells her pupils about her quest for the 1972 Olympics. "I built my life around my Olympic quest. I had one particular image, one vision that sustained me. I pictured myself walking into the Olympic stadium in Munich, Germany, wearing the United States uniform I had admired since I was in junior high. On days that it was cold and rainy and I was tempted to crawl back under the covers, I would lie back in bed, close my eyes for a moment and envision myself at the opening ceremonies as a U.S. Olympian. After just a moment with that image, I would be excited again. I would pop out of bed and dress warmly for my morning run, happy to be training for the Olympics."

More pictures, more images, more scratch sounds on the blackboard. Marilyn's hard work paid off. "I made the Olympic team by one-tenth of a second and qualified for the third and last pentathlon spot. But I didn't get quite what I expected. Yes, I did get to march in the opening ceremonies as I had envisioned, but my left ankle was heavily bandaged. You see, I chipped a bone while practicing long jumps in the Olympic stadium. My injury was severe enough that I was unable to compete in the Games. What I had imagined on all those cold mornings, however, had come true: I was on the team and I did march in the opening ceremonies."

Now the kicker, a pivotal point in Marilyn's history lesson. She lets her kids in on a big secret about disappointment, loss, and letting go. Not everything in life works perfectly and we have to expect the unexpected and bounce back from our losses. She continues with a healthy dose of reality, as she stares into some disappointed faces. She lets her kids look into that deep hole of despair and imagine the worst, when expectations are shot and we feel rejected. Her kids have been there before, she's up to the challenge.

"The disappointment forced me to re-examine why I had wanted to be an Olympian in the first place. I soon realized that what truly mattered to me was to push the upper limits of my ability and find out how good I could be. I wanted to be the best I could be and test myself against the best in the world. I vowed to do that at the next Olympic Games. I threw myself into training for the 1976 Olympics in Montreal. I was more determined than ever. I trained daily and kept the vision of competing in the Olympics in the forefront of my mind.

"Again, my hard work paid off. I placed thirteenth in the pentathlon in Montreal. I was proud but knew I could do even better. While competing in Montreal, I had watched the highly trained Russian and East German athletes. They performed at a whole different level. Their training and scientific approach to the pentathlon were obvious. If I had the opportunity to train like the East Germans, I was sure I could be in the running for a medal. I took a year's leave of absence before Moscow, the 1980 games."

All went according to plans for Marilyn King until nine months before the Olympic trials. In November 1979 she was ready and on schedule for the Olympics, but the universe wasn't ready for her. "I was in a terrible automobile accident and injured a disc in my back. During my long rehab period I was forced to lay on my couch month after month unable to get up, to shift positions or turn over. For four months I was in pain from the back of my neck down to my heels. What about all my plans and dreams? Had I come this far to end my career this way? No. I was determined to continue my Olympic quest. So I started training from my bed. I got films of the world-record holders in each of my five events. Every day, in my one-bedroom apartment, I propped myself up, and, when the pain subsided, I looked at those films. Day after day, over and over again, I watched them flicker on the wall—at normal speed, slow motion and frame by frame. And, when I had enough, I lay back and mentally rehearsed what I had seen, going through each event, step by step in my mind. I told my muscles what they should be doing and sent them the signals they'd need later.

"When I could finally walk, I went to the track. I couldn't jog yet, but I set up the hurdles and imagined myself going through each part of my training program, one step at a time, all in my mind. Then one day I jogged a little; the next day a little more. Later I ran. Then I jumped the first hurdle, every day pushing to do just a little more. During that entire time I had one desire: Never in the history of the Olympics had there been a three-time Olympian in my event. I would be the first. And, what's more, I would do it against all odds, against all reason. In spite of my injury, somehow I would be one of the top three at the Olympic trials. I would make the team!"

King competed in the Olympic qualifying meet and took second place at the Olympic trials. "I won't say what I did is impossible, because I did it. But anyone who knows what it takes to train for a pentathlon—the sheer, overwhelming physical effort—knows that it's unlikely to be done from where I had been just months before—on my bed, unable to move. For me, capturing second place at the Olympic trials was probably the greatest achievement of my life. It was way beyond what I was physically capable of, beyond what was possible given my injuries and lack of physical preparation."

King has made her points. None of her kids are falling asleep, they are alive, animated, and a few are moved to tears. King is softer now, not as intense, and she feels the energy of the classroom. She senses the emotion, the pain, the trauma that these kids experience daily, the uncertainty that awaits them at home each afternoon. Marilyn challenges this uncertainty and adversity and takes her kids on a new journey. She gets them to that other place in their mind's eye, to a new visual, a new movie set, where they can take control of their lives. She gives them the goods, the recipe for empowerment. She dares them to imagine a new life that can cope with fear and anxiety. She dares them to imagine a new day of higher expectations for themselves and a reshaping of their goals for a healthier life.

Major Willie D. Davenport has a different take on mental practice, a different focus for his imagery in life. Davenport was only the second American ever to compete in both the summer and winter Olympic games. Eddie Heakins, a boxer and a bobsledder, beat him to it in 1932. Davenport is, however, the first African-American with that distinction.

Although a great 110-meter hurdler, Davenport was coaxed, cajoled, and harassed into becoming a bobsledder. He even had to overcome his fear of speed and heights. "I never went to the amusement park; I was deathly afraid of rollercoasters. So how they got me on that bobsled course is beyond belief."

Davenport does not talk about victories or medals or the fact that he is a five-time Olympian. He talks in terms of competitors and images of an event. Even today, many years later, he speaks as if the race took place yesterday. He is great at calling and visualizing the race. His voice gets animated when he goes into his personal memory bank. "Charles Foster's coming out of the blocks quite good today, better than he's been doing, so I know that he's practiced his form and technique all week. His form over the hurdles is excellent. He is approaching the hurdles properly and his balance is good. If he hits the hurdle, I always know why. Normally, these guys in my race will do what I expect them to do. For example, Guy Drut patterned himself after me, so I know what he's going to do and when he's going to do it. Charles Foster runs a consistent race and that's his strong point. If he comes out of the blocks at eighty-five, he's going to keep it at eighty-five all the way. Leon Coleman was another one that I used to watch. He never won, but he was always there as a burr in your saddle, always irritating you."

Davenport is a race encyclopedia for the 110 hurdles in nearly every major competition in the past twenty years. He doesn't just report the facts and the data, he gives vivid detail and lucid recall of each event, each competitor. "I guess the best example that I could give you is that you get a guy like Earl McCullough and he could not run in traffic. If Earl McCullough was next to me or in the middle of the pack, he was in trouble. If you put him in lane seven, you had a race on your hands. In the 1976 Olympics Guy Drut was running like a computer. I think he was in lane one. James Owens was in lane two. Owens hit the first three hurdles beautifully. Drut accelerated off that last hurdle, because that's what he did best and knew how to do. Casanas, the Cuban, was on the outside, so Drut really didn't see him and really didn't pay that much attention to his races coming off the last hurdle. I could out lean all of these guys over the last hurdle, so as long as I knew their position on the track, everything was in sync."

With Davenport, it's like "Wide World of Sports" revisited. His pictures during a dialogue are that clear and riveting. His visualization work is so strong that even today each race is part of a permanent imprint. "When I got in the starting blocks, the first thing I put in my mind was the image of the perfect race. You have to visualize the perfect race. Like a thrower, you visualize the perfect throw and then everything else just clicks. The one race that I ever ran that I thought was perfect was in the 1968 Olympics. Of course, I won that baby! When I came out of the blocks, I swear to God, that was the only race I ever ran in my life that I knew I had won from the start. When my lead leg left the starting block, before it touched the ground, I knew I had won that gold medal. When the starter yelled set, I didn't hear him. I saw the others come out and get set, I did the same, and when that gun went off, I hit that first hurdle perfectly, and from then on I had it in the bag. It was cruise control. I hit the eighth hurdle and that race was mine. I just coasted in and the rest was history." With Davenport, it's not boasting, it's clear and factual!

Davenport defies the laws of running and competitive racing. He does something that is considered an absolute no-no! He watches everybody in his race. He watches them start, hit their stride and go for the hurdles. "I see somebody in back of me. I don't know how, but I can visualize these people and where they are. If I'm out in front of them, I can still see them. I tried to explain this phenomenon of my 360-degree viewpoint to somebody and they thought I was a nut case. The only thing that I believe is analogous to my full race vision is to a famous guy on the basketball court. If you watch highlights of the NBA and the magic of Earvin Johnson, you can see what I am saying. Magic is going right to the center of the court and he just throws the ball, a no-look pass, and never sneaks a peak at the guy. It just goes right over his shoulder, back to somebody else, and they slam dunk it. Now, how in the hell did Magic Johnson see that guy? I don't know. That's what I see. I see all the hurdlers on the track, and I can envision the complete scene. I'm sure that Magic would tell you the same thing."

Not everything in Davenport's life is smooth sailing or should I say clear vision. He has had his ups and downs and very serious injuries, in between all of this great high achiever success. He does keep a clear perspective and a positive attitude throughout. It was 1975 and the scene was The Athletics Congress championships. Davenport tore a patellar tendon and had to be taken to the hospital. Dr. Stan James, a renowned orthopedic surgeon, told him it was time to hang up the spikes, that his running career was over.

During a prolonged hospital stay due to a secondary infection including phlebitis, Davenport made the best of it. "I had all these friends coming to see me, including my buddy Kenny Moore, who kept sneaking smoked salmon and imported beer into my room daily. Then one day I was spaced out from the pain medication and I awoke in a stupor to find some buddies just hanging out in my room. I looked up, gazed out at the flowers all over my room, and I see Ollan Casell and Stan Wright and some of my buddies talking... and I thought I was lying in a casket there, having a bad dream, the ultimate bad dream. I jumped out of my stupor, hurt my knee in the process, and we all laughed as I told them my bad dream. They reminded me that I was still living and that if I had died, they would all have been long gone!"

Davenport spent more time in the hospital than he'd like to remember. He also started to get bummed out. His doctors told him that he would never be able to run again, certainly never be able to race. He certainly never expected to be an Olympic high achiever again. The patellar tendon was broken and to save it they had to cut a piece of it off, and then drill holes in the knee cap so it would grow back again. Davenport is not one to take no for an answer. No is not in his vocabulary! Faith, hope, optimism, and imagery are!

"From day one I did isometrics. I just kind of squeezed the muscles, flexed them, and began to imagine myself back on the track. That's what I did with my leg in the cast, all day, every day. And while my cast was on my leg for the entire six weeks, I'm sitting there watching television, or reading, and I'm flexing the muscles and visualizing the strength coming back!"

The day after he got his cast off, Davenport started to walk, all over the house. Within days he started jogging, at a fourteen- or fifteen-minute per-mile pace. Each time he got up to walk he kept imagining himself going through the motions that would eventually get him back to the track. "And when I started going to the track, I would jog through the straight-a-way and walk the curve, jog the straight-a-way, walk the curve. And I started picking it up, doing a little speed work, and then going into a full-blown comeback."

His tendon blew out in June, and by September he was competing again. The wise sages of the orthopedic world, stumped again! He attributes a big chunk of his recovery to a competent physician, but a bigger chunk of the attribution goes to his mind, his will, and his discipline for imagery practice. "When I first went over the hurdles in late September, I really wasn't pushing it. I trained twice a week for the winter indoor season, and after that is when I started cooking, almost seven months after my surgery."

Davenport still had pain, but he also had a greater desire to compete and he desperately wanted to make the 1976 Olympic team. He would set up his hurdles and train when no one was around. "No pain, no gain" was his motto before it was fashionable, before it made the t-shirt logos. He was in pain and he didn't want anybody to see it, so he trained privately. "The pain was so bad that hair on my head would stand up!"

Davenport's story is now documented and is part of Olympic history. He did make a successful comeback and has secured a place in Olympic folklore, a five-time Olympian, even with a life threatening, career ending injury. The best part of his comeback, however, was never really told. His mission was to get out of the hospital and get his leg well so he could be in the next Olympics.

His real moment of glory came just a few months before the Olympic trials when he got a long-distance phone call from his surgeon. "Dr. James called me and said, 'Willie, there was a misprint in *The New York Times* today. It says you ran in the Melrose Games in New York City this week.' I told him it wasn't a misprint, it was correct. He asked me if I was pulling his leg. I said no, I was healed and in great competitive shape. There was a long pause on the other end of the line. I think the doc fainted. He just couldn't believe I had come back to competitive racing."

Whether you are a weekend warrior, recreational athlete, or have secured a place in history as a five-time Olympic repeater, the mental practice game is an important one. The use of imagery and visualization skills is no longer considered counter-culture among those who take their sport seriously. Mental practice for any sport is a useful and constructive tool for preparation and enhancement of any skill. The use of these techniques is now being implemented in elementary schools (as both of my daughters will confirm) so that our future athlete achievers are up and running when they hit the big leagues! And as Marilyn King reminds us, imagery work

can be used to challenge us at all levels of development
so that we might go beyond our wildest dreams.

CHAPTER 7

IN SEARCH OF THE PERFECT MENTOR

*"The mentor relationship is a delicate one and one that
evolves over time. Each of my mentors was right for my
development, both emotionally and athletically. It is so
important to have a trusting relationship with someone
who fits that developmental time frame. Often we grow
up and the chemistry is no longer there between coach
and student. So I was very fortunate to have the influence
of three great human beings, three great mentors from
distinct backgrounds and cultures.*

Tim Daggett
1984 Olympian
Gold Medalist, Gymnastics

Athlete achievers Bob Beamon, Harvey Glance, Tim
Daggett, and Bill Toomey all have important messages about
the role of the mentor, in particular their mentors. I wanted
to know from all four of these great achievers, some of
whom are presently coaching, what the essence of mentoring
is and how mentors, past and present, affected their lives.
In the following pages, each one of these achievers offers a
sense of their mentor, their trusted counselor. All of these
champions had different needs, different wants, and strong
opinions about their relationships to a particular mentor.
We begin with Bob Beamon.

Born in 1946 and growing up in a severely dysfunctional
family in the projects of Queens, New York, Beamon looked
to his mentor as the one person who saved his life. Larry
Ellis was the guiding light for Bob Beamon. Ellis, who
coached Beamon in high school, went on to become the
track and field coach at Princeton and then head Olympic
coach for the 1984 Olympics.

Beamon is a quiet man. He gets even more soft-spoken
when he reflects on the history he had with Ellis. It is a
powerful history! "He made me realize that there was more
to life than crime. He made me realize that all I needed to
do was concentrate on a couple of positives in life and work

with them and I would be able to reap the benefits of those attributes. And it definitely happened. The benefits to sticking with positive things in my life led to some great achievements."

For the past ten years Beamon has worked as a counselor and role model for troubled inner city youth in Florida. For Beamon, life today has much more meaning. It is not a life that just struggles and copes with the addiction of crime. While growing up in the projects in Queens, Beamon was moving toward becoming a statistic in the community. He could have been one of the many stories that come to a sad halt from drugs, crime, or even murder. "I was heading in that direction, so I knew I must make some positive decisions in my life. Growing up disadvantaged, I was forced to move quicker in life and have values that were different than those from middle class families. I had to grow up a little faster and think about some of these things that were out there and could prove fatal to me."

Bob noted that long before he even engaged in athletic achievements, he had to start feeling good about himself. He had to find that inner strength, self esteem, and a secure place away from the subculture of street gangs. "I went to the edge a couple of times and then I found some self-confidence which led me to a path of healing."

Larry Ellis, his coach and mentor for life, taught him that sport has nothing to do with a guy who lacks a job and is staring at despair and no hope in his family. "When you have a mother who is unemployed and she is out there in the streets selling her body to get some crack and the kid takes on a job of being the lookout person for the drug man, then there is little future. When the drug man gives him a certain amount of money so he can give it to his mother, so she can get high, then the future looks pretty dim. It's a hard, hard way to grow up. I don't think that some children know any better. They only see and copy what other people are doing."

Beamon explains how Ellis helped him break the cycle of despair in his own family environment. "When you have a Larry Ellis who comes into your life and says, 'Let's take that energy, that high-powered paranoid energy, or the high-powered hyperactive energy, and we're going to go over to Central Park and race around the water reservoir,' then things begin to happen. The scenery changes and lights get brighter.

Larry Ellis was a caring human being, and that's all it takes. If you care about someone and check in to where they are going, then you have it made. Ellis had a tremendous insight and knew that I needed special attention. He was tuned in to me. Coaches can play the role of parents when they're not around, and Larry Ellis played many roles for me."

Beamon today is an important mentor and role model for thousands of kids stuck in that same cycle of despair. He provides an important balance for those who are caught in a cycle of family violence and dysfunction. He knows about pain, he knows about taking the wrong turn, and he knows that he went right to the edge.

Today, Beamon attributes his success as a top achiever both in sport and in life to his mentor, Larry Ellis. He is clear that without the guiding hand and firm convictions of Ellis' good judgment, he would be just another crime statistic. Today Beamon is proud of his achiever statistic, especially the one that has been on the books for many years. In 1968, Beamon captured a gold medal in the long jump, shattering the world record by almost two feet to achieve a distance of twenty-nine feet, two-and-a-half inches. Beamon's record lasted twenty-three years and is widely considered one of the greatest achievements in modern Olympic history. "Again, if Larry was not in my life, that number would have had a different meaning."

Beamon doesn't like to talk about his other statistics. He doesn't like to talk about his educational pursuits, including attending the University of Texas at El Paso and Adelphi University, earning bachelor's degrees in sociology and anthropology. He would rather give credit to Larry Ellis. He also doesn't like to talk about his autobiography, *The Perfect Jump*. He would rather talk about the special relationship that he had with his mentor, one which gives youngsters a model to strive for. When he works in the inner city with youth at risk and youth on the edge, he rarely tells them that he won the prestigious Sullivan Award or became a charter member of the United States Olympic Committee Hall of Fame.

He prefers to talk about his mentor, Larry Ellis!

Three-time Olympic sprinter Harvey Glance is passionate about the concept of the mentor. In fact, he is absolutely passionate about *his* mentor. Glance has deep respect for the role that Mel Rosen played in his life. Rosen, the 1992 Olympic coach and former track and field chief at Auburn University for thirty-two years, is one of the greats. "He is undoubtedly the guy that I have always admired as a coach and as a mentor. He means a lot to me because I've learned a lot from him. He taught me the ability to relate to people and I think that is a key issue in any mentor relationship. He is a free-spirited man, but I knew that his door was always open. Mel is a people person, and when you are coaching Olympians you have to be able to communicate with your athletes on all levels. I think I acquired many of his unique qualities and hopefully I've learned how to apply them with my position as his successor at Auburn. Rosen has accomplished great things in his career and that's my main goal right now. If I can just accomplish half the things that Coach Rosen accomplished as a coach, I will consider myself successful."

Harvey spoke specifically about two lessons that may have been pivotal in his athletic career. He chose to describe a time, a place, an event, that is now part of his mental imprint. It is one that reflects how his mentor got involved in his psychological and emotional process. Rosen once told Glance that he was too nice of a guy to be a winner. During competition coach Rosen would chastise then-athlete Glance for signing autographs all the way to the starting blocks of his race. Glance usually would defend this practice by saying he would never, ever, refuse to sign an autograph for anybody. Rosen would say that he was simply amazed that he had the ability to just focus on a race and at the same moment act as a celebrity.

Although sensitive about this issue, Glance said that this reminder from coach Rosen did teach him an important lesson. His lesson was that sometimes those kinds of external pressures do distract you, and give a subtle advantage to those people who are your competitors. Rosen used to stress absolute focus well before a race and urge Glance to learn and incorporate that process into his training. Glance also learned that even though he never felt distracted as an athlete, he finally understood that his coach and mentor was feeling distracted. "Even though it didn't affect my performance, it affected him as a coach because he felt that my competition was getting an advantage over one of his athletes. It also upset the delicate balance that exists between coach, mentor, and athlete."

Glance says that this example was an important revelation for him. The second lesson was about goal setting. "For years and years and years we have gone to the track every day and have worked hard and dedicated ourselves to a commitment for training and excellence. I say *ourselves* because we both knew what the goals were. My goals were his goals and he was there to try to help me reach them. We put countless hours of training in on the track every day, and that involved much blood, sweat, and tears. And each time we trained, his favorite comment was, 'I expect you to win every race and I don't expect to be there when you do, but when you expect to see me is when you lose the races.' And that is the one thing I remember about him the most. Rosen was never really there to share in all the triumphs that I had. But if there was a period when I was down or I finished fifth in a race and I wanted to make a relay team, he was always there and he was there because he wanted to boost me up. He was there at the critical times and said certain things like, 'You can make it, big guy. Come on, you can do it.'"

Glance recalls that at small races and at the big ones, Mel Rosen, his mentor, was always there for him and knew what to look for. "Once at the Olympic trials when I was getting ready for the finals and I wasn't looking very sharp and I had my head drooping down, Coach Rosen walked over to me. I looked up at him and knew at that very moment that his strength was there. That *is* a special moment when your coach is there as a teacher, as well as being present as a real mentor."

One great quality of mentors is their willingness to step out of the limelight, and recede into the background at the winner's podium. "Rosen always knew when I wasn't finely tuned. He had that sixth, intuitive, sense about me. He was always there to help me pick up my head so that I could be proud and achieve my goals. Rosen had that insight, that emotional antenna to assist his athletes. He was always sensitive to my moments of disappointment and he provided me with that shot of self-esteem, that lift, at the critical moments in my career. That is the subtle difference between a coach and a mentor. That is the quality that I hope I inherited and I try to bring to my own athletes today."

There is a fine line between the coach and mentor. The coach might put in the hours and get the guys pumped up. It is the mentor that goes beyond punching the clock and takes a deep personal interest in his or her athletes. It is having that intuitive sense about a kid who is struggling. Rosen would tell Glance, "I expect you to do well. It's when you don't do well is when to expect to see me." According to Glance this is the diagnostic period. This is when the therapist comes in to try and diagnose and understand the dynamics of a situation or a problem. "He was always trying to find the answers to why I didn't do well. It made a lot of sense to me and it wasn't about ego gratification or trying to get publicity as a coach. He was just more in the background trying to understand the dynamics of his individuals and trying to understand the chemistry of his team."

Gold medal gymnast Tim Daggett had more than one mentor, a troika of important teachers, in his life. He explains that he had three primary coaches throughout his career and each was extremely important. Bill Jones was his high school coach and he started Daggett on his quest for elite level athletics. He was the man who found a place for Tim to work out at in the off season. Tim told me that Jones was the most dedicated coach he had ever known in the sport. When Daggett went to UCLA, he met a man named Makato Sakamoto who became his second mentor. "He was one of the most remarkable men I've ever met. He taught me a lot about life and laid the foundation for me in my career goals. He told me that training is going to be hard. You don't hear that reality check from too many people nowadays. He would stress the point that if you want to be the best gymnast in the world, you have to work harder than everyone, and experience a lot of sacrifice. Everyone is a lot of people!"

In the true eastern philosophical tradition, Sakamoto

challenged Daggett to objectively look at his career goals. He asked each athlete to take off the rose-colored glasses and write down all their short- and long-term goals and keep asking the question, do I still want to do this?

His third mentor, Yefim Furman, came to UCLA from Kiev, in the former Soviet Union. Prior to 1979 he was one of the top Soviet gymnasts. Daggett explained that Yefim was a little bit of everybody rolled up together. "He came from a very different system, politically, economically, and gymnastically. He came from the Soviet system. He looked at technique in a very different way. He's a good friend and he coached me for the last four years of my career when I was much older and, I would like to think, more mature."

Daggett explains that the mentor relationship is a delicate one-and-one that evolves over time. He notes that each of his mentors was right for his period of development, both emotionally and athletically. He explains that as one matures as an athlete and develops a new level of confidence, it is important to have a trusting relationship with someone who fits that developmental time frame. "Often we grow up and the chemistry is no longer there between coach and student. And so I was fortunate to have the influence of three great human beings, three great coaches, with distinct backgrounds and cultures. I had the influence of an African American in Jones, an Asian in Sakamoto, and of course, Furman, a Soviet."

Daggett was not only blessed with having the combined chemistry of three fine coaches as his mentors, but generational longevity as well. "The eastern Europeans, former eastern Europeans, and Asians have a constant knowledge base that is always growing. You have a culture that breeds athletes and coaches over many generations so that when athletes retire, it is part of their cultural expectation that they move to the profession of coaching and nurture the next generation along. It is an unselfish system, something we Americans have a lot to learn about. It's a data base of experience that you just don't put on paper. It lies in the unconscious learning of many generations of athletes and their mentors. Indeed, I was lucky to be exposed to this phenomenon."

Bill Toomey, known in 1968 as the world's greatest athlete because of his gold medal success in the Mexico City Olympic decathlon, attributes his winning and success to two important people. His coach at Worcestor Academy, Dee Rowe, was more than just a coach, he was an important role model and mentor for Bill. He was Toomey's very first coach and had an important impact on him throughout high school. Bill subsequently reconnected with Rowe after many years of just living with the memories of his fine mentorship qualities. "He's a guy that continues to do great things for people. It was over thirty-five years ago that I graduated high school, and he was my coach and he was unbelievable. He was a terrific mentor then, and continues to be there for young folks today."

Toomey explains his special relationship with Rowe and the coaching profession in general. He told me that coaches have a longer period and a more consistent exposure to youngsters than any other adult. "Coaches are usually people with a passion. And when you combine passion, interest, activity, adventure and humanity, you have all the rich dimensions of a fine mentor. And when you have a coach that follows that passion with his athletes, then you have a special situation that offers a kid a terrific role model for achievement!"

There's something special that goes on between a coach and an athlete that probably could never go on between parents and a child. Toomey agrees and takes it to the next level. "One rarely travels with an economics teacher. You rarely go to a math conference somewhere, and when the debate team travels, it is a very small group of kids. But when you get on a bus with a bunch of kids from your football or gymnastics team, and you are traveling four or five hours to the state championship and you're going up against a major competition, it's a special circumstance. That's where special people are bred. This country starts to lose that if we don't have trained coaches and sports programs. We will just become another group of ordinary folks."

It was later in life when Toomey met his second mentor. He was studying secondary education at Stanford when a unique person offered important guidance for him. "Dwight Allen headed up the education project at Stanford and he personally watched over me. Our daily contact was in the classroom and he was one of the few teachers who ever made sense to me. And he would talk about the reality of teaching and the things that you had to watch out for. His strength as a mentor was in daily assessment and how to check in on a regular basis. I started looking at how I trained, and I kept asking the question; Am I really doing this right? Then I would take this method of planning and self-assessment from the classroom to the decathlon field and continue to develop my strategy. Probably the greatest lesson I learned from Dwight was not to be afraid to spend time on my weaknesses."

Toomey, who received a bachelor's degree in education from the University of Colorado and a master's in education from Stanford University, emphasizes the importance of a having a mentor in life. "This is a person that sets the agenda and gives you a road map." Toomey's comments were unique because, among all of the high achievers interviewed, he was one of the few who noted that an academic professor was his guiding light. His mentor interfaced both academics and the science of sport by giving him one of the tools in the classroom to apply to the playground. "I became my own student. Mr. Allen gave me a matrix. Nobody ever tells you what life is all about, and this guy was an inspiration about the reality of what was really going on and how you dealt with things. He made me a great teacher in life."

Toomey taught English for six years in junior college and wants to go back to the classroom someday. Today he is still teaching, in his own informal way, as he continues to go on the lecture tour for his various projects. Toomey is always on the move and is constantly reminded of his mentor from Stanford. As he speaks to youth groups about sports or gives a formal speech to a corporate audience about fundraising for the new Olympic training center, he recalls the lessons of Dwight Allen. "He was such a great thinker. He got me excited about academics and learning for the first time in my life because I could apply it. He set the stage for my next set of achievements."

Their lifestyles and origins are worlds apart, but these achievers found guiding lights in their respective mentors. These were mentors who did more than just provide energy and practical knowledge of sport; these were men and women who offered skills and coping strategies for the future.

Tim Daggett was blessed with three mentors over different "developmental phases" of his athletic career. Sprinter Glance had the fine graces of Mel Rosen bestowed on him, and Bob Beamon has incorporated the greatness of his teacher when he shares those qualities in his mentorship role. Each achiever has his own special relationship with a coach. Each seeks to establish that subtle, yet delicate, balance between teacher, coach, and perhaps ultimately, the mentor.

CHAPTER 8

DRAMA OF MUNICH:
A CRITICAL TURNING POINT

"On Tuesday, September 5, 1972, tragedy struck the Olympic village and the world at large. Eight Arab terrorists from the Black September group, a violent arm of the PLO, infiltrated the Olympic village and stormed Building 31, a three-story structure that housed the twenty-one members of the Israeli team. I awoke to a loud commotion. Two Israelis coaches had been killed, the body of one pushed into the street for the entire world to see. I knew then that the Arab terrorists meant business. It was the longest day of my life and the most tragic day in sports history."

U.S. Congressman Tom McMillen
1972 Olympian
Silver Medalist, Basketball

"It was the longest day of my life and the most tragic day in sports history." These are words that have been spoken and published most prolifically over the past twenty years. These are words and images that I have heard over and over as I interviewed athlete achievers for this book. They are thoughts, images, and feelings that will stay with all of us forever. This chapter will explore the harsh images and dark recollections of two athletes, Tom McMillen and Mamie Rallins, and one coach, Bill Bowerman, who were there, and had first-hand accounts of the tragic moments in Munich. This chapter will relive those television images projected worldwide with the solemn voice of ABC's Jim McKay. These three interviews revisit the unspoken horror of an athletic festival turned into a game of terrorist bloodbath. These achievers went to Munich with a singular focus; to pursue the intensity of sport and competition. They came back from Munich changed people. Their perspectives on life, coping with loss, and their outlook for the future, were shaped forever. The festival of sport and its players changed forever in the summer of 1972, never to be the same again. We begin with Tom McMillen.

Tom McMillen was traumatized by the events of 1972. He was a college superstar, a member of the Olympic basketball team, and a great achiever in many other areas of life. He was destined for the big world. His life changed dramatically in the summer of 1972. The terror of Munich and the horror of murdered athletes caused him to look at life differently. He returned home that summer and wrote copious notes of his experience in Munich. He wrote about his involvement in a festival of sport tarnished by the dreadful events that unfolded in view of the entire world. These feelings were captured in his book, *Out of Bounds.*

Tom relived the tragedy of the terrorist attack on his brethren and recalled the horrific imagery of those traumatic events. He watched the tragedy of the Olympics unfold before him, just like a bad dream. He remembers the thousands of German police and sharpshooters in sweatclothes surrounding the Israeli compound. He remembers with horror as the terrorists demanded the release of 236 Palestinian prisoners from the state of Israel.

McMillen's mood travels from fear to disgust when he recalls the decision to let the Olympic games continue twelve hours into the bloody massacre. He heard athletes suggest with great insensitivity that they should just blow up the building regardless of the hostage situation. "I often thought I was trapped in a surreal nightmare, I could not believe my eyes. Every hour or so a masked terrorist stepped onto the balcony in plain sight of thousands, and before a television audience of millions."

McMillen speaks with deep emotion about the juxtaposition of the German police trying to protect Israelis on German soil some quarter of a century after the Holocaust. "There was this incredible irony of having the Germans, so intent on removing all vestiges of militarism from the Olympics, now forced to flood the compound with twelve thousand troops. I could not shake from my mind the visit our USA basketball team made to Dachau only a week earlier. I feared the horror of more Jewish sacrifices."

Tom thought that maybe there would be some success with the hostage negotiations and that the Olympic festivities could return to normalcy in that dreadful summer of 1972.

It was not to be! "Around midnight I heard helicopters and watched in horror as the terrorists herded nine hostages bound and blindfolded onto a bus. I knew then that the terrorists had won! I could not sleep, I waited anxiously for a report on my fellow Olympians. On Wednesday at 3:00 a.m., I was sickened by the official word that all hostages had been killed. Just as the Arab terrorists were about to board 727 jets for freedom, the German sharpshooters opened fire on them. As retaliation, the terrorists lobbed grenades into the helicopters holding the Israelis who were destined for safe passage. In all, fifteen people were murdered."

The following day was another horror show for McMillen and his Olympic buddies. It was almost as sickening as the terrorist attack itself. "The Olympics were over, the spirit of the games was dead. Events were resumed after a brief delay. Avery Brundage, the infamous octogenarian and IOC president, led a brief memorial service for the slain athletes in the Olympic stadium. Brundage in his remarks linked the death of the slain Israelis to the expulsion of the Rhodesian team. He said that the two events were both savage attacks on the Olympic games, as if they were equally as important and traumatic. He basically converted the memorial service into a pep rally." Tom was appalled by Brundage's insensitivity and unwillingness to terminate the games.

Later that week, McMillen and several other Olympians placed a wreath on Building 31, the home of the slain Israelis. As he did, he noticed the bullet holes in the walls and doors of the building. "Death, destruction, and depression hung like a cloud over the once-joyful Olympic village. Gone were the laughter, the fun, and the camaraderie. Now there was only this bizarre sense that we had to complete some history, finish the games and go home. There could be no happy ending to the Twentieth Olympiad, Munich, 1972."

McMillen declared the summer of 1972 as the most tragic event in sports history. All memories of winning basketball championships in high school, college, the pros, and now images of the Olympic games, will be forever overshadowed by this horrendous international incident. "It is important that we not forget... so that such an atrocity will never happen again."

Tom McMillen's life changed that summer. As an athlete he will never forget. As an individual, an achiever in the global scale of things, he will always remember. McMillen's life took a sharp turn that summer, his future actions undoubtedly shaped by those frightful images of the past. Tom came back to America in the summer of 1972 wanting to make some changes in his life, and in the world around him.

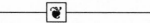

Mamie Rallins revisited the imagery of the 1972 Olympics as well. Her perspective of terror and tragedy had a bit of a different twist. She had made her second Olympic team when she competed in Munich. "I thought I was going to compete well, and then the shooting started. I saw the tanks and the SWAT teams, and then I felt it was time to go. I could be home in Chicago with the blacks rioting and arrange this kind of chaos, rather than getting killed over here by somebody I don't even know." Mamie ran in the semifinals of the Olympic sprints and then the Olympic Committee made an announcement that they had a plane heading for the States. She recalls that Mark Spitz was secretly rushed through the back door of the plane because of his vulnerability as an American Jew. And as soon as he was on the plane, they took off with a group of athletes who felt it was unsafe to continue. "I was one of the few athletes that came home early."

Rallins memory is vivid when she talks about the shootings and even the bomb threats that continued after the Israelis were murdered. "Our dorm faced the parking lot and helicopters were coming in and out all hours of the night. Then they brought in all these tanks and machine guns and army guys and I thought, this is not for me. I can get slaughtered in Chicago just as easily." Her survival instinct told her that this is history repeating itself. She realized that being a great athlete and winning medals has little meaning when human suffering is everywhere. For Rallins, a sense of purpose in life and being on her home turf superseded her need for athletic stardom.

The morning of her semifinals, Rallins got up early to eat breakfast with her friend and coach, Ralph Boston. He suspected that something strange was going on because they weren't allowed to go past a certain spot in the village. "Right after our meal there was this loud booming announcement in English that told people not to move, to stay where you were. We looked out this window and saw army tanks and machine guns everywhere. Then the guy on the balcony with a hood over his head appears. We knew there was trouble when we saw this character."

Rallins' event was held up for two days before she could run the semifinals. She ran the preliminary heats well and moved to the next round of competition. "And then I lost in the semifinals. I think that maybe my concentration was off a bit." Mamie Rallins knows that when you compete you can't be thinking about being somewhere else. You can't be coping with fear and survival and then in the next split second visualizing yourself as the fastest woman on earth. The brain doesn't function that way.

Mamie Rallins believes they should have stopped the Olympics. "I don't think the Olympic Committee knew who to trust and who not to trust at that point. There was a lot of fear in the village. You know after you have lived in Chicago for a while and they burn up half the city when Martin Luther King dies, you know enough about danger and destruction. And you know the images and feelings and if you're in the wrong place at the wrong time, some things can happen to you. It brought back a lot of bad memories for me!"

Rallins chose to go home early the summer of 1972. She and others invoked a survival mechanism, a feeling of being with family and friends. It is a coping strategy that has been very good to her for many years.

Bill Bowerman felt a lot of pride in being chosen as the head U.S. track and field coach at the 1972 Munich Olympics. He deserved the honor and the glory; he had worked hard to get there. He didn't anticipate the agony that was to follow that appointment.

Bowerman reflects on those difficult days over twenty years ago as if the images were part of last night's television news. Visualizing Munich and the whole experience of the Israelis being murdered is very painful for him. He feels that he was personally involved in the tragedy that befell the community of athletes worldwide.

Bill Bowerman describes in vivid detail the layout of the physical plant, the housing for athletes, as if he had been there last week. He explains that the U.S. Olympic athletes were housed in a small building about three stories high. "Having been in combat in World War II and having known the rules of security, the first thing I did was check security when I got to Munich. The security that the Germans gave us was a group of young boys and girls. I don't think any of them were over seventeen years old. They had blue alpine-type uniforms, they were hired by the Olympic committee and the German federations to protect our kids. That's our security!"

Bill Bowerman had a big responsibility that summer and he clearly had some major concerns for his athletes! He went to the American officials, our U.S. Olympic Committee, and asked to have real security in the building. They asked him why he needed security. Bowerman responded to the question from the perspective of a coach and world traveler as well as someone who had spent time in war zones. He told the powers that be that any time you get this many people together, you have petty thieves. "I don't want people wandering around in our quarters at night or any other time when we don't know who they are or what they're doing."

The very next day Bowerman got called on the carpet by the International Olympic Committee for upsetting some of the German officials. He was told that his behavior was outrageous and that he should not be running a military operation. So Bowerman and his staff went back to the dormitory and set up their own security. "We just assigned our people, our athletes, to security—to secure the place. Anybody that came in that building was watched by our team. There were two entries, a front one and a back one, and one where an elevator came up. And we even set up laundry security so they wouldn't rip off our equipment and USA uniforms. I had everyone mad; even the newspaper men were incensed that I would put up security. They wanted to go in there and interview my kids before their events. I told them they would have to clear the interviews with our staff. If an athlete doesn't want to see you, you're not going to get in. They thought I was being a little ruthless, protecting my athletes and keeping them focused before the biggest competition of their lives!"

It was a rocky start. There were ongoing days of controversy, power plays, and ego battles. Bill Bowerman just wanted to make his athletes safe. He was being called on and off the carpet and alienating everyone, including the international media. But Bowerman, no stranger to controversy, said that the commotion didn't interfere with his eating or his enjoyment of the Olympic competition. Thank goodness! "I felt that my behavior was appropriate and my conduct was in line with my coaching philosophy."

As Bowerman begins to explain the drama that unfolded on that infamous night in Munich, his eyes shift focus into a cold stare. He describes the buildings and the view from their window and notes that the Israelis were housed directly across from the American delegation. Bowerman recalls vividly what happened next. "I'm sitting there talking to another coach and I hear this rap on the door. It's an Israeli athlete and he's wondering if he could stay in the American quarters tonight. I looked at him and asked, what the hell for? He looked horrified and muttered something about the Arabs are in our place, they have killed some of our people." Bowerman went into military mode. He reached over and picked up the telephone and called the U.S. Consulate. "It was about midnight but the staff woke the senior officer and got him on the phone. I told him I wanted a squad of U.S. Marines to secure our building and protect our kids— and in thirty minutes we had two squads of Marines." Bowerman personally stationed the troops. By this point several Israelis had been killed.

Bowerman recalls the next series of events with shock, horror, and absolute disgust. He got a call several hours after the troops arrived from the president of the International Olympic Committee who had no idea that there was even a problem with terrorists. "You've done it again, Bowerman, you've called the Marines in to secure your building." Bowerman was appalled and subsequently invited an official delegation down to assess the seriousness of the situation. IOC officials were downtown, miles away, in a fancy five star hotel and had no idea what was happening with the athletes in the Olympic village.

By now the German police and sharpshooting anti-terrorist units were out and the Olympic Committee knew nothing about the situation. Two Israelis had been killed in the dorm at this point and the other nine athletes and coaches were taken to the airport as hostages. American athletes were watching this drama unfold right before their eyes. Bowerman has a look of great disdain when he tells me that the Olympic hierarchy, the IOC, declared a one-day suspension of the games so they could have a memorial ceremony for the eleven Israelis murdered in cold blood.

"I was so disgusted with the leadership, our Olympic people, and the directors of the IOC that, as soon as the last competition was over, I joined the American contingent and went to Lausanne, Switzerland. I resigned from the Olympic Committee that day and have never been to another one of their meetings since Munich. It's a rotten organization. The Olympics should have been suspended to honor the memory of the Israelis, but we have a number of bigots and aristocrats in that Olympic movement."

He looks sad, almost beaten up over this thing. It's over twenty years later and yet his feelings about 1972 and his tenure as an Olympic coach, still carries a difficult burden. It was an event he had worked toward his whole life. His words were simple and straightforward. "It was the worst experience of my life. When you stop to think about what happened to these kids and what the Olympics is supposed to mean to the world—a celebration of diversity, of achievement—it was horrendous."

Citizen Bowerman was invited to testify at the international hearings about the terrorist attack and asked to explain his position on his response to the tragedy. He felt that there was a brief spirit of reconciliation, although a number of committee members continued to challenge his judgment call on maintaining security in the Olympic village. They told Bowerman that he should have stayed out of it and not taken the authority into his own hands. They told him that the committee should have been notified first and that proper protocols should have been followed.

Today, Bill Bowerman reflects on his judgment call. He is clear that the U.S. Marines could have saved more lives. He is also clear that if the Germans had adequate security in the first place, the outcome would have been very different. In fact, four years earlier at the Mexico City Games there was very tight security! Did Bowerman, an educator, a military man, and someone with great insight about motivation, have any intuition that all was not right in Germany that summer? He mentioned earlier that when he got off the plane in Germany he first went to the embassy to introduce himself to the authorities. "I went to the U.S. Consulate to introduce myself because the consulate general knew my sister—her husband had been a United Nations official. And after we got acquainted, he said to me that if you have any problems in Germany, please give me a call. I, indeed, gave him a call, and I got through right away. It was the middle of the night when the Arabs attacked!"

Bill Bowerman wore many hats during the summer Olympics in Munich. He went to Germany as the preeminent track and field coach and came home an ordinary citizen, feeling frustration and anger at the world at large. He maintained his integrity as the U.S. Olympic coach while preserving a human dignity for his athletes and their survival. His instincts were to protect and rescue, using all of his knowledge and skills as a former military man. Yet, in the end, he walked away knowing that athletics is just one small piece of the puzzle when one copes with life on the big screen.

Throughout the many hours of interviews with noted achievers for this book, nearly everyone had, at the very least, a comment, a recollection, or a vivid memory of the 1972 Olympiad. Nearly all expressed their grief at the loss of life and the dramatic shift that occurred in their own personal struggles. Tom McMillen, Mamie Rallins, and Bill Bowerman offer us a brief glimpse, a snapshot of emotions that seem to pervade the reflections of all who revisit that summer in Munich. These three renowned achievers offer insight into the sheer terror and feelings that accompany that trauma. These three note the coping and resiliency skills that were called into action in order to deal with this tragic event. These are emotions that most of us only remotely felt from the safety and security of our living rooms and television screens.

Of all the interactions, however, I came away from Bill Bowerman with an uneasy, almost eerie feeling. I can't help but think that somewhere, down deep on an unconscious level, perhaps our United States Olympic coach had a feeling, a premonition, that things were not all that safe and secure in Germany in the summer of 1972.

SECTION
3

LIFE AFTER
THE WINNER'S CIRCLE

CHAPTER 9
FROM SPORT TO THE WORKPLACE

"You really need to take that passion and groom it into a vision. The vision is like creating a movie of what you want your life to be, as if it has already occurred. It is using the mental skills of vision and imagery to create a picture of what you want. What we know about peak performers and high achievers is that these are individuals that are able to imagine what they want before they ever get it and can balance the priorities in their life in the process of reaching it."

Mary Osborne Andrews
1980 Olympian
Track and Field

This section—life after the winner's circle—is precisely that. Here our interviews with athlete achievers explore the various paths and journeys individuals took when they transitioned from the rigors of sport to the world of academics, work, and their new careers. For many it was a struggle. Some had enormous amounts of energy but didn't know where or how to re-focus the passion. For some athletes, the transition to a new goal and new level of achievement was graceful and quite natural. We now take a brief glimpse into several athletes' transitions to the real world and begin with Mary Osborne Andrews.

Mary Osborne Andrews is not your average run-of-the-mill jock or for that matter high achiever athlete. She knows about discipline, she knows about perseverance, and she knows about toughing it out. She has had a vision for herself and her achievements since she was a young girl. She actualized that vision as a 1980 Olympic javelin thrower, but then got confused about how to reach her next passion. She wanted to work in the corporate arena, be a top flight management consultant, and maybe even move up the corporate ladder. She got sidetracked, her vision got cloudy, and her focus shifted slightly.

Mary decided long ago that she could balance work, play, and athletics, although perhaps not in that order. She has no limits to her work ethic, at least not when it comes to the psychological dimensions. Well into her career as a management consultant to Fortune 500 companies, she shifted gears and wanted to take a shot at the Olympics. Again, for a third time, this time for the gold! "I'm glad I didn't know how tough it would be in terms of getting into shape, maintaining shape and getting an injury at age thirty-two compared to being nineteen again. Healing from an injury took a lot longer and I had to go a lot slower. From a mental standpoint, it was easier because I knew what the whole experience was about. Spiritually and emotionally it was more rewarding because I was more conscious of what I was going through." She had to give up a lot. It was more than a balancing act to go back and train in midlife, it was a huge sacrifice. "It was difficult in terms of maintaining energy around career and marriage and social obligations. That is the hard part when you train at a later stage in life."

Andrews is quite the exception to the typical rule about athletes who win, withdraw, and then re-enter the Olympic rat race. Her training goals and Olympic quest covered a spectrum of nearly twenty years. Trying to make a comeback in her thirties, Andrews had to make some adjustments in balancing her life. Her first obstacle was dealing with her employer, a large nationally known insurance company. She had to get it to buy into a new time commitment so she could train adequately.

Mary needed flextime so that she could train. She made it clear to the corporate hierarchy that her training would allow for more productive work in a shorter work day. "I was asking for flexibility both in terms of my hours and my availability to the company. They didn't buy everything I asked for and wanted me to play by the same rules as everyone else. They told me that in terms of career and upward mobility it was important to be visible within the company during regular work hours. I wanted them to look at the notion that since I was training for my third Olympics, perhaps there was some corporate payoff or public relations angle that would benefit the company."

Although her company wouldn't agree to her proposal, she learned a valuable lesson in the process. She uses this experience as a springboard to encourage companies to promote flextime for high achievers or anyone else pursuing a worthy goal. In her management consulting business, she promotes the idea that companies will achieve higher productivity levels by allowing employees to have more flexibility in their lives. "For example, when you have an Olympic athlete working for a company and you've got a company newsletter, you can create a story that can inspire people to great performances and achievement. By encouraging creativity and discipline, you build in corporate loyalty and excellent morale."

Mary Osborne Andrews has a philosophy, one that has emerged from years of discipline and hard work on the track. It is a philosophy that has developed into a work ethic and way of life that she now carries into the work force. The philosophy is quite simple. It is a series of lessons that she takes with her everywhere. She calls her lessons a "model for success in the workplace."

She teaches people first and foremost to go beyond goal setting. The first step in her model is passion. Olympians, corporate executives, and anyone in the workplace, must identify what their real passion or desire is. The passion is the energy that keeps you going. "It's what looks on the outside as willpower and discipline, and is really passion or desire blossoming from inside. When you get people to believe that they can have what they want without having to go through so much sacrifice, it really empowers them. The most difficult thing is to get people to imagine or to start to identify with what they want. Most people don't know what they want."

Osborne's second step is to take that passion and groom it into a vision. "The vision is like creating a movie of what you want your life to be, as if it has already occurred. It is using the mental skills of vision and imagery to create a picture of what you need. What we know about peak performers is that athletes are able to imagine what they want before they ever get it."

The third step in her model is the risk/reward analysis. Going after what you want has to be a conscious decision. This is a critical point in the process. "This is the point where people get to make a conscious decision and then they try and do a risk/reward analysis. Invariably, this equation creates a bad movie. You have on the one hand this wonderful movie about life and what I want. Then there is the dichotomy and a bad movie that follows that decision. I got what I want, I am a '92 Olympian, but I'm running around the track in Barcelona with an oxygen mask on because we've blown the ozone layer and there's no air to breath." Mary explains that we often create the worst case scenario of what we need in order to fulfill our goals.

The fourth step is assessment. "Now that you've really taken an honest look at what it is you really want, it's time to take an objective, nonemotional look at who you are. Look in the mirror. What are my current needs? What are my current fears? Strengths, weaknesses, education and experience. Then and only then can you look at the gap between where you want to be and where you are. And that gap is called dynamic tension. If you can set up the dynamic tension by holding simultaneously in your head here's where I want to be, and here's where I am, you're going to be prompted into action. There are some people who will get nervous because that gap is uncomfortable, and lower their vision. I didn't really want that. That's just a dream and a fantasy. There are other people who will go into denial about their current state. Yeah, I'm an Olympian. I'm going to be there in '92. My back's OK. I don't really have to lift those weights. I'm going to be there anyway. So, it's that dynamic tension between step two and step four. Here's where you want to be. Here's where you are. That then leads you to step five."

Step five is goal setting and being receptive to the previous steps. "What do I need to do to get from here to there? Who are the people I need to get to support me, to coach me? Who are the people I need to articulate my vision to so that I can receive from them, because I believe very strongly that in order to get from where you are to where you want to be, there's got to be a very strong balance between being proactive and being receptive to other people helping you get it. Visions don't have dates. Goals do."

Step six, the last step in the model, is the one that makes the model a dynamic one and it includes feedback and support groups. This last piece suggests that people will find out information for themselves through a feedback loop that will plug right back into the first five steps. "I may find that being an Olympian in '92 isn't what I really wanted. What I really wanted was to be known around the world for something. So that plugs me back in and tells me more about what my real passion is. Or I might get some clarity about my vision. So it brings you closer to your goals and it allows you to go back to any one of those steps and keep it alive."

Mary Osborne Andrews never looks for the easy way out. She works her tail off in any commitment she makes. She seems frustrated and a bit let down at this moment. "Most people always want the magic pill. Most Olympians want the magic pill. I don't have the prescription for the one-dose job, and if I did, I'd throw it away." From her own experience, the six-step model, she says, is one that works. Her passion right now is to give corporate folks a model that makes sense, one that might even frustrate people into looking carefully in the mirror. So far, her lessons and visions of passion have paid off. She's a player in the Olympic arena and has scored big with the Fortune 500 corporate world.

Mitch Gaylord left gymnastics in 1984, after the dramatic men's team sweep of the gold medal over China in famed Pauley Pavilion at UCLA. He was riding high on great success and achievement as one of the world's premier gymnasts. It was the perfect time to transition from sport to a new career. The time seemed right but it was a difficult move to make. "The transition wasn't easy. It has taken me a long time to get on track with my life. The thing that is tough for me is not missing the sport, but the purpose that sport gives you. It is the day-to-day intensity, the focus, the self-worth that is attached to your accomplishments and achievement of goals. That is hard to replace; I really struggled with that transition."

Mitch got stuck in the California coasting mode for half a dozen years. He was frozen in time, with no purpose in life, and no place to put his focused energy to fulfill new goals. He drank, got depressed, drank more and got more depressed. "I partied a lot because I was trying to fill that void. I had a passion for gymnastics and I had a disciplined routine and I knew exactly how and where I spent my time. Without that passion, without the disciplined schedule and focus, I was really lost." Gaylord tried acting and got into the celebrity status thing, but found no fulfillment there. Being left in the lurch with all his energy and passion and high achiever mentality scared the hell out of him.

"I have seen a lot of athletes come off the podium with a medal or two and then crash. They have gone heavily into alcohol and other drugs, to try and fill the space. It is very sad and very scary. The frightening part is that when you take my high achiever personality in sports and you transition into a high achiever personality with drugs, and then mix in some competition, the outcome is disastrous. I knew that I would party harder and longer than anyone else, that is just me, my nature. And let me tell you that was a scary time in my life, being stuck in a destructive world of substance abuse!"

Gaylord got off the rollercoaster of destruction and turned his life around. He met a lovely lady in acting class and in 1992 they married. He put that passion into romance and now feels committed to starting a family. Things started to happen for him. President Reagan appointed him to the Council of Physical Fitness and he began to tour, speak to youngsters, the military, and corporate America about the benefits of fitness and well-being, including a drug-free lifestyle. He spent time in Washington consulting on fitness programs. He felt like his old self again, his old positive self-image revisited. Gaylord was touched deeply by the L.A. riots of 1992. He sees sports as a way to reach out and get youth involved, as part of a team-building effort to share community responsibility. He is presently doing outreach to inner city youth in an attempt to turn kids on to sport and off to drugs and gang recruitment.

Mitch Gaylord had great success in the gym. He was completely focused on one thing: being the best gymnast in the world. He was not focused on the responsibilities that attach themselves to gold medalists. He was not prepared for the limelight, the role modeling, the media exposure. It caught him by surprise and he struggled with his fame. "I feel that your ethical responsibility is to yourself. If you want to be a Michael Jordan, a Mary Lou Retton, a Bruce Jenner, fine. If you can handle that responsibility, the community role model, putting yourself on that healthy lifestyle pedestal, that is great. But it didn't work for me. I had to stay focused on my goals and nothing else. If you become a role model because you think you owe it to somebody, then you are doing it for the wrong reasons."

Mitch is passionate about one thing, know thyself. He knows what his struggle was in making the transition from sport to the real world. He knows that certain athletes are cut out to be on the Wheaties box. Most are not. His fear is that too many of our young elite achievers are looking beyond the training and discipline of sport and focusing on the end results, the endorsements, the big bucks. "Too many of our talented and gifted athletes are worrying about the day-after-the-medal ceremony and all the great material opportunities coming their way. They have tunnel vision with all their agents and corporate sponsors chasing them. They have this image of how beautiful life will be when they win the medal. That is complete bullshit! I tell kids that I work with to stay focused on their work ethic, their routines, their sport, and listen to their coach. Don't worry about the other stuff, it will be there if they want it later. It is such a waste of energy and a major distraction to be caught up in the riches and spoils of the commercial aspect of sport."

Gaylord wants kids around the country to get turned on to the sport of gymnastics. He loves to talk about the grace, the beauty, the aesthetic quality of floor routines, the drama and intensity of horizontal bar maneuvers, and the excitement when you hit the perfect routine. He once gave a motivational lecture to young rising stars of the Joffrey Ballet. He envisions a day when ballet and gymnastics perform together, each providing a delicate balance of movement and grace. In his work as a motivational speaker, he focuses on the here and now. He reminds his audience of aspiring young achievers to do their best in whatever discipline they choose. He reminds them that sport is just one component of the big picture, but a good way to begin setting goals and objectives.

Gaylord loves his sport and the feelings of accomplishment that he found in gymnastics. He has tried to make the transition from sport for years, yet his passion keeps bringing him back.

Lynn Gautschi retired twice, each time a year just prior to the Olympic games she swam in. She fooled herself, her friends, and family. It was her way of preparing for the grueling psychological and physical training regimens of Olympic-caliber training. She finally walked away from swimming with a bronze and a silver, but she wasn't gone long.

Gautschi grew up with strong, proud, working-class parents who devoted their lives to her swimming career. Her mother got up at 4:15 every morning to drive her to swim practice. Lynn trained under the famed George Haines of the Santa Clara Swim Club. Swimming was her life. It was in her blood. She did the eight-hundred laps a day, the doubles, the morning and afternoon workouts.

Lynn had a vision, a discipline about her sport, and she had her idols. "Donna DeVarona was my idol in life. I adored her. She was my role model and later in my athletic life she was very kind to me. Donna helped me get to be a great swimmer and, when I broke her world record in 1968, she interviewed me and made me feel special." Donna gave her a special ethic about swimming for herself, for her heart and soul, and not for the media.

Gautschi bristles at the Olympic image and its out-of-proportion desire to make teen idols out of athletes. She finds the hype, attention, and financial incentives offered to gold medalists sickening. She prefers Olympians to spend more time on their self-esteem and less on enhancing their media image. Anyone who medals or, for that matter, makes the Olympic team, is a true winner, she emphasizes. "Donna helped me grasp my self-concept, my self-image, and a positive ethic about sport. There is too much media hype about the second and third place finishers being failures, being losers. It is disgusting and getting worse each year. Anyone who finishes is a winner!"

Today, Lynn coaches at Morgan Hill High in northern California. She travels and gives swim clinics as well. She likes to emphasize the positive components of competitive swimming; the character building, the discipline, and mental focus. She clearly de-emphasizes the hyperbole around winning, the glamour, the media, the pot of gold at the end of the rainbow. She coaches athletes from dysfunctional homes, those who are trying to escape the pain of the alcoholic and abusive parent. She knows why they are there, in the pool, learning to cope with their family dysfunction. She knows that they are dealing with a tough family situation, and she supports them in a healthy, positive way.

She also coaches the kids who are being pushed into swimming so that their parents can live vicariously through their winning, even a shot at the big time. She takes these kids into her office, closes the door, and lays out the options. "You can either swim for your parents or you can swim for yourself. If you swim for your parents, you will most likely fail, and never live up to their expectations. If you swim for you and find that passion within, then you automatically win."

Lynn reflects back on her career and some of the issues that keep coming up with her student athletes. "I felt stupid when I was a kid and I wasn't very attractive physically, or at least I didn't think I was. So the pool was where my self-esteem came from. I was in total control in that environment. I was a hotshot, nobody could touch me there. I was brilliant and beautiful in the pool, but I also really loved this sport, it was my complete passion. I try and instill that or at least explain that issue to my kids. They have to love it to be here."

Lynn looks at her transition from athlete achiever to coach as a natural ongoing learning process. She seems comfortable with herself as she gives something back to the sport that gave her so much.

Bob Seagren vaulted to a gold medal in 1968 and then vaulted into a series of career moves. His move was so swift that he didn't have a chance to graduate from USC, so went back to finish the three classes he missed and graduate at the same ceremony with his daughter. Seagren had talent as a businessman even before the Olympic games. He worked for PepsiCola during his youth, building displays for their products in supermarkets. After college, he moved around to different jobs and then settled into the sportswear field. He became vice president of Puma, the company that spun off from the giant Adidas group in Germany, and put in eighteen years there building its reputation. He now consults with Fortune 500 companies around the world, assisting them with their image building.

Seagren thinks of his brother when he considers his success in the athletic achievement arena. He counts his brother as one of the most positive motivators in his quest for great achievement. "My brother was a good pole vaulter and I always wanted to be like him. Once I achieved that goal and went on to win major competitions I still looked up to him. He was my idol, he was someone I always wanted to be like, he was always a strong supporter."

Seagren is good at setting goals. When he speaks to young athletes he reminds them that they have to set a short-range goal and a long-range one. And with sports achievement or any other success in life you have to have the right mixture of success and failure. "I call it climbing the ladder. If you climb straight up to the top, then it's too easy. You must have certain things that affect you, that motivate you and some of these things might be obstacles or setbacks in your development. But they definitely motivate you. You have to be flexible along the way and set realistic goals. That is part of climbing the ladder."

Seagren struggled with a number of big climbs in his life, but the biggest perhaps was a bizarre event that happened in 1972 at the Olympic games in Munich. It was just a day before his pole vault event and some international sports officials decided that they were going to ban and then disallow certain types of poles from being used in his competition. Bob tried to argue with American and European officials, but to no avail. He lost the battle and had several of his personal poles confiscated just prior to the Olympic event. He was upset, frustrated, and knew that politics were involved with the decision. When he got back to the States, he and his dad sat down to assess the situation and considered a lawsuit. He knew that he was on solid ground, but his dad gave him sound advice that has remained with him, both in sport and in business, many years later. "Dad told me that win or lose in a courtroom on whether they had the right to confiscate my pole, the public will perceive this event as sour grapes, that you are just a poor loser. I also knew that, because of the politics, it would be a hard, expensive fight." Seagren today reflects on his evaluation and his father's solid advice. He had to swallow some pride and walk away from a situation that was painful. But in his heart he knew that he was a winner.

Seagren looks at sport as a training ground for the real battles in one's life. When he transitioned from athletics to his business career, he took with him the principles of good sportsmanship and a sense of ethical standards. He reminds us that sport is just a microcosm of the big picture, and a place to learn the fundamentals. "If we don't get the rules down early in life, then we are in for some rude awakenings."

Herman Frazier is an achiever who brings a refreshing perspective to the table when he talks about leaving sport and re-entering the community. He has transitioned from the pinnacle of Olympic sport as a great competitor and now is part of an athletic administration that is setting the policy for future athletes. He believes that athletics is not the ultimate solution to society's problems. But through participation and the learning experience, athletics can build character and solid values.

Frazier, the gold medal sprinter and two-time Olympian, is now associate athletic director at Arizona State University. He is championing a new event in his community. He is unhappy with the under-representation of African-Americans in the administration side of sport and wants to do something about it. "When you go to a USOC meeting of 120 directors and there are only six African Americans in the room, something isn't quite right. We need to look at the reality of the situation and consider for a moment who is bringing home all the gold medals to America!"

Frazier believes that race relations among athletes have improved over the years, but the work hasn't even scratched the surface with athletic administrators. He is incensed when he talks about the media's role in racial issues. "When you consider a Gail Deever and her phenomenal contribution to sport while overcoming a life-threatening injury, it is hard to imagine that she won't get the attention that a Shannon Miller gets. Society is awkward with having a black superstar who is also bright, articulate, attractive, and a true competitor both in sport and off the playing field. I think Madison Avenue and all the corporate sponsors are more comfortable with a little gymnast that white America can relate to."

For Frazier, the issue of racial prejudice goes much further and much deeper than the sporting arena. Frazier is living in a state that until November 1992 was frozen in time. Arizona did not have a Martin Luther King Jr. holiday, and in fact, it had been rejected by voters in a state-wide referendum. It was defeated by seventeen thousand votes in 1990 and, consequently, the state lost billions in tourism dollars, including the Super Bowl (which was later reinstated for January 1996). Frazier sees a new wave of racial injustice re-emerging in the 1990s. "I think affirmative action is a part of it. We have tried to recruit more black faculty to come to our university and yet we haven't been able to give them the kind of salaries that they are getting elsewhere. So they leave and go to another institution."

Frazier is not one to sit back and take a good long academic view of things from the ivory tower. He is disgusted with the lack of progress and how we have actually turned back the clock on some racial issues. He came from the inner city of Philadelphia to the lily-white desert of Arizona with a population of 3 percent black. Indeed, there is work to be done. In 1991 he helped form the Victory Together organization, a group of multi-racial clergy, corporate citizens and athletes. They came together to promote voter registration and higher turn-outs at the polls to overturn the ban on the M.L.K. Jr. holiday. His worked paid off: It was passed with a strong mandate in the 1992 election.

Frazier has been offered some plum jobs, some of the top spots at the big gun athletic powers. He could easily pack up and head for greener pastures in Los Angeles, Seattle, or back east, pick up more money and maybe some added prestige. But he feels that his life's work is now focused in Arizona. He is one of thirty African-American administrators at Division I institutions in the country, and he knows that his work is not just confined to the athletic arena. "My goal is to get out on campus, into the community, and get some change happening. Let's not roll back the progress in racial issues to the Sixties. It is time to move forward and make positive changes. Sport is a place to start, and then the rest of the community will follow."

Peter Kormann is one who knows about discipline. He left the sport of gymnastics after a stunning career and moved into the second half of his life as a premier coach. In

1976 he won the bronze medal in the floor exercise and became the first American gymnast to medal since 1932. He retired from the Olympic games, went on to Southern Connecticut State University for his degree and then on to the Naval Academy as head coach of their gymnastics program. Today, he is head coach at Ohio State and very successful.

Kormann is a dreamer. He sees gymnastics from the perspective of dreams and images that translate into movement and tricks on the apparatus. He explains that gymnastics is a constantly evolving sport with new tricks on each event emerging every year. Unlike the long jump or the high jump that have been studied and analyzed in slow motion for decades, gymnastics is constantly changing, it is never static. "Gymnastics is incredibly diverse. The skills are always changing from year to year, from competition to competition. To have athletes repeat as two-time Olympians in this sport is phenomenal. You are not racing the clock or surpassing the world-record height from year to year; you are performing, accomplishing, and perfecting a skill level on an apparatus. You have the influence of the Russians, the Chinese, the Romanians, all gifted athletes, who are all bringing new skills and new performance levels to the sport. It is terribly exciting to see the growth and complexity of the sport."

Peter loves his sport and his coaching responsibilities. It was a natural transition for him to leave the sport and enter coaching. It is his passion and it is part of his dreams. "Ask any of my student athletes and they will tell you that I come to practice with a new idea, a new skill that I developed last night in my dreams. It is always clear, vivid, and I know that it works." Peter should know about dreams and the human potential. In 1976, one of his nightly images commanded him to try out something new, something daring, and a skill never performed before. He took his dream into the gym and created a reality by being the first American to ever perform a full triple back somersault on the floor exercise. Today he uses his dreams to encourage his athletes to visualize a new skill. He is excited about this learning and developmental process. He sees it more than just applying to sport but as a creative process that can be nurtured throughout one's life.

Peter was a dreamer way back when, maybe from birth.

His dream was to be the best you can be before that became a media slogan. He left high school early to train under Abbey Grossfield, the two-time Olympian who went on to coach at Southern Connecticut. Kormann was not only a gymnast, he was obsessed with gymnastics and being great. At nineteen and finishing up his sophomore year in college, he was disappointed that summer would break into his year-long training schedule. He saved some money and decided to go to Japan for the summer so he could train with some of the top Japanese athletes who were dominating the sport at that time. Peter came home to the states with new skills and greater motivation than ever. He wanted to be the best in the states, best in the world.

Today, as coach, he reflects on the mentoring and great teaching skills of his college role model, Grossfield. "Abbey had this great knack for keeping us involved, motivated and not stale. If you were fatigued or burning out, he would pull a new trick from his bag. Literally, he would stop practice and give us a new skill to try out, always something fresh and innovative. We never got bored. He always had something cooking so that we would stay motivated."

Peter takes his work seriously. He is a bit of a scientist and a philosopher about his role in coaching athletes. He struggled for many years with a "balking" problem, not wanting to throw a maneuver on the floor that he had done millions of times before. He had just switched to a new type of tumbling mat and it threw off his timing and balance. He took a fall and it almost crushed his neck. He tried to get back to correcting the problem and yet he found that he struggled with a simple tumbling skill. He finds that his athletes today get into the same dilemma and often they need to back up the videotape and take a good hard look at their technique. In addition to the physiological component, he also feels that there is the emotional aspect that can distract and distort an athlete's mental image and personal visualization screen. "In my case, my hesitation or balking problem was tied to my relationship with my girlfriend and soon-to-be wife. I really wanted to spend more quality time with her and not be at a particular training camp. I got my wires crossed and my emotions seemed to interfere with my mental focus and gymnastic routines."

Peter is careful not to get too psychological, too analytical about the problem. He reminds me that the art of gymnastics is also about rhythm, timing, and a certain amount of innate ability and control. "We are all animals, and remember what happens when you see a squirrel jump from one branch of a tree to another. They jump, they leap, they fly through the air and they barely make that other branch, but you never, ever see them miss. Now how did that little creature know that it could make it with the wind blowing, the branch shaking, and the vertical angle of the jump? He or she just looked at the damn branch and said, by goodness, I can make it. So it is just a natural learned response. And my point is when you *unlearn* that response, or interrupt it, you are screwed! You have big problems as an athlete if you interrupt that natural motion and elegance."

As Peter evolved from athlete achiever to coach and mentor, he brought with him his gifts of imagery and visualization training so that a new generation of athlete could share in his dreams of performance and success.

When Kathy Johnson was young, her grandmother gave her a coin collection that featured former Olympians, including Jesse Owens. In fact, she went to the movies and saw black-and-white footage of the great sprinter in the 1936 Berlin games. It was inspiring. She actually wanted to be a runner, and she dreamed of being in the Olympics. Only half of her dream came true, however, but she's not complaining. Kathy made the 1980 gymnastics team and then repeated in 1984, winning silver and bronze medals in Los Angeles.

Johnson uses an interesting metaphor when she describes herself. She is a bit of a race horse, a highly competitive, energetic, race horse. A coach once told her that like all competitive athletes, you have to be careful when training a race horse. "When training a competitor, especially a spirited one, it is easy to break them. It is easy to break their spirit and then they won't run again, they absolutely will not race again. They can still be talented and gifted, but they will never race to win again if you break their spirit." Johnson remembers being broken during her athletic career, but not dispirited. She got hurt, broke bones, and was pushed to the edge by tough coaches over her long tenure in gymnastics.

She also went through the 1980 Olympic boycott, which was the major disappointment of her life. She trained and dreamed all her life of making the Olympics, only to have those dreams shattered when President Carter declared that the United States would boycott the games in the Soviet Union. But through it all Kathy Johnson never broke. Her body might have been in pieces, but her spirit was always intact. "I think that is the single most important component to my success. I was so hard driving, so strong willed, that come hell or high water I would still maintain my focus, perseverance, and continue to fulfill my dreams as an Olympian."

Johnson now works as a commentator for several of the networks. She also travels as a spokeswoman for international gymnastics. She shares great stories with young up-and-coming athletes. They are stories laced with pride, frustration, and incredible emotional fortitude. She is probably the only athlete ever to compete internationally who had her music tape break during a floor exercise routine. Not once, but *twice*. "I was competing in London and they set up my tape incorrectly. The person who runs the tape machine had fast forwarded it to a part that came later in my routine. So here I am starting to do a tumbling pass which takes a good deal of concentration and, puff, I stop dead in my tracks. It is the wrong music! I walk over to the head judge and very quietly say this is not the right music, it's wrong. I was pretty scared. Here I was just five-hundredths of a point behind Nadia, and I have to negotiate with the head judge. This was not fun! It turned out to be no fun at all. I over-rotated on my double back and dropped to fourth place, out of the medals."

Johnson reminisces about the awards dinner later that evening. "At the banquet that night, the moderator said, 'This is Kathy Johnson and she would have been our winner except that we messed up her music.' So it was a tough one. But like I said, I was down and maybe out but I was never broke. The spirit was always there."

Today, Kathy is still a race horse. She has an enormous amount of energy and still wants to be a competitive athlete. She is studying dance and wishes she could be twenty years old again. She wants to do all the moves, and be as limber as that two-time Olympian of the 1980s. She has also run three marathons in respectable times. She is a true competitor and one who gives 110 percent. Once, after an international competition in France, her brother wrote her a letter. He said that he had watched Kathy perform on television and he saw extreme pain and happiness, joy, and grief all in one floor routine during the international event.

"I am an extremely emotional person and I brought deep emotions to my sport of gymnastics. During this event I told a particular story. My choreographer and I worked on the story of my athletic career. In the beginning, I was supple and free-flowing, and every motion was easy, it was effortless. I was like a bird. Then later in my career, as I got older and more fragile, I had an injury. So in the second portion of my floor routine, I told the story of the injury using the bird as the metaphor. I spiraled down to the floor as if I was shot out of the air. I showed the hurt, the pain, the agony of not being able to fly with grace and style. I was expressing my transition and evolution in the sport, my vulnerabilities. I used to fall in love with telling the story through gymnastics, and not just getting up there and putting on some music and going after a good score from the judges. I really wanted to move people, move myself, express something of my life through gymnastics. It was very powerful that my brother saw that through the tube ten thousand miles away and wrote to me."

Today, Kathy lights up the air waves with her lively commentary of gymnastics competition for ABC and ESPN sports. She calls the action and brings her viewers into the dynamics and beauty of the sport. She educates television audiences by describing the techniques and yet offers them a glimpse of the personality behind each routine.

Many athletes waltz out of high level competition and transition gracefully into a new job. Louise Ritter didn't find herself dancing through life, but jumping lots of hurdles when she retired from sport. She was thirty, had just won a gold medal in the 1988 Olympics, and she was out of work and lost. In every job interview she responded to questions about experience by saying that she had traveled extensively and was very good dealing with people. "Nearly every interviewer was unimpressed with my Olympic credentials. Most said that they didn't want to hire someone who was still a pampered kid with no experience. Many employers think that being an athlete is easy street and they resent the lifestyle of athletes. It was real hard for me to change that perception."

Louise Ritter knows preparation. She spent twenty years of her life preparing for her most important jump, the big one in 1988. She did all the right stuff. The diet, the stretching, the weight work, the proper coaching. She used imagery day and night, especially right before bedtime. She and her coach made training films of her jumping technique. They would role-play situations on the field during major competitions. "My coach would call out the meters and tell me, 'This is it, Louise. If you don't clear the height, you are out of the competition.' He would pretend there were two other European athletes ahead of me. We would build in tension, intrigue, and get me to think and feel in terms of the real live situation."

Ritter wanted to be prepared for the real thing, no matter what the conditions, what the circumstances. She would make a great jump and her coach would say that she now had the lead. He would also up the ante, build in a bit more suspense. "Just as I was getting my height up in practice, he would turn up the heat. 'Okay, it's now raining in Korea. Let's flood the track and jump under a hose so we can simulate slippery conditions.' Then he would turn the pit around and tell me that we had a wind change. 'It's time to jump into the wind, Louise.' I mean, we had a regular weather station out there."

At night, Ritter would go to bed with a videotape machine on watching the perfect jump. She would fall asleep to the perfect visual, the perfect image and motion of the high-jump body, always clearing with ease and perfection. When she woke in the morning, she would take that image with her to the track and repeat it many times during the day. It was her mantra!

Her preparation for sport and the high-jump event was obsessive, meticulous, and absolutely flawless. Her preparation for life after the big jump and the big medal was not so thorough—she has struggled.

———————————| 🍷 |———————————

Anne Cribbs had an unusual career as a high achiever in sport. She won a gold medal at the Pan American Games at fourteen, and then a year later a gold medal at the Olympics. She retired from sport at the ripe old age of fifteen, went back to high school and started to look at life with a different perspective. One view she found not very attractive was the perspective on women in sport. "Now this was the early 1960s and women didn't really have a public persona in sports yet. In fact, in my case it was almost like being Casper the Ghost. Four years after I graduated high school, I got a call from a friend who said that they just announced to our school in Menlo Park, California, that we had our first Olympian, a guy. So my friend's sister gets up in the back and says, 'No, I'm sorry. We had Anne Cribbs here back in 1960 and she won a gold medal.'"

Gender bias rubbed Cribbs the wrong way and got her plugged into her next rude awakening. When she arrived at Stanford she did a project tracing women athletes back to the 1920s. What she found was quite disturbing. "In researching all of the media and sports articles, I found without exception that writers would always classify women athletes as pretty. Yes, a bit muscular, but always pretty. Or a fast swimmer but very feminine. Can you imagine if they used those qualifiers on every line about men?"

Cribbs has always had a sense of her own self and maybe even her own destiny. When she was three her parents wrapped a lifejacket around her and popped her into the water. "And this woman came over to my mother and said, 'You should be ashamed of yourself. This child will never learn how to swim. She will always have a false sense of security.' My mom desperately wanted to find this lady right after the Olympics in 1960." Anne suggests that she was coerced into swimming instead of tennis because little girls in those days didn't get hot and sweaty. "Not only did we have to look clean and fresh, but we had to act the part. We were required by the AAU until 1974 to wear those funky racing suits with skirts across the front. They had to be double paneled. It was a vanity issue for the sport. They were so cumbersome and buoyant that you could literally make them into a flotation device. In 1974 when the

Belgrade racing suits came out, they changed the rules for women and, wow, we shaved at least two seconds off our racing times by wearing the new swimwear."

Today Anne Cribbs is a partner at Cavalli & Cribbs, a Palo Alto advertising, public relations, and events agency. Founded in 1983, the firm manages high profile events such as the Stanford Centennial Celebration, the East-West Shrine Football Classic, the San Jose Sumo Basho, and World Cup Soccer '94. Her agency is no stranger to pro bono work for schools and colleges that want to promote sports for all, regardless of gender or race. Anne is also the president of the northern California chapter of U.S. Olympians, a group of past Olympians who draw upon their athletic experience to inspire youth in their region to reach for Olympic ideals in sport and academics. They meet regularly to support each other, as well, and to offer outreach to the community at large.

Anne Cribbs took out the old "vanity, double paneled suit" and put it on her young daughter last month. They all had a terrific belly laugh. Cribbs realizes now that she has come a long way since her early racing days!

Mike Eruzione has a saying that he loves to use when he speaks to corporate executives. "Ability and a dime gets you a cup of coffee." This comment typifies the essence of Mike Eruzione. He still gets excited when he reflects on his days as an Olympic hockey player, and the dramatic win over the Russians at Lake Placid. But he doesn't live in the past, he doesn't hang out with images that might carry him through the workplace. He believes that no matter what you do, you have to work at it. And hard work means dedication.

Eruzione is no stranger to a work ethic that supports long hours and complete dedication to a task. He attributes his desire to be a great achiever to his parents and the family's Italian heritage. "Nobody ever gave me anything when I was young. I had to work for everything. I had to appreciate the value of hard work at a very young age. My dad worked three jobs. He would come home, eat with us, and then go off to his third job. He would work weekends to get extra money to pay the bills. We weren't poor; he just had to work hard to make ends meet."

Mike grew up in a rather unusual household that instilled

the work ethic but also a sense of cooperation, perhaps even team cohesiveness. "My mother and father and aunts and uncles all lived in the same house. We lived in a three-family house; my parents, five siblings and I lived on the middle floor; my mother's brother—who married my father's sister—lived on the top floor with five kids, and my father's other sister lived below us with three kids. Altogether we had fourteen kids and six adults under one roof. You definitely had to get along with everyone. We never went out for dinner, never took vacations. There was just hard work to pay the bills."

Eruzione wanted to do well both in sport and in life after sport. He wanted to have more opportunities and greater options available when he raised a family. Now that he does corporate motivational speaking, charity benefits and lectures on the national circuit, he does get to see the world from a different perspective. It upsets him when his child asks for seventy dollars to buy a pair of Nike Air Jordans. He knows what his dad had to do in the 1970s to scrape up the dough to get him a pair of skates. He wants kids to understand where they came from and not take life for granted. He wants to maintain that work ethic in his home and in the community.

Eruzione donates a big chunk of time every year to community work. And when he does motivational speaking, he reminds the CEOs of Fortune 500 mega-corporations that money is not power, dollars and cash flow are not the answers to productivity. It's teamwork, cohesiveness. "If I were a boss, I would want my people to be just like the mates I had on the 1980 gold medal hockey team. These are guys who worked hard, who believed in themselves, and believed in each other. You can have all the talent in the world, but if you are not willing to work hard at it, the guy who has the same talent as you and the strong work ethic is going to do the job better. It is a very simple philosophy." Eruzione likes to end all his speeches with one thought: "ability and a dime gets you a cup of coffee."

Terri Stickles Strunck is a woman with a mission. She swam in the 1964 Olympics, joined the Peace Corps in '65 and went off to South America to spend the next two years coaching youngsters who were on their way to elite athletics. She learned a lot about coaching, but her real passion was to help others, others less fortunate and those in crisis.

Strunck came back to the states and went to the police academy in northern California. In 1977, she became a police officer during a time when women were not part of that job market. Being a woman in a male-dominated law enforcement world was stressful, but Terri wanted to up the ante. She was a risk taker and she wanted to stretch her boundaries and grow. She became a specialist in hostage negotiations. Her philosophy about difficult situations was to mediate first and then bring in the firepower. She believes that women don't use or depend on brawn when they do their work. "They tend to use their intuition and verbal skills to solve problems. Guys on the other hand just jump into the middle of the violence, try and arrest a person, and use their force before they talk through a difficult situation." In 1984, she won the Officer of the Year award for San Mateo County.

Times changed and Strunck came under the supervision of a new police chief. She felt the stress of trying to prove herself and at the same time burning out from the stress of job-related fatigue. She left the force after eight years and has been searching for a new profession. She wants to help people. She wants to reach out to families in distress and make a difference.

Winning a medal in 1964 was a great achievement for Terri. But for years she put the trophy away, out of sight, out of mind. "It's as if the athletic conquest was no big deal. It was expected that I would do well in swimming and then get on with my life. I wasn't going to win the medal and then cruise through life showing it to every employer or client that I ever met. Remember, in the 1960s, international sport had some sense of perspective. You received a few press reviews and went to some parties with your friends and then it was time to get back to business, to reality. Agents didn't call and sign you to four zillion dollar endorsements in those days. Life was simple, uncomplicated. You just swam, won a medal, and got on with your life. There was more important work to do out there than just relive the past."

Terri Strunck recently took her Olympic medal out of her drawer and had it framed. In fact, several of her buddies from the Olympics got together to relive the glory days of sporting achievement. Most had forgotten how monumental the experience was. A large contingent of Olympians were recently honored at a professional football game at Candlestick Park in San Francisco. It was quite a flashback to the glory days. "To have a soldout stadium of eighty thousand screaming fans cheering for you during halftime was a great feeling. It was like reliving the opening ceremonies of the 1964 Olympics; it was very exhilarating! Thirty years ago there wasn't much prestige attached to the Olympic games. But now, with the media coverage, the endorsements, all the public awareness globally, it really is a big deal. And the fact that we are getting older, I guess it was important to take that little medal out of the drawer and put it around my neck and march in the parade. Every once in a while a little reminder, a little acknowledgment of the past, is important."

Terri Stickles Strunck is a child of the '60s. Sargent Shriver was one of her mentors. She believed in him and his ethic of public service. She thinks of herself as a giver, not a taker. "After all, I grew up during the Kennedy years. We all learned a lot about giving something back to our country, our neighbors, our communities." Strunck got burned out on the politics of law enforcement, but she hasn't forgotten the lessons of mediation and conflict resolution. She is now looking forward to her next career challenge.

Ed Burke had an amazing experience in 1984. He was riding on a bus on his way to the Los Angeles Coliseum with a group of teenagers. Some were twenty years old, they were athletes, and they could have been his children. Typically it is not so unusual to be in Los Angeles on a bus with youngsters, but when you are all competitors competing in the same Olympic games, that is quite a different story. "I was the oldest athlete at age forty-four in the L.A. games, and here I am hanging out with these adorable little gymnasts and swimmers. Even some of my fellow hammer throwers who were thirty seemed like children to me."

Burke had done it all: three Olympics, American and world records, and then a successful business career. He felt quite accomplished until one day when his daughters asked him about his athletic career. They had no idea about dad. They had never seen a hammer, let alone a big sweet guy like dad throw the thing. "I took the rusty hammer out of the closet and drove over to the San Jose State track and took a few throws. It was weird, sort of like getting back on a bike after you haven't been riding for years. It was a natural and comfortable feeling. I started to have this vision, it was almost mystical. I kept seeing myself entering the Los Angeles Coliseum as part of a team of athletes getting ready to compete. You know, the adrenaline thing, and then my wife encouraged me to go back and set a new record. I could feel the energy of the crowd in my vision. I could hear the applause. My hair would stand up on my neck and then with the vision came the tears. They just started to flow. I knew that I could do it. It was a wonderful, joyful set of emotions. I just knew all the parts were there."

Ed Burke had an old record for the hammer throw: 235 feet, 11 inches. He eventually threw 244, but that was later as an adult. He did change his training style using different strategies. "I got into using a sensory deprivation tank with a warm saline solution. You float in the epsom salts and they pipe in the music and you learn deep relaxation. Then they give you a videotape, a Cybervision tape, and you watch it over and over in this very relaxed state of mind and body. The idea is to get the imagery out of your head and into your hard-drive, your subconscious. This imagery is something that has to come naturally, without force or struggle. So you just see things happening and then you relax. I first did this with my golf game and then used it for all my sports. The results are beautiful. I encourage all young athletes to try it out. It is a wonderful way to get out of your head and get into your soul, a complete refocus for your game."

Ed Burke has done it all. He has two credentials, both in political science, and he has even been a university professor. He brings his astute awareness and political savvy to various track and field committee meetings and to his prestigious

ob Seagren – *Pole vault; 1968, 1972.*

Photo by USA Gymnastics

Julianne McNamara –
Gymnastics; 1980, 1984.

Herman Frazier – *Track;*
1976, 1980.

d Etzel – *Marksmanship; 1984.*

ck Fosbury – *High jump; 1968.*

Kenny Moore – *Marathon; 1968, 1972.*

Photo by Brian Lenton

Frank McKinney Jr. – *Swimming; 1956 1960.*

Lynn Vidali Gautschi (left) – *Swimming;* 1968, 1972. Also pictured: Olympic Coach George Haines.

Alexander Tarics (right) – *Water Polo,* 1936.

nne Warner Cribbs – *Swimming; 1960.*

Mary Osborne Andrews –
Javelin; 1980.

Photo by Monica Davey

Nancy Hogshead – *Swimming; 1980, 1984.*

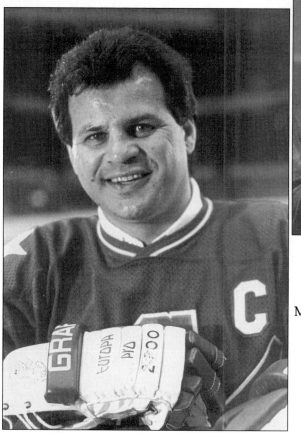

Mike Eruzione – *Hockey; 1980.*

ott Hamilton – *Figure skating; 1984.*

Ed Burke – *Hammer throw; 1964, 1968, 1984.*

appointment to the Olympic Committee. He is founder and CEO of the Aerobic Sports Corporation and is a big supporter of young athletes moving into the nonglamour events of hammer and shot. He has a lot of pride and deep concern for the future of his sport. At age forty-four he was honored at the 1984 Olympics by being the U.S. flagbearer during opening ceremonies. He still remembers the tears!

Kim Carlisle is an individual who puts her best foot forward and doesn't dwell on the past. She was thrilled to make the 1980 Olympic team and then momentarily disappointed when the Soviet boycott robbed her of the chance to compete in the Moscow Olympics. Many athletes are still bitter about the situation that occurred over a decade ago. Kim was eager to get on with her life, so she didn't stay stuck with the bad feelings. "I kind of made the best of a horrible situation when I went to the White House to meet President Carter. He wanted to honor all of us and still keep some integrity with the political boycott, so I felt okay about it. After all, I'm still an Olympian. Nobody can ever take that away from me."

Carlisle kept that same positive perspective when, one year later in 1981, she became a two-time NCAA swimming champion and athlete of the year at Stanford. That was her icing on the cake. She did not have a burning desire to make a second Olympic team and prove herself again. She was ready to graduate college and get on with her life. Enter the real world! She went from a high-powered, intensely motivated college career to starting over, to ground zero. The transition was difficult. She struggled, going from job to job trying to find herself, reassessing her self-worth, her self-esteem.

She landed several jobs as a freelance journalist, but settled into steady work in advertising sales at the *Stanford Magazine*, an alumni periodical. She was asked to manage a staff and head up a team of sales personnel. She hated it, she didn't feel comfortable in the traditional leadership role. The position brought back some unfinished business with her junior year at college and her obligations as captain of the Stanford swim team. "I have always had a hard time working with people who don't agree with me. I am a consensus builder and it's tough for me when I can't get everyone together. My dad used to say half the people will always agree and the other half will disagree. There will always be some dissension in your world. Dad was right, I just wasn't cut out to be captain."

Carlisle swam poorly her junior year, distracted by problems and expectations associated with being a captain, a consensus builder of a team with strong egos. Her fellow athletes were needy and demanded a lot of her emotional time, thus interfering with quality workouts in the pool. Her senior year she stepped down from the role and had a great swimming year, completely focused, no politics to worry about.

"I have learned both in athletics and in the workplace that I do better as a team player and not as the captain. I do better going my own way and setting an example than by trying to fulfill some prescribed role. The negative stuff is too painful for me!"

Carlisle stays in touch with fellow Olympians, especially the swimmers. She is deeply committed to her friendships and the camaraderie that created permanent bonds between them. She explains that swimming several miles a day in workouts tends to create a nonverbal connection among athletes. "You don't touch each other physically, you don't pass the ball around, you don't even speak to one another. But you do see these bubbles coming to the surface and when you look at each other through a blurred goggle vision, you know that each one of you is putting out, training hard and committing themselves to the team effort. There is this spiritual connection among swimmers; it is nonverbal yet very powerful. Maybe that's why we all stay in touch so many years later."

Julianne McNamara made two Olympic teams. She had five perfect 10s, the highest score given in the demanding sport of gymnastics, and finished her career with a silver and a gold. She capped off a brilliant career by having an uneven bars maneuver named in her honor. Even with the McNamara mount, Julianne wanted more.

Her peak experience in sports had nothing to do with the awards or the medals or being part of the history made in women's gymnastics. Her peak experience had to do with a bad fall she took in the team competition in the L.A. Olympic games. "I lost my concentration and fell on the beam. There I was on the floor with points being deducted, ruining team chances for a medal. It was devastating, and yet I knew I had to rise above it. This was the Olympics. I had to get beyond the hurt, the disappointment, and turn this negative mishap into a positive experience. I had to learn from this!"

McNamara looks back on that fall ten years ago and is proud. It was a pivotal event in her athletic career and maybe a pivotal event in her life. She is the ultimate perfectionist. She left home at thirteen and moved thousands of miles from home to train with the notorious Romanian coach, Bella Karolyi. She knew from day one that gymnastics was her life. To arrive at the Olympic games and have a critical fall, this was sheer terror. When Julianne reflects on that nanosecond of time, she smiles with confidence and contentment. "I knew that I had spent a lifetime perfecting a routine, doing this apparatus thousands of times in practice. I also knew that I wasn't going to let a fall or a slip or a few tenths of a point psych me out. I was going to turn it around and make it a learning experience on the spot."

Julianne looks at life mostly in terms of turning negatives into positive experiences. She subscribes to the "blessing in disguise" school of training thought. She believes in growing from mistakes, no matter how big or when they occur. Julianne left her passion in 1986 and officially retired from gymnastics. She still hasn't left the gym, however. She does broadcasts for NBC, CBS, and ESPN. She is the expert commentator in the broadcast booth. She has left her sport, but she stays fairly close to the action.

Kenny Moore is a two-time Olympian and present day senior staff writer for *Sports Illustrated*. He originally left sports and was on his way to a career in the practice of law via the Stanford Law School. He got side-tracked with a master's degree in creative writing and ended up as one of America's preeminent sports writers. He has one book already published, and his second, which chronicles the life of Bill Bowerman, is on its way. For the past fifteen years he has traveled the globe interviewing some of the greatest athletes of our time. Moore says that writing fits his personality; it is his way of looking at the culture and ethnicity of sport. "If I can capture an experience, an event or the essence of a person, and transmit that essence into the mainstream, then I have fulfilled my goal. It is important for me to touch people through my writing, to get to their souls."

In December 1992, Moore received a call from his managing editor at *SI* who asked him to fly to New York City to write the "Sportsman Of The Year" feature article. Kenny Moore, whose office overlooks the blue waters of the Pacific from a hilltop in Kona, Hawaii, said that he really didn't want to go east. "My editor knew that I was allergic to New York City, but when he told me that the honor was going to Arthur Ashe, then there were no second thoughts. I was on the plane that afternoon."

Although they had never met, Olympic marathoner Moore felt an immediate rapport with Ashe, the tennis star, author, and human rights activist. "We were both the same age, had been in college at the same time, and shared much of the same literature. His library looked like mine. I felt an immediate connection with the man; he put me immediately at ease." Moore often approaches his work with a good deal of research in advance, a preparation that carries over from his marathon training. "I read his books and a volume of material about the man. He was a giant, both in the world of athletics and as a scholar and humanitarian."

Moore, who claims that he is shy, felt immediately comfortable with Ashe, his wife Jeanne, and daughter Camera. As a journalist, he is careful to retain that objective look, that critical, yet sensitive eye, for the core issues. He is skillful when getting beyond the small talk and chitchat to the real issues at hand. He goes beyond the scores, the matches, the mental preparation strategies, to really know and understand his subject. He is part psychologist, sociologist, and anthropologist, all disguised as a philosophy professor wanting to engage his students in dialogue. Moore wants to learn about the athletes' culture, their community, their family, the parts that make up the whole.

"I don't think that I could have interviewed Arthur Ashe at any other time in my life. There was a sense of destiny about being called to do this interview in New York. Earlier in my life, I was not able to get a grasp on racism, on sexism, on stereotypical behavior. I wasn't mature enough, both as a person and as a writer. Journalism is about personal growth, about evolution. It is not a static process. Writing is a dynamic, constantly evolving process."

As an athlete and now as a journalist, it was important for Moore to approach this interview with a sense of history. He needed to learn about Ashe being barred from tennis tournaments with whites. He needed to know why Pancho Gonzalez became Ashe's role model and tennis idol. It was not because of his furious backhand, but because of his struggle to break the minority barrier in a very white sport. Arthur Ashe explained that in 1970 he tried to get a visa to play tennis in South Africa so that he could lend moral support to those oppressed by the violent times of apartheid rule. In 1973, he finally was granted his papers, traveled to South Africa, and soon became a mentor to Yannick Noah. Ashe offered an autograph to Noah that simply read, "Maybe someday we will see each other at Wimbledon." Six years later they played on a doubles team together in that elite venue. His imprint was so powerful on the anti-apartheid struggle and subsequent breakthrough that the first person Nelson Mandela met with when he voyaged to the U.S. was Arthur Ashe. These are parts of the high achiever that Kenny Moore gets turned on by.

Moore has reported on hundreds of high achievers over the years. In Ashe, he was struck by the sheer joy of life and incredible energy that this man possessed. His life read like a who's who of humanitarian missions. In his brief forty-nine years of life he found time to start the Arthur Ashe Foundation for the Defeat of AIDS, and the Safe Passage Foundation so that youths could achieve a productive life by combining sports and academics. Within the foundation, he initiated the Athlete Career Connection program which is an organization committed to improving the graduation rates of minority athletes. He also started the African American Athletic Association which counsels minority athletes in New York City. In an attempt to battle both discrimination with race and gender, he founded a players' union known as the Association of Tennis Professionals. His work did not end there.

Moore was also struck by something else when he met Ashe, a sense of commitment to fatherhood and the precious time he had left due to his terminal AIDS condition. "He was concerned about leaving a special gift for Camera. He had such a clarity about his love for his daughter. He was so lucid in saying goodbye to her, his tenderness was so rich." For Moore, the experience of interviewing Arthur Ashe just months before his death was more than just a professional obligation, an assignment. It was an honor, a duty, and a responsibility to transmit greatness through the written word.

After the December 1993 Sportsman of the Year Award, Moore was again tapped for another piece on Arthur Ashe. This time it was the obituary which was written shortly after his death on February 6, 1993. Kenny Moore chose to focus his piece not on death and the scourge of AIDS, but on the rich memories of life and accomplishment. Moore focused his essay on the family, with particular attention to the relationship between father Arthur and daughter Camera. "For me it was a reflection of my own childhood, the fond memories of my dad, being patient, accepting, and always there for me when I raced. Dad told me he would always be there regardless of the outcome of the race. There was unconditional love."

When Kenny Moore wrote his first piece on Arthur Ashe, it took him a while to get all the pieces together. He needed some time to sort out his thoughts. "I wandered down Lexington Avenue and looked in department-store Christmas windows. I saw these things in the shops, but the images were not items for sale or *things* ready to be purchased. They were images from my own mind and heart, images that had been collected in the unconscious, etched by Arthur's compassion for the human condition."

Kenny Moore needs to reach people through the written word. He takes pride in transmitting a message that might go beyond the mundane and touch some inner core. He usually keeps a cool, objective demeanor when he interviews his athletes. With Arthur Ashe, he felt something different— it was a difficult and painful relationship. "I felt his vulnerability, yet he had such incredible energy for the week we spent together. We agreed to stay in touch after I left New York. He even called me in between flights from the Minneapolis airport to clarify a thought he had about our discussions. He promised to bring his family out to the islands to spend some quality time with me. I felt anger and resentment that we didn't have a long-term relationship, we were just getting to know each other. It was painful to write his obit because this was such a caring and wonderful person, a man with such charisma."

Moore suggests that it was more than coincidence that the two of them met. He speaks with deep affection of the brief time they had together.

Kenny Moore is a trained professional, he is a journalist, an author of books and hundreds of magazine articles. He makes a living understanding the depths of humanity, the sense that we are all here together for a purpose.

The governor of Indiana noted that Frank McKinney Jr. was a man who viewed problems as raw materials that could be converted to opportunities. McKinney served on the board of trustees of more than twenty nonprofit organizations and in his lifetime had been associated with more than thirty agencies. He was Mr. Community and he was now being eulogized by the governor and many of Indiana's top officials. Two days before I was set to meet with Frank McKinney, he died in a tragic plane crash with four other business colleagues. They were on their way to a community development meeting.

Syd Cook is the senior vice president for Bank One Indianapolis and Bank One Indiana Corporation. He spoke with me about the late Frank McKinney who at the time of his death was CEO of the corporation and a leading force in the banking business in the country. "Frank was the most disciplined person I ever knew. When he said the meeting is from 10:00 to 11:00, then you had better be there because it started precisely on time and the hour was a productive one. Not much idle chatter. There was always a structure, an agenda. I guess you could say that it was like a swimming workout. You get your lap assignment from the coach, you get in the pool and get your workout done."

Frank McKinney Jr. was a modest man, almost shy. He never displayed his Olympic medals to his colleagues. It wasn't his style. "Everyone sort of knew his reputation, so he didn't have to trade on it. He had a quiet and commanding presence and a competitive one. He always wanted to be the best bank, have the best bottom line, the most efficient staff, and he was extremely competitive in the business world. I'm sure that style of management and success-driven personality was a carryover from his being a great athlete. But at the same time he wouldn't impose his will on us. He would set up an atmosphere where we could be self-motivated and empowered for the corporate team. He was not what you might call an authoritarian CEO."

Syd Cook smoked for thirty years. For twenty of those years he worked closely with Frank McKinney Jr. and would often light up in his presence. "Several of us would take out our cigarettes at meetings and Frank never batted an eyelash. I'm sure that—the specimen of health that he was—he didn't like secondary smoke in the room, but he never imposed his will on us or told us to stop. Just recently we moved to a new building and we were encouraged to go through a ten-week SmokeStoppers program because the building owners kept a smoke-free environment. But McKinney never sent out a memo that mandated you shall not smoke! It wasn't his style."

The Cooks were being entertained at the McKinney home a few months before his death when Frank McKinney Jr. announced that he was going to retire early. "He was just short of fifty four, and he wanted to get more involved in charity and civic causes. So my wife said to him, 'Frank, you should reconsider. Don't leave the bank quite yet.' He was so touched by her comment, he smiled and seemed genuinely moved by that statement. We think about him every day; the bank runs fine, and we are not struggling from a management perspective. But the guy was such a visionary in the state and on a national level, that his energy, his lust for life, and creativity is deeply missed. It was a profound loss to us, to his family, and to the business community."

Life after the winner's circle is not always a piece of cake. Those athlete achievers who make the successful transition into a new career path and establish their "new" identity as a professional in the work force always reflect on their previous life. Athletics was a great training ground for life! For those who struggle with that transition, sport was and still is their life. It is their self-esteem, their self-worth, and a place where they are safe and secure—the risks are calculated.

CHAPTER 10

GIVING SOMETHING BACK TO THE COMMUNITY

> *"Olympians who came from the projects went into detention centers to work with kids who had come from some tough neighborhoods. Our Olympic volunteers went in and told their story to these tough, dysfunctional kids. We had a great number of tools that we used, but the speakers were usually our best. We taught them how to do job interviews, fill out job applications and how to do public speaking. The first couple of days the kids hated us and, at the end of the week, it was like they had discovered each other. We had kids who were in gangs that wanted to turn their guns in. They wanted to surrender themselves for having been involved in a shooting fatality. All of a sudden somebody cared enough and it was through sport. So don't tell me that sport is not an important access point."*
>
> Bill Toomey
> 1968 Olympian
> Gold Medalist, Decathlon

Some people say that athletes are spoiled rotten, overindulged, undersocialized *brats*. Not everyone agrees. As part of the interview process for this book, I asked each athlete achiever to reflect on their involvement in community service. The responses were varied and quite different in form and substance. The spectrum of outreach covers the work of athlete achievers from all walks of life. Some achievers are highly visible and move into government and public policy; others are making their mark on society in quiet, less public ways. As achievers related their commitment to the community in terms of money, time, and heart, it became clear that these individuals wanted to say thanks for all the memories, the strokes, the acknowledgments, and the awards. Many, however, are stumbling and are still learning how to express it.

Everyone I spoke with gives something back to the community, with different degrees of involvement, and with varied beliefs about the ethic of giving and receiving. In this chapter we examine the outreach of four noted achievers: Bill Toomey, Nancy Hogshead, Bob Beamon, and Bill Bowerman. We begin with 1968 gold medalist, Bill Toomey.

Bill Toomey has never left sport. He graduated from famed Olympian to community organizer, activist, and fund-raiser overnight. He is passionate about his love and commitment to sport for both the serious athlete and the recreational person. Toomey is presently director of the San Diego Olympic training center which will eventually provide training facilities for thousands of future Olympians. Prior to his appointment with the training center, Toomey had been part of a community outreach effort for high-risk youth. The program, under the sponsorship of the U.S. Department of Labor, took place during the summers of 1980 and 1981.

Toomey and fellow athlete achievers Barry King and Dr. Leroy Walker (the chief of the USOC) were all involved in the concept as well as the implementation of the community outreach project. The DOL project offered over one hundred week-long courses in nine cities around the country. Under the federal contract, the Sports Directions Foundation was initiated. The purpose was to administer a series of thirty-hour intensive motivational and career development classes for inner-city youth age fourteen through twenty. More than one hundred and twenty former and current Olympians worked in the program, alongside teachers and administrative staff.

King and Toomey were high on the experience. "Thousands of young people across the country were connected to the Olympic experience. We had programs running simultaneously in Albuquerque, New Mexico; Birmingham, Alabama; Indianapolis, Indiana; Los Angeles, California; Miami, Florida; Newark, New Jersey; Raleigh-Durham, North Carolina; Richmond, Virginia; and Santa Ana, California."

Toomey knows young people. He also knows that they face an extremely high risk of unemployment when they first begin to look for a job. He knows that there is a great need for skills and attitudes that will help them overcome difficult environments. Toomey also understands basic economics. "Unemployment is draining the economic vitality of our country's inner cities. Both business and society benefit

by improving the communities whose stability is the essential condition for growth." In this program, Olympians drew on both their athletic and life experiences to demonstrate the value of setting realistic goals and making a sustained effort to achieve them. The program presented career choice and personal development as expressions of the same incentives.

Toomey explains that a specific curriculum was developed to provide labor market skills to the participants of youth employment programs supported by the Department of Labor Prime Sponsors. The curriculum specified twenty-four to thirty-two hours of programming for each participant. For youth enrolled in the Summer Youth Employment Program, the schedule matched one workweek.

Barry King, now an executive at the USOC headquarters in Colorado Springs, laid out the objectives of the program along with some of the long-term goals. The goals included:

- self-awareness and improved self-esteem;
- greater confidence in potential and ability to achieve tasks and objectives previously perceived as difficult;
- improved goalsetting, assessment and decision-making skills;
- improved communication skills;
- improved self-discipline, self-reliance, and persistence in working toward goals;
- improved knowledge and understanding of the job market, realistic choices, and the skills and education required;
- improved job search and job interview techniques; and
- improved attitude and motivation in seeking, acquiring, and maintaining productive careers.

The first year costs ran about $600,000, with the second-year budget jumping to $800,000. *The Washington Post* gave it rave reviews, noting the following accolades: "In Miami, a teenage girl anxious to complete the last day of training sneaked out of the hospital a day after giving birth. In Los Angeles, a Chicano gang leader turned his gun over to a program leader. Most are inner-city youth. Some are dropouts. Others are pushouts. Athletes interviewed today said most of the youngsters want handouts and believe the world owes them a living."

Toomey was delighted to be part of this effort. He and his distinguished colleagues believe there is room for something like this in the Clinton Administration. He was joined in the program by former Olympians Wilma Rudolph, Ralph Boston, Tommie Smith, John Smith, Wyomia Tyus, Milt Campbell, John Carlos, Charles Foster, and Bob Beamon. Toomey also believes that the private sector needs to pick up the slack in doing community outreach.

The Toomey/Olympic project set a new standard for community outreach. Athletes who are high achievers who came from the projects went into detention centers with kids who had come from pretty tough neighborhoods and had fought their way out. And they went back and told their story to these tough, sometimes dysfunctional, kids. They had a great number of tools to influence positive decision-making, including the athlete role model.

Toomey had 125 Olympic volunteers in eight cities to teach the kids how to do job interviews, fill out job applications and how to do public speaking. "We did this in a week. The first couple of days they hated it. At the end of the week, it was like they had discovered each other. We had kids who were in gangs that wanted to turn their guns in, that wanted to turn themselves in for having been involved in a shooting fatality. All of a sudden somebody cared enough, and it was through sport."

Toomey had a lot of naysayers. His critics claimed that he couldn't do anything in a week. As an athlete and an achiever, he knows that learning is part of a cumulative effort in life. It's the amount of good things that happen to you that help you make the decision to be an honest person. "We didn't have the expectation that we could change a criminal into a productive human being in one week's time. It may be, however, that when this kid is about to inject himself with heroin or pull the trigger on somebody, that he remembers something from our program. He might remember our program where there was a moment of humanity where people actually touched each other, which is what they don't do when things get tough."

Like any community effort, Toomey's project was an experiment at first. It wasn't easy. The kids were highly suspect of the athletes and the people who were brought in to teach. "Toward the end of the program they understood that nobody was trying to get into their heads to change anything. They were just trying to make them think about who they were, what they were doing, and what they could really be."

Toomey's roots go way back to community involvement. He is steeped in a tradition of giving, pro bono, something to people with less. "When I worked for the Peace Corps as an adviser we went around the world to these countries that had struggling economies. One of the things they wanted more than anything else was sport, because they felt that what that did for their youth was to create leadership. Even though they were struggling for food they wanted to have a sports program because they wanted to have an identity, a morality, and an integrity to who they were. They wanted to have this identity for themselves and their own people, as well as an identity to show to the world. I think we need to accept responsibility for this ethic of sport, especially at the high school level where it's a minimal cost to our society."

Toomey gets emotional and feels distraught when he talks about budgets cutting out sport programs in our public schools. He has data from a major study that looked at the costs of maintaining athletic programs. "I can't remember the numbers, but it's ridiculous. We are cutting out things that absolutely address the greatest problems we have, which is the breakdown of society and family. And sports are really a unique adventure that Americans have always had. It's been part of our daily regimen. And most important it is education and the only place where you can learn how to be a team member. It's the place where you first learn, whether it's the tennis court or on the football gridiron, that there are rules. And regardless of where you play (on Astroturf or on a bunch of rocks in the inner city), there's no cheating. And if you cheat, then your friends let you know about it. Classrooms are, in an abstract sense, an extension of this concept where education can become a formalized process. But we really need to have the playing fields so that our kids can learn the ethics of fair play."

Olympic champion, high achiever, and community activist, Bill Toomey went one step further. His philosophy of health care and prevention was not solicited by Hillary Rodham Clinton, but he will give you the spiel anyway. It's a good spiel; it's rational and makes clear sense! "Spiraling costs don't need to endanger our country. Sport is an adventure in fitness. And fitness is probably the most important thing in this country where our health care and well-being is involved. You can't remove these components from the early learning stages of our youth and expect that all of the other things are going to take care of themselves. Sport is social ecology, it is part of our mental health and well-being curriculum. It is all linked to productivity—it is all related."

Olympic swimmer Nancy Hogshead subscribes to the same philosophy as Bill Toomey. She's an activist, a community fighter, and a key player in the world of women's sports. She is a serious advocate for ethics and a single standard of conduct in all athletics. She is a swimming champion who realized early on the benefits of sport to enhance one's human potential.

As director of the Women's Sports Foundation in New York City, Nancy is committing her entire professional life to community outreach with a specific focus on women in sport. She describes her journey and personal awakening to the role of women in sport. Hogshead got started with her work in 1984 when Olympic champion Donna DeVarona came and talked to all the Olympic swimmers about Title IX. She had never heard of Title IX and didn't know what it was, but remembers thinking that legislation to allow women to have college scholarships was pretty damn important and not to be taken for granted. She remembers thinking that she had gotten a college scholarship to Duke because she had worked very hard. It never occurred to her that this was due, in part, to federal legislation.

Hogshead explains that Title IX was not just a cultural awakening that led people to suddenly start giving money to women in sports. It was a whole political movement. "I was a Women's Studies major in college and we were examining women in third world countries. By my junior year, I realized that for my life's goals this was something I wanted to do. I wanted to be a part of this movement that impacted women and sport."

Nancy broke down the components and gave me the specifics of how the Women Sports Foundation gets involved with sport and, in particular, women's issues. The foundation responds to simple requests for information about scholarship programs and where women can get a good education but also be an athlete. The foundation promotes opportunities for women in sports, and supports gender equity. It's a nonprofit educational organization that seeks to enhance the sports experience. They answer 250,000 phone calls a year that range from career guides for women to coaching or officiating. They also enhance Title IX enforcement. They put together people who will assist with legal needs in processing violations of Title IX requirements.

Hogshead explains that the bottom line is that women deserve the right to have a women's sports experience, both in recreational and in competitive sports. She cites research indicating that kids who play sports do better in school than kids that don't play sports. "Young women in sports are three times more likely to graduate from high school than nonparticipants. They are 92 percent less likely to get pregnant. They are 87 percent less likely to do drugs compared to their nonathletic peers. All of these numbers belie another important social dimension. These statistics don't give the full picture of a young woman struggling with upward mobility and self-esteem issues."

Nancy is big on empowerment issues and how women see themselves in society vis-à-vis sport and competition. She plays hardball when it comes to the legal aspects of protecting women's rights on campus and beyond. "Probably the most egregious case in 1992 was at the University of Massachusetts. They had the most cuts for women's sports while the men's program was getting a lot of gains. They even had a new arena for men's programs and the male athletes were flying first class everywhere. We knew that there were Title IX violations going on there and we knew it was time for an EOC investigation. There was even a quote in Sports Illustrated that said women don't matter. They don't think we mind getting cut and we're not as dedicated as the male athletes."

This kind of stuff gets to Nancy Hogshead. It gets her juices flowing; she has no tolerance for nonsense! The Women Sports Foundation provides the sounding board to all sorts of inequities and violations. This is the 1990s; there is no room for nonsense. "In some cases when we do provide an athletic director or an administration with the data and show them that they are in violation, we sometimes get a twenty-four-hour turn around—anything to avoid a lawsuit." The foundation works at all levels of sport, from developmental to Olympic caliber. At one end of the spectrum it works with younger kids in middle schools and at the high school level. The other extreme might be to provide travel and training award grants to up-and-coming athletes. Kristy Yamaguchi (of 1992 Albertville Olympics fame) is a good example of how the program functions. She received money back when nobody knew who she was.

Hogshead is also responsible for fund raising and making sure that the Women Sports Foundation has money available for these training programs. Some of the corporate contributors to the foundation include Sudafed, a subsidiary of the Burroughs Wellcome Corporation, which gave $150,000 in 1992. Tennis superstar Martina Navratilova also gave $150,000 to get the fund started. Continental Airlines and Budget Rent-A-Car are also corporate players. Nancy Hogshead in her spare time is also quite renowned for her Jockey underwear billboards, including the larger than life one in Times Square in the middle of Manhattan. A portion of her underwear poster contract goes to fund women's sports as well.

Nancy is passionate about sports, but even more so when she talks about women in general getting a bum deal. She is devoting her life to giving something back to the community. She has deep appreciation for her education, her sports experience, and all the pieces that led up to her gold medal Olympic experience and her life's achievements.

Bob Beamon didn't have the luxury of growing up with after-school recreational sports. Or for that matter, taking up competitive sports because it was cool and the right thing to do with your peers. Sport chose him by default—he had to survive. Bob Beamon is a legend, and the tough, harsh environment he grew up in is legendary. His work has taken him back in time and returned him to his roots and to a community in poverty and emotional distress.

He lives in Dade County, Florida, and is working as a special projects coordinator for the Metro-Dade Parks and Recreation Department. His ultimate goal (after making

Olympic history) was to provide a role model and mentorship for dysfunctional kids who were struggling with their identity. Beamon sees himself as a liaison between private enterprise and local government in trying to fight crime through recreation and education. His constituency is high-risk kids who might be on the verge of dropping out of school and those at-risk for becoming institutionalized for behavior that is not socially acceptable. Beamon recruits these kids from areas in Miami that fit the high-risk profile. Beamon knows the single-parent families, those struggling with unemployment, low education, and housing distress. He is sensitive to their needs. He was there himself at one point in his life.

"We try to give a child a well-rounded program. Of course, sports is one of the themes. We also have an art department, which could be for those that are more inclined to be artists, dancers, musicians, and actresses. We try to give these kids a sense of opportunity and availability of options in their lives. We let them know that any child can be in baseball and basketball, but also can pursue dance. They can focus on one discipline or they can choose from a menu of opportunities. And that is a word that we allow them to use and exploit—opportunity."

Beamon also wants these kids to enjoy the process of growth and exploration. "We have kids that have never been on an elevator. We'll take them to a building so that they can see how people live on the tenth floor and let them joyride on an elevator. We want to give them something to shoot for other than just shooting a gun or shooting up drugs or shooting off their mouth. We want to reframe their experience so they are doing things that are positive to the community. We are trying to prevent them from becoming a statistic; thus we are encouraging and supporting them to end up in the column of success." Beamon is articulate, philosophical, almost theological.

He reaches out to dysfunctional youth in an attempt to deal with the demons of his past. He is in therapy, with himself! His work is a reflection of his own struggles. Since he won the gold in that ever-famous 1968 Olympic record-setting long jump, his focus has been to take that passion, that energy, and move it into a place that is equally exciting and rewarding. "I'm still finding myself, I'm not finished yet, I'm still learning. Just now, I'm probably in the third quarter of my apprenticeship for life's achievements. Hopefully, soon, I will start enjoying life to the fullest. I'm just really starting to come around into understanding how each day becomes significant as opposed to dealing with weeks or months or years. Days are definitely key elements for me. There is not enough time in one day to do the things that I want to do. In addition to my job, I am constantly doing interviews, or promoting a program that the Olympic Committee is behind. There is just not enough time for all of that. I wish I had more time." Easy does it, one day at a time: these are familiar mantras in the life of Bob Beamon.

Working with kids and families at risk is his passion. He is terse, almost arrogant, when he begins to respond about the needs of his community. "This is not a fad or a do-gooder thing with me. This is something that is in my blood and that will always be there. It's not something that is going to go away. I'm always going to be there for these kids."

Beamon articulates his goals with ease. They are really quite simple. He wants to reach a few kids through sports and get them to focus on academics and the arts. Beamon uses his own experience growing up in Queens as a springboard for allowing kids to imagine their own potential. He has been giving speeches to schools and communities on a regular basis since 1968 and he is perpetually bombarded with questions about his great success in jumping. "I kind of use the jump as a metaphor—it's there, but it's not really there. You see it, but you don't really see it, because every other factor is more important. So my message to kids using drugs, gang members, child abuse victims, and everyone else is that jumping has done this for me. You can use your abilities to jump into something that you like, and the same thing can happen to you in a different aspect of life. It doesn't necessarily mean that you have to be on the sports page in the newspaper. You might find a great discovery as a doctor, or you could work on a great case as an attorney."

His voice changes, there is a new inflection, a new tone, a quality of uncertainty. He continues. "Or, you could basically be the greatest father and mother and give birth to a wonderfully healthy child. I want you to have a positive, productive, and healthy life." He repeats that line, as if he wants to convince his audience, and himself, that we all have that potential.

The dynamics of sport are such that great athletes and their achievements can have a real impact on the wellness of a community. This sounds like a piece from the American Medical Association. No, in fact, it came from the mouth of educator, sometimes professor, and universally known Olympic coach Bill Bowerman. He demonstrated the power of community health over twenty years ago in the great Northwest, when he brought together a bunch of University of Oregon jocks, the medical community, a private hospital, and the media, for a most unique experiment.

Bill Bowerman has a covenant with the community. He has made education, sport, and the environment (in that order), a priority in his life. Now, into his eighth decade, he is able to reflect on the ethic of sport and his commitment to giving it back to the people, to his community. Bowerman's community experiment began after a trip he took with his University of Oregon track team in the 1960s. Some of his athletes were merely NCAA champions, most were Olympic hopefuls. They were all high achievers!

"We had just taken the entire team to New Zealand to train, to race, and to have some fun. When we got back to Eugene, a local newspaper guy asked me what we had learned down there. I told him that I saw lots of people exercising and engaged in a thing called jogging. The media wanted to know if I thought this type of 'physical' activity would fly in our community. I told him we should give it a try."

Bowerman, the inventor of the Nike waffle shoe that eventually led to his co-founding of the four-billion-dollar athletic sportswear company, went on to describe the process of community sport. "We got the local newspaper, the *Register Guard*, to run an article about getting people together for some community exercise. We told people to come out on a Sunday behind famed MacArthur Court and the first week we had twenty-five people out there. We put them through a simple little introduction on jogging and spent about half an hour on the basics with them. We came back the next week and there's nearly fifty people out there ready to go. Next thing you know the television people are there taking pictures of these people jogging and the whole community is plugged in."

Bowerman becomes animated when he describes what happened next. "After a few weeks we go out there on a Sunday morning and I'll bet there were five-thousand people out on that field. There wasn't room enough to move. And I looked around and thought to myself, 'We may have some real problems; somebody's going to die out here.'" He told everyone to go home. Bowerman decided he had to back up, go to square one, and find out how to introduce large numbers of people to an exercise program. He needed to learn about boundaries and how physically qualified participants were.

Bowerman, eighty four and a tower of physicality, moved to the next phase of the community project. He asked a friend of his, Dr. Ralph Christianson, to help out. Dr. Chris, as he was known, later became the University of Oregon track team doctor. "I told Ralph that I didn't know exactly how we are going get control of this thing. I don't want to be responsible for getting somebody out there competing, have them fall down, and having a coronary. So he recruited a cardiologist, Dr. Waldo Harris, to consult with us."

Bowerman decided to start over, this time with only fifty people, give them a complete physical exam (compliments of the local hospital), and offer them a six-week program, three times a week. "We charged them ten bucks because you know Ralph was a good psychologist, and he knew that if it was free, people wouldn't believe that the program was worthwhile." Bill Bowerman started this program in 1970 when recreational running was virtually unheard of. Looking over at some faded pictures on the wall, he notes that his track stars from the university were out there leading the program. "Everyone knew who they were, so it was a good role model for community health. We divided our groups into one athlete per ten participants, so we had close monitoring and supervision. And when someone was screened out of the program for a bad heart, we had the cardiologists work with them so that they could build up slowly and work into the program."

The whole community experience was positive. The training program was successful and considered by some to be one of the initial models of a public health prevention program. In fact, some of the physicians from the project went back to Chicago to a national AMA meeting and presented the data as a pilot for community public health.

Bowerman, who is known as a legend in competitive track circles, was quite instrumental in shifting the emphasis from competitive sport to community recreation at large. At a time when health promotion, corporate wellness, smoking cessation, and weight-loss programs were unheard of, Bill Bowerman founded a movement that has changed the complexion of leisure time. His movement does not get huge federal research dollars, but has raised a consciousness that is pervasive throughout the United States and beyond.

Every city in America has a road race honoring a major holiday or just a fun run to raise money for a local charity. The jogging for personal health "industry" has given way to creative fund-raising for drug-free communities and schools, heart and lung associations, and the American Cancer Society. The whole recreational running movement is an outgrowth of some "old coaches and a group of young jocks who wanted to give something back to the community." Bowerman smiles and his eyes light up. He is proud of his accomplishments, and he takes pride in this particular achievement. "After we had our athletes out there, it was a snowball effect. We had our doctors, the hospital, the specialists, and then young and old—anyone who wanted to start an exercise program. We had good records of what we did and, invariably, we were paid a high compliment by the director of the hospital. He said that this community exercise program did more for wellness in our state than any of the other medical health promotions had ever done."

Bowerman had fun with this project. He still gets tickled when people read his book, *Jogging*, a testimony to a bunch of jocks who wanted to make a difference in their community.

The lives of great achievers are usually measured by their stature on the winner's podium. Little do we know about their role off the podium, outside of the sports pages, and in the low-profile day-to-day drudgery of community service. It is curious to examine the outreach efforts of Toomey, Hogshead, Beamon, and Bowerman. All had their passions on the field, in the gym, and in the pool, and are now converting energy and love to those families and communities who need something extra, something special. The same passion that drove these achievers in athletic pursuits is now driving these individuals to a higher calling, one that doesn't reward with money and medals, prestige and shoe contracts. It is a higher calling to community service so that their protégés can compete on a level playing field, and someday, hopefully, be great achievers themselves.

CHAPTER 11
TWO OF THE BEST GIVE A GIFT

"No matter how good the team may be, it won't win the championship without the owner fully in the game. I am disappointed that you have dropped the ball, Mr. President."

Earvin Magic Johnson
1992 Olympian
Gold Medalist, Basketball

This chapter discusses the work of two important high achievers. Both are well known to the consumer imagery of television viewers and both were, at one time, amateur athletes who transcended to stardom as Olympians. Both of these individuals have also had the title of "professional" athlete bestowed upon them. Both are now achieving stardom as leaders in the forefront of AIDS education and awareness efforts, giving time, energy, love, and lots of money to the cause of saving lives. Scott Hamilton, a 1984 Olympic figure skating champion, initiated The Friends of Scott Hamilton Foundation in order to reach kids in distress and families traumatized by the AIDS virus. Earvin Magic Johnson retired from professional basketball in 1991 and then re-emerged as a gold medalist in the 1992 Olympics.

We begin with the work of Scott Hamilton. Scott was in between whirlwind tours of benefit skating performances when his agent called to say that he would be available for an interview. He was tired from all the jet lag, yet he managed to retain that bubbly, upbeat persona as we talked. As a segue into his work with children and families in distress, Scott opened the door to his life and started talking about his childhood and some of the medical problems he suffered as a kid. "I never really had consistent exposure to kids my age. I was underdeveloped, so I had no muscle tone at all. I was the smallest in my class, sick a lot, and consequently spent little time in school. I was in clinic hospitals in Boston, Toledo, Detroit, and Bowling Green, and I really didn't get to play much of my childhood. The only exposure I had to other kids were with sick kids. I don't know if it was obvious to me, but I'm sure that being the last one chosen on any football or softball team tends to make you feel down on yourself. I was always picked last because I had the least muscle development, lacked coordination, and I was the weakest one. I was always kind of the last one on the totem pole or the last one to be considered. It was always, 'OK, we'll take him.' And so when I started skating, I found that I could skate circles around these macho guys. I finally started to feel pretty good about myself and I turned around a lot of the negativity and low self-esteem that I had. I think every kid has to have something that makes them feel good. For me, it was knowing I could skate as well or better than anybody in my class."

Scott's openness and candor is refreshing. He is like an old friend that you connect with after a long time. You just pick up where you left off. Hamilton's mother had an important influence over his life. She helped him out a great deal. "She was just this incredible source of strength. She was suffering from cancer, and yet she knew she had to get a better job to keep me on the ice, with skates and the right equipment. While she was fighting for her life, she was going to school and teaching full time. She really went through an ordeal in order to get a better job. She went from being a second grade teacher when I started skating, to being an associate professor at Bowling Green State University. She died when I was seventeen and didn't see a lot of the success I had with sports. She was a solid source of strength and a role model for me."

Scott's mother was and still is a great inspiration to him. He often reflects on his mom and the meaning of her short life when he does outreach to kids who are fighting life-threatening illnesses. "As I got into different parts of my life, several people came forward to help me. There was a family in Chicago who started to help me pay for my skating. They were not only sources of financial stability, but also of emotional strength. My mother and the extended family that came into my life after her death gave me a deep sensitivity for the human condition."

Clearly, Scott Hamilton is one who understands and lives with a feeling for human suffering. His words are thoughtful, reflective, and spoken with great compassion. He started his own group, The Friends of Scott Hamilton Foundation, in order to dedicate and focus his energies to helping others who are medically in distress. The foundation is a charity that mainly assists children. "Anything that I can do to help children and their afflictions, I'll be there for them! It was formed so that several of us athletes could raise money to help kids with their medical problems. We also wanted to educate athletes about their sense of responsibility in giving something back to the community. We wanted to let them know that they are the haves and they can make a difference in someone's life, especially among the have nots."

The foundation has been doing major fund-raising for children's hospitals, the Children's Miracle Network, and pediatric AIDS research. Recently, Scott and his colleagues have been showing up at television award ceremonies and skating events and making as much noise about AIDS prevention as possible. Scott is sensitive and compassionate when he refers to kids who are HIV positive and those who may be suffering. "I was in a hospital for a long time when I was a kid and I know what that's like. It can be very lonely and terrifying, and if I can help some kids feel a little bit better or raise some funds that will make their stay in the hospital or their illness shorter, I am more than happy to be a part of it."

Hamilton becomes deathly serious when he speaks of AIDS and the skating community. There is no hesitation in his voice when he speaks of this dreaded virus. "AIDS is a very serious social problem that needs more attention and should be addressed more directly before it is too late, before it has devastating effects in all walks of life. I think the powers that be, including the Olympic federations, understand that. Personally, I have lost some pretty close friends to AIDS. In 1990, Rob McCall, a Canadian Olympic medalist, fell to the disease. We just had a huge benefit for him. 'Entertainment Tonight' was nice enough to do a long piece on Rob and they raised $500,000 for AIDS research in one night. Rob felt very strongly about this issue even before he knew he had the illness. AIDS took his life in just a little over a year. He went through it big time. You could see the effects physically on him. And he was bigger than life. This guy was one of the funniest, most outrageous, energetic people I've ever met, and he weighed eighty-five pounds when he died. When you see something like that, it tends to make you understand that we have had enough of this crap!"

Scott was touched and in the same breath outraged by his friend's untimely death. He was emotional when he reflected on the scourge of AIDS. "This is a disease and it's real and this is something anyone can get. And whether it be from a bad blood transfusion or unsafe sex, or whatever, it's not just something that happens to gay people. It's something that can happen to anyone, including children. Wonderful people are victimized by this thing. It's not just gay folks, it is all folks. You just don't put a label on this disease and pop it into a specific type or social category. This is something I've learned about recently, because when I turned pro in '84, I was very homophobic and it was a big adjustment for me."

Hamilton, initially frightened and wanting to keep some distance from the AIDS story, is now outspoken and urges everyone he meets to get educated. "Get up to speed on this virus, learn about its transmission, learn how you can prevent the spread. I have seen what AIDS does to children and I've seen what it's done to a lot of close, close friends. It's tough. It's really, really hard, so whatever you can do, however you can do it, you get involved and you try to make some noise. I don't really think I'm an activist or anything, but if I can talk about it in a way that may reach other people, I will."

Scott has the same passion when he talks about the cancer that overcame his mother. He senses that we are making some progress with cancer, but he has that reserve in his voice which suggests that we haven't done enough, that we are not targeting our research money correctly. He becomes frustrated and sad when he reflects on preventing breast cancer, the malignant melanoma that conquered his mom. "If there were different ways of detecting or earlier warning signs, maybe she would have lived longer. You have to get out there and get involved and make some noise about these issues. If you sit back and you watch all the time, everything is going to pass you by."

Hamilton has the attention of the athletic community. He also has the eyes and ears of millions of television viewers. Between charity benefits and pro skating events, he is not shy about making his public health pitches. He makes no bones about grabbing the microphone from colleagues and interjecting his plea for more sane health care for our children. He is not shy and certainly not timid about the issues that really matter in life! When it comes to his future, his skating, his politics, his exposure in the bigger global scale of things, there is an ambivalence that filters through his voice. His inflection changes, there is a reserve. Scott Hamilton is an athlete. He sees himself on the ice, in the broadcast booth, touching and feeling the essence of other athletes. He doesn't envision himself on a commission somewhere in the ivory tower, isolated, stashed away from the children who are suffering and friends who are dying a slow death.

Scott does not shy away from the notion of public stature, but feels that there are athlete achievers who are better suited to go to Washington and make some real noise about public health issues. There are those who know how to walk softly and carry a big stick, and make themselves heard in Congress. Scott likes Magic Johnson! He has deep respect for his stature, both in and out of the athletic arena. "The man has incredible clout in any universe. Whether he serves on or off a Presidential AIDS Commission, the guy carries the power and prestige, people are just so moved by his persona! The bureaucracy and red tape of the AIDS Commission is slowing down the progress of a time-critical issue for AIDS victims. Earvin can chart his own course and set in motion any political wheels that need to assist the cause."

One senses that Hamilton would make a great spokesman for any cause, and yet he is just as comfortable taking a supporting role to the big guns, the guys with the moves and the power plays, the ones that can kick some butt on the political court.

Earvin Magic Johnson is frustrated with the politics of AIDS and now has more than a passing interest in getting things moving, at fast break, full court speed.

I met Magic Johnson and many of his teammates in Barcelona, the site of the 1992 Olympics. This was a special event, no doubt, with images of great athletes against a backdrop of extraordinary architecture, culture, and very cordial people. I was struck by a few powerful events that occurred at the 1992 games, both in the athletic arena and outside of it.

Magic Johnson, an unlikely figure in an Olympic uniform, came with his colleagues of the NBA. In fact, the twelve superstars of the Dream Team commanded the limelight and caused a great distraction to the true ethic of amateur athletics and achievers in Barcelona. The games seemed awkward and shamed by the media spectacle and presence of these "giant" superstar professional athletes. I think basketball was on the minds of most of these twelve competitors; however, one athlete came to Barcelona with another agenda.

Earvin Magic Johnson came to Barcelona to play with the USA Dream Team, but his real purpose for being in Spain at the Olympics, I believe, had a greater meaning, a deeper sense of purpose.

The T-shirts read "No Pain, No Gain!" Magic Johnson came to Spain *with some pain*! He came to play basketball, his love and passion, but he also came to make a statement about his condition. On November 7, 1991, he announced his retirement from the NBA and the Los Angeles Lakers due to testing HIV positive. From day one of his diagnosis, he has let the world know that he will continue to lead a normal life. This normality would include working out in the gym, shooting some hoops, paying close attention to the advice of his medical team, and most importantly, reducing the stigma surrounding the AIDS virus.

The brief history of his well-publicized AIDS diagnosis has not been without controversy. When Johnson announced his desire to play in the All-Star Basketball Game in February 1992, some of his colleagues said he shouldn't be there, that he had already retired and the all-star slot should be made available to others still active in the league. When he announced his desire and willingness to play for America and be a member of the "Olympic Dream Team," the Australian Olympic Team, led by a misinformed medical staff, threatened to withdraw all Australian competitors because of the risk of HIV transmission from Johnson's bodily fluids.

Johnson did travel, train, and compete with the Dream Team in Barcelona. At every stop, he was met with world-wide adoration, both in the foreign press and in huge crowds waiting to greet him. NBA commissioner David Stern said, "It was like traveling with the Beatles and the Rolling Stones all in one package on a concert tour." Of course, the only difference between a rock star and an NBA athlete is that NBA athletes are afforded the opportunity to be physical on the court and then verbally abusive in the media twenty-four hours later. Charles Barkley, who set out to offend his opponents by physically assaulting them during one Olympic contest, embarrassed most of America by writing and defending his actions in a daily *USA Today* column the very next day. Fortunately for sport and international diplomacy, Magic Johnson was in Barcelona cleaning up the mess and learning how to become a foreign diplomat and statesman.

Magic spent an afternoon at the Barcelona outlet for Toys 'R Us, and gave out toys and autographs to underprivileged and disadvantaged children. With little fanfare, he managed to show up at the gymnastics venue, USA women's basketball competition, and at the track and field stadium. When the NBC cameras spotted him in the audience and tried to project his face across a billion screens, he told them to go away, he didn't want to distract them and their viewers from the competitors and their moments of glory. He told the media that he was there to honor and show respect for other Olympians. He told me the night of the women's gymnastic competition that he was absolutely in awe of the grace, beauty, and athleticism of these young bodies. "I am blown away by how hard these young kids work. They are the essence of amateur sport, they are the core of the Olympic games."

Later in the week, Johnson found himself in a personal (one on one) meeting with Juan Antonio Samaranch, the Big Daddy of the Olympiads, the CEO of the IOC. He asked Samaranch to assist him with his quest for better education and more awareness of AIDS prevention. He asked Samaranch to use his clout with the Olympic movement to secure financial assistance for AIDS sufferers and their treatment needs. He asked the IOC chief to do community outreach in Spain, in America, and extend his reach to all 172 participating Olympic nations. Samaranch said he would help: in what form, it is still unclear. Samaranch, in turn, did make a request of Magic Johnson. He told him to keep playing basketball and spread the gospel according to the

NBA. And then he thanked him for coming to Spain with his NBA colleagues.

I initially spoke to Earvin Johnson about a drug prevention evaluation project my colleagues and I had done in connection with the Laker organization several years ago. He thanked me with that ever-engaging smile. "Good work, you done good work. That was an important project." He pre-empted me just as I wanted to thank him for his contribution to the video outreach project. He did not, however, want to talk about another prevention effort, one that has far more serious consequences.

Magic didn't want to talk about the National AIDS Commission in the summer of 1992. He was struggling with his role in that arena. He was frustrated. Things move so slowly in Washington, even if you do carry a big stick. He commented that he had a lot on his plate right now and that he needed to sort out the politics of the Commission when he got back to the United States. He subsequently resigned on September 25, 1992, citing President Bush's incompetence with the AIDS issue.

Earvin Johnson was originally appointed to the Commission by President Bush back in November of 1991, shortly after his press conference about retirement from the Lakers. Since late 1991, Magic had met with President Bush on several occasions in his capacity as a member of the National AIDS Commission. He appeared on many national television shows discussing the work of the agency. On one occasion (January 14, 1992) when he met privately with the president, he carried a special letter that had been carefully worded by AIDS experts. The letter articulated a precise request for action and dollar amounts for funding research and treatment. The letter and the face-to-face confrontation with George Bush was published in Johnson's book, *My Life,* and became a pivotal issue in his decision to become a serious social activist and not just some former jock trying to make a name for himself in the real world.

"I met with Mr. Bush in January and told him that as president he could do more than anyone to fight the battle. I asked the president to provide the missing AIDS research money for NIH with a specific demand of $400 million in 1992 and $500 million in 1993. I also asked the president to fund the Ryan White Care bill for treatment which consisted of $300 million for 1992 and $600 million for 1993. Finally, I asked that Medicaid pay for people with HIV which would cost another $500 million in 1993. I told the chief executive in the Oval office that we cannot afford to lose this game. I'm a fighter and so are you, let's do it together."

Magic served on the AIDS Commission for nine frustrating months and then on September 25, 1992, he sent the president of the United States another letter saying; "I cannot in good conscience continue to serve on a presidential commission whose important work is utterly ignored by your administration. No matter how good the team may be, it won't win the championship without the owner fully in the game. I am disappointed that you have dropped the ball." This letter of resignation made headlines around the globe. In fact, during one of the three U.S. presidential debates in the fall of 1992, one of the moderators raised the issue of Earvin Johnson's resignation.

In addition to playing in the political arena, Earvin Johnson has established his own organization known as the Magic Johnson AIDS Foundation. It was formed in 1992 and has raised many millions of dollars. Some of that funding has come from the NBA, and $600,000 has been raised by the Laker organization alone. Although Johnson's endorsements with 7-Up and Converse shoes have been put on hold (presumably due to his HIV condition), his visibility for community outreach is everpresent. Hardly a week goes by that there is not a television report or national newspaper/ magazine story about his career and how he is managing his life in this uncertain "time of AIDS." Johnson went to the public (again) in March of 1992 with his Nickelodeon For Children program about prevention and the spread of AIDS. He was interviewed by noted correspondent Linda Ellerbee, surrounded by a group of culturally and ethnically diverse children, about the whole concept of AIDS prevention. Some of the children were HIV positive and some were actually in the advanced stages of fighting the virus. The program addressed the issues of contact in school, how AIDS is transmitted, prevention measures, and how best to talk among our peers about the virus and its effect on the family and the community at large. The program was deeply sensitive and touching. It was perceived as an experiment on national television and was considered such a success, according to Nielsen ratings, that PBS and other networks ran the show several times.

Magic Johnson's good health, athletic conditioning, and positive attitude, are working wonders on his T-cell count. His count is up, a sign that AIDS researchers suggest is critical when counterattacking the disease. Johnson would like to be a spokesperson for everybody that is suffering from AIDS. His charisma is untouchable and his compassion for the human condition is off the scale—it can't be measured. One senses that his altruism, his charity work, his love of family and his son are the pieces that make him human. But what he really wants in life is to transcend that humanness, move to another plateau, and ultimately to be back on the court with his buddies. One senses that there is this terror, this feeling of inadequacy, and vulnerability within his soul. It's a terror that can only be dealt with on the open court, in the lane, making those no-look passes and assists. The ones that make him look good but also make him feel even better, about himself!

Earvin Johnson, Scott Hamilton, and countless other prominent athlete achievers, are making their mark in public health and prevention issues around the globe. Their styles are, indeed, quite different. Their approach to the media, to the political system, and to public policy have their own distinct, personal imprint. It is clear that their words are being broadcast, seen and heard by millions. Whether their messages are being heeded or falling on deaf ears, we will not really know the outcome of for many years to come.

CHAPTER 12

A VIEW FROM ABOVE: THE IVORY TOWER

> *"Physiology is just a small part of the equation in the total makeup of the elite athlete. It is mainly psychology and a particular understanding of the personality characteristics that leads one to identify the high achievers in sport. If you factor in stress management, resiliency factors and coping responses, the whole package is there. The research and application has to be from the psychological court so that we can get a better handle on personal focus and those individuals who really want the recognition. That's the driving force that will make an individual do whatever it takes to get the job done. If you take those ingredients and mix up the batter with someone that knows what they're doing in the coaching field, then your recipe for success and achievement is on the table!"*

> *Peter Snell, Ph.D.*
> *1960, 1964 Olympian*
> *Gold Medalist, Track and Field*

In reviewing and summarizing all the faces and personalities of these great achievers, I chose to examine closely the views and perspectives of a few noted and gifted individuals. They not only achieved a high level of commitment and excellence in sport but also in academia as well. Ed Etzel excelled in the Olympic arena as well as the educational one. He has a doctorate in counseling psychology, was a twelve-time national rifle champion, and won a gold medal in shooting for the U.S. at the 1984 Olympics. Peter Snell earned a Ph.D. in exercise physiology and became the director of the St. Paul Human Performance Laboratory at the University of Texas Southwestern Medical Center in Dallas. An eight-time world record holder in track and field for his native New Zealand, he won a gold medal in the 800 meters in the 1960 Olympics, and won gold medals in both the 800 and 1500 meters at the 1964 games.

Dr. Alex Tarics, a Hungarian-born achiever, was on the gold medal water polo team for his native land during the 1936 Berlin Olympics. He completed his Ph.D. in Budapest, only the forty-seventh doctoral degree ever granted at that point, and subsequently moved to the United States in 1948. After receiving citizenship, he joined a prominent architectural and engineering firm of which he later became chairman. Today, the firm of Reid and Tarics is known internationally for its prominence in the design and building of structures that are earthquake-proof. Steven Gregg, a 1976 Olympic swimmer, felt there was a reason for his great physiological success. He went to Berkeley to try and find out, earning a doctorate, and then left to pursue a career in exercise physiology. He still isn't satisfied with his achievements and wants to push the envelope of corporate America.

Peter Snell, Ed Etzel, Alex Tarics, and Steven Gregg are high level achievers who have interesting views about motivation, psychological preparation, and the transitioning phase from sport into the real world. We begin with Dr. Ed Etzel.

Ed Etzel says that his athletic training often interfaces with his psychology background when counseling athletes. In his sport of rifle shooting, use of mental practice skills was essential. "Those are very helpful skills for any athlete, but in this sport, stress management skills are particularly critical. I learned progressive relaxation, autogenic training and diaphragmatic breathing, and I attribute whatever success, especially during the Olympics, to having those anchors."

He should know; he coauthored a book, *Counseling College Student Athletes*, about this practice. Etzel is clear about the analogies from sport to performance in the classroom. You really need to be focused in both places. You have to be completely there to shoot one moment at a time and not be distracted. Etzel learned imagery skills to assist this process. He practiced daily over a considerable amount of time. "Visualizing and mentally rehearsing each shot is essential because it's more or less the same thing each time, although there are changing environmental conditions. There are wind flags, and imagery work is critical in assisting you with the management of stress when the conditions change. Most sports call upon a particular psychological and physiological demand where you have to monitor different types of arousal, and it's tough when your heartbeat is cranked up. You have to have the skills in your toolbox to deal with the stress of competition!"

Etzel explains the art of letting go, saying goodbye to sport. He has become an expert in this arena. He was thrust into it and realized that transitioning out of athletics and into the work force was a necessity, it was survival. It wasn't easy, and he had a serious battle with it. His personal struggle led him on a journey of self-discovery, reassessing his confidence, and believing in himself again. "I think that it has been a very useful experience to look carefully at my transition from seeing myself as an Olympian to a coach (which I did for thirteen years) and now to a psychologist. All three lives have been part of my identity and it has taken a good bit of effort for me and a considerable amount of time to make that full transition into my career path. I think my transition is something that will continue on for the rest of my life."

Etzel doesn't shoot anymore, not for fun or competition; he is burned out! He lost interest in it. He has all the equipment and knows exactly where everything is, but he never touches the stuff anymore. "I distanced myself from it and I think that's been useful in a lot of ways. I think that's growth. You have to know when to hold them and know when to fold them! I think part of what athletes need to learn is the letting go of certain parts of their psyche and then holding onto other parts that allow that new transition to take place."

Etzel's struggle in making a complete transition from sport has to do with the gold medal myth, the one myth that everyone seems to make so much out of. He notes that it is difficult to sort out your own autonomy, the "who you really are" part of that experience. "People make an extraordinary accomplishment out of something that was really quite ordinary for me in terms of my sport. Within the context of the Olympics, it's kind of a big show and our culture tends to blow reality way out of proportion."

Many Olympians in the 1990s are now turning back the clock and reflecting on their accomplishments of the 1950s, 1960s, 1970s, and 1980s. They seem to be reliving the past decades through the media hype of 1990s culture. Etzel suggested that all of us should examine the renewed interest we might have in identifying with our accomplishments from the past. Olympians of yesteryear that take the medal out of the drawer and start doing press conferences and speaking tours might be experiencing another developmental shift in their lives.

In working with college athletes as a faculty member and psychologist, Etzel often gets a referral of an injured and disabled athlete. In his textbook he talks about the delicate nature of intervention with this type of athlete. "It's a critical area. Injury can be a very useful experience for an athlete, especially for those who have foreclosed on their identity early on. They see themselves as an athlete and maintain a fantasy, a gratifying fantasy when they become a professional and don't think much of anything else. Sport is a lifestyle they live and want to play out to the fullest without much prior planning.

"I recently worked with a person who had a career-ending injury and had to make the decision to stop competing. This person went through the denial, anger, grief, isolation, and shift in social status, and now had to confront a major lifestyle change. Injury is tough for most but seems to be additionally hard on athletes who have so much of their physical and emotional self-esteem tied up with their body and their athleticism. Once we did the grief work, evolved into the letting go phase, the career and vocational goals started to emerge for this person. I believe there is a silver lining or blessing in disguise in many injury situations, because this process of self rediscovery is quite instructive for people. Athletes need to learn how to cope—it's part of the growth process." Spoken like a true psychologist, Etzel is one who practices what he preaches.

Alex Tarics, after becoming a great athlete, decided to finish his formal education and become an engineer and architect. He fulfilled his dream in the United States and today is well known for designing over five-hundred schools across the U.S. His firm is responsible for designing and building subway stations under the streets of San Francisco, stations that are tough, resilient, and can take a California licking. He is noted for buildings at the University of California Medical Center in San Francisco—award-winning, earthquake-proof buildings that have people scurrying from the around the world to investigate structurally.

Tarics' work came into national prominence with his introduction of the "base (or seismic) isolation" concept of earthquake protection for major structures. Using this technology, buildings are mounted on earthquake shock-reducing pedestals that prevent most of the ground-moving damage from being transmitted to the structure during an earthquake. He was in charge of the earthquake-resisting design for the first building constructed on base isolators in California. In fact, a hospital using this concept survived the dramatic earthquake in January 1994, centered in Northridge, California.

Dr. Tarics' achievements have brought him major accolades, including the Goethal's Medal and being nominated for the National Medal of Technology, which is given to the most outstanding engineer by the president of the United States.

Alex Tarics has a unique understanding of the relationship between training and discipline in athletics and that which is carried over into the discipline and training in the world of work. "I have learned in athletics that you don't win all the time; many times you lose. Now if you don't correct the feelings attached to those heavy emotions expressed by losing, then you might have some severe consequences in life. You have to adjust immediately when you experience loss, because one day you lose, the next day you win. If you can learn to keep coming back and work harder than you previously did, then you develop a positive attitude. That attitude, which is part of your mental blueprint for life, suggests that if I lost, it is no big deal because I can also turn around next time and win. It has created the philosophy in me that the road to success is paved with failures. It was important for me to learn that lesson. Because in real life there are a lot of disappointments, jobs that you don't get, contracts that fall through. It is part of the game and you have to learn how to shake it off and keep on going."

Athletics taught Alex Tarics something else: the desire to excel, a desire to do better, to outdo others, and to do as well as he could. His philosophy is a sound one. "If the best doesn't succeed, at least you have the satisfaction that you tried everything that you could. Intrinsically you know it is not because you are lazy or that you gave up or have a weakness."

Tarics explains that today's athlete achievers are faced with a new model of success, one that is quite dangerous. "The whole athletic model must change; the attitude is always about winning and losing. The winners are always named; the losers are never mentioned. There are no first and second in this country, there is only first and last. And that's a very bad image, a very bad precedent for our children. The model for athletics as well as any great achievement (including engineering) ought to be the fact that you got to compete in the first place. You are already winning because there are dozens and dozens of people who never even got there. That for me was a very important component in my life, both in sport and in engineering. It is all part of the game of life—you lose or you win, but if you keep on doing it well, then at the end you win because of the great satisfaction you get from being part of the process. Just being part of the system is a victory."

Steven Gregg has a unique view from the ivory tower. After a successful swimming career including a silver medal at the 1976 Olympics, Gregg moved swiftly into academic competition. He worked hard and finished up with a doctorate in exercise physiology. He now runs a team of scientists at the Gatorade research lab, a division of the five-billion-dollar Quaker Oats giant. He loves his work and feels like there is still a lot to learn.

Gregg is concerned about sport and those who exercise properly. His company has collected data on a disproportionate number of deaths in the southeast, in both Alabama and Georgia. During late summer and early fall the temperature exceeds one hundred and ten degrees and 100 percent humidity. It's a deadly combination, and many kids have suffered heat stroke and death due to dehydration during football practices. He has a concern that the media is not doing justice to the issues around athletes' workouts and problems associated with fluid replacement. Gregg says that advertising, including television, print, and radio ads need to say more in an attempt to educate the public.

"Corporate America in conjunction with our media campaigns need to be more proactive in our position about products that help and those that don't contribute to healthy workouts. There is a lot of false and misleading information about diet, nutrition, and liquid supplements. A lot of the fluid replacement products are complete garbage, but the public buys it anyway because it looks sexy on the tube."

Dr. Steven Gregg, scientist and concerned athlete achiever, notes that part of the problem is that everyone wants to be like Mike. They see Jordan holding his cup of Gatorade after playing forty-eight minutes of competitive NBA basketball and they want to imitate him. "Most kids think that's cool. Mike likes Gatorade, Mike has monster dunks above the rim, so we better just drink it, so we can jump higher and get better hang time in the air. It's only a small part of the real story."

Gregg claims that this type of television ad imagery is a disservice to kids, especially those in extremely hot and humid regions of the country who are experiencing problems with fatigue and heat stroke. He feels that Jordan and his NBA colleagues could do more to alleviate the problem. "Anything that these superstars could do would help. It would be more productive if Michael would follow up in his little TV promo with a word about the product. The product is healthy and useful for such and such a reason, that it might actually work with electrolyte replenishment. We happen to know that it does work. We have spent millions in our lab doing research to support this claim."

Gregg feels that being part of the corporate establishment carries a certain amount of ethical conduct and social responsibility. As a sports and exercise physiology scientist, he wants to see the best and most optimum conditions available for all competitive athletes. He knows that along with discipline, perseverance, and a heavy dose of passion, all athletes have to have proper nutrition and constant fluid replacement in their systems. As a former Olympian, he has a moral obligation to ensure safety and healthy training products for all athlete achievers. Gregg and his colleagues work closely with the National Athletic Trainers Association in trying to make sure coaches are educated about training and dehydration problems. He interacts with those setting the standards for health and fitness from the American

Physicians Association and those experts from the American Medical Association and the College of Sports Medicine.

He gets irate when he talks about standards and the violation of a training ethic in sport. "You are supposed to start athletic practice with a combination of the dry ball temperature and the wet ball temperature and there is a specific formula for how much humidity is allowable for these kids to experience during heavy exercise. If it gets to a certain point there, beyond the window of allowable thermal heat load, all coaches are required to cancel practice. This is often not the case. Last year, a kid at Texas A&M University— a walk-on—died right before practice."

This incident is upsetting to Gregg. He knows that such an event is senseless and is avoidable. He also knows that coaches want to exploit the hell out of their athletes in the guise of toughening them up. They want the fittest to survive so they can do combat in any weather condition. He also knows that he and his team of scientists can contribute to a greater awareness level, intervene with educational seminars and lectures. He wants to see athletes, coaches, and trainers clean up their act. It's risky business out there.

"If college-age kids do what college-age kids do—drink coffee, stay up late, drink beer—the signals for disaster are all there. If the coach is riding your butt because you're overweight, and a kid is trying to lose weight by sitting in the sauna all afternoon and then hitting the practice field already dehydrated in one-hundred-degree weather, then the handwriting for crisis is on the wall. Most of the time there is no dialogue between the coaches and players, everybody assumes that the rules are being followed!"

Gregg wants his company, Quaker Oats and the Gatorade division, to get more involved in the educational process. He has already placed himself at the forefront of a lecture and educational tour to reach coaches and trainers. He travels for his company, promoting health, fitness, and preventive training measures. Steven Gregg has responsibility, he gets paid well, and yet he doesn't feel completely fulfilled. He has this urge to help shape public policy and get health and fitness into the proper training regimen. He knows that we can do better!

Peter Snell had a lot to prove, not only on the track, but in the educational arena as well. His dad wanted him to be a cricket player and his mother expected stardom on the tennis court. Snell rejected both ideas in the long run, but was a good boy, and ended up with a decent grasp of both of those activities. Running was, however, his passion and something that he had to discover for himself. "My dad had a stroke when I was seventeen, then another one when I was eighteen. That left him with right-sided paralysis and impaired speech, so he really wasn't too much of an influence in my athletic career."

Snell's dad was somewhat responsible for his desire and motivation to be successful, even though he was unable to communicate because of the strokes. He couldn't speak, yet he could understand. This was painful for Snell. He wanted desperately to please his dad, to somehow get through and share some love with his father. "In my success as an athlete, I took quite a lot of pleasure in realizing that my winning gave him some pleasure. He died five years after his stroke, so I didn't get to finish my business with pleasing dad."

Peter Snell had to overcome some other demons as well. As a teenager, he recalled his dad saying that he was disgusted with his performance in school. "He often compared me to my older brother who was quite successful academically. He told me that I would never measure up to my brother." Snell bristles at that one. There's a visceral reaction to that emotion; it is still tender and bothers Peter Snell today. He not only had to overcome a family stigma of poor academic performance, but one that seems to pervade the culture in New Zealand. "It's a major disappointment to me that New Zealanders have not thought of my doctoral studies and my research as a big deal. People still think of me as a runner. It just seems that for a guy that failed in school and has been able to turn around his educational goals, that's got to be a message of hope for a lot of people that performed poorly early in life."

Peter explains that the transition from sport to the real world is about setting new goals, having new passions, and maybe burying some stereotypical behavior. Snell competes as a master's orienteering athlete, but his real identity is with his teaching and research job at the University of Texas.

Snell works with elite athletes every day and has an interesting insight about high achievers from the biochemical/physiological perspective.

"I think you have to have some genetic goodies in your system and an ability to compete to achieve the elite status, to make the top level. But I think there's a lot of people that have that God-given talent and the potential to be great but could not incorporate the love and passion into developing it. I think that's where the distinction is made. You have to pair the physiological gifts (the genetics) with a deep, deep passion and motivation to train hard and succeed." Snell feels that the perfect athlete, the ideal model, is found in a delicate balance, somewhere in the middle between the most gifted genetically and those with a huge heart and soul for discipline.

As an exercise physiologist, Snell has spent most of his professional career attempting to identify the delicate balance between the genetics and the big heart. But it may be a useless exercise scientifically. Snell takes off his athlete persona and puts on the research scientist cap. He begins to expand on that notion. "Many athletes are written off early because they have an average physiology, nothing spectacular in the body department. So a lot of young aspiring athletes fall through the cracks because they are not coached properly and there is no one to nourish the creative discipline and motivation. We can measure only so much from an oxygen intake, glycogen depletion, and biomechanical assessment perspective. We can make calculations on percentages of intake based on our fancy scales, but ultimately we need to factor in the motivational assessment. We need to know what is going on with this young man or woman from a psychological perspective, from a discipline perspective, and from a passion perspective. This whole business of saying that so-and-so is just genetically superior to so and so is a total copout. It's a bunch of crap!"

Snell offers additional insights about this dilemma. When he began his doctoral work he concluded that physiology was just a small part of the equation in the total makeup of the elite athlete and high achiever. "It is mainly psychology and a particular understanding of personality characteristics that leads one to identify the high achievers in sport. If you factor in stress management, resiliency factors and coping responses, the whole package is there." Peter Snell was a great and gifted athlete. He did extremely well in competition, he had the ability to focus, stayed completely tuned in to his race and could defer any distractions. His first wife used to say that his concentration was so strong that he tuned everything out, including her.

Snell offers up some apologies when trying to understand this model of success. "I still feel that physiologists don't have too much to offer in assessing elite athletes. The research and application has to be from the psychological court so that we can get a better handle on personal focus and those individuals who really want the recognition. That's the driving force that will make an individual do whatever it takes to get the job done. If you take those ingredients and mix up the batter with someone that knows what they're doing in the coaching field, then your recipe for success is on the table!"

Athletes Ed Etzel, Peter Snell, Alex Tarics, and Steven Gregg—from the Olympic podium—offer intriguing insights about desire, motivation, and ultimately elite performances. Dr. Ed Etzel, Dr. Peter Snell, Dr. Alex Tarics, and Dr. Steven Gregg—voices from the ivory academic tower—offer a unique perspective on psychological and physiological functioning, factors that may contribute to the winning game. Ultimately, they all agree on one thing: passion! Without it, there is no such thing as a great achievement.

EPILOGUE

The quest for success is about passion, identifying your goals and following your real desires. It is about perseverance and stretching your limits. *Quest for Success* is Kathy Johnson pushing through obstacles and disappointments and maintaining her focus to fulfill her dreams as an Olympian. It is about Russ Hellickson teaching through experience that "the athlete who gets beat is the athlete who rises above and performs better in the next competition." It's about discipline and "doing what you don't want to do when you don't want to do it."

Quest for Success is a snapshot of fifty-one high achievers; and a glimpse from their early childhood experiences to life beyond the winner's circle. It is Ken Matsuda imploring his stars to define their goals as a "dream with a deadline." *Quest for Success* is about parents, siblings, peers, and community support. It is often about overcoming hardship and dysfunction. It is about Bobby Douglas, Theresa Andrews, and Norma Hilgard battling trauma, emotional turmoil, and deep wounds. It is about Ben Nighthorse Campbell overcoming emotional voids, inferiority, and adapting through his street smarts to become an important policy maker in the U.S. Senate. *Quest for Success* is the glory of Jeff Blatnick beating Hodgkin's disease and simultaneously whipping his athletic opponents!

Quest for Success is swimmer Stephen Clark, who focused hate, anger, and aggression into images so that he was "able to create the tingling feeling that allowed him to compete well and finish strong." It is the words of Russ Hellickson, declaring "success is not so much an occurrence as it is an attitude." It is about mental rehearsal and visualization strategies employed by skiers Holly Flanders and the fabulous Mahre twins.

Quest for Success is the delicate balance required in coaching an athlete, which is more than just acknowledging someone who is physically talented and gifted. Olympic Coach Mel Rosen and his protégé, three-time Olympian Harvey Glance, suggest that there is a nonverbal understanding between the two parties. "There is an unwritten communiqué with the expectation of winning races and being there for the athlete, during both the highs and the lows," says Glance. The love and acknowledgment from *his* coach is a legacy that Glance shares with his own athletes today.

Quest for Success is about the concept of mentors and mentoring. Nearly every high achiever spoke of the influence of their mentors and how that relationship changed their life. Bob Beamon, Tim Daggett, and Bill Toomey, all three great Olympic champions in their own right, had completely different, yet important, mentor experiences. Beamon explains how mentor Larry Ellis helped him break the cycle of despair in his own family and the surrounding environment. Larry Ellis came into his life and shifted Beamon's "high-powered paranoid energy into a productive focus." Ellis' guiding hand and firm convictions led to many positive outcomes. Beamon is clear today that "without Larry's direction and mentorship, I would be just another crime statistic."

Tim Daggett was blessed with the mentorship of three unique individuals with distinct backgrounds and cultures. He had the influence of an African-American, an Asian, and a Soviet. Daggett was not only blessed with having the combined chemistry of three fine coaches as his mentors, but generational longevity as well. Daggett was exposed to three cultures that breed athletes and coaches over many generations. "It is part of their cultural expectation that after athletics they move to the profession of coaching and nurture the next generation along. It is an unselfish system, something Americans have a lot to learn about. It's a database of experience that doesn't just emerge from the written text. It lies in the unconscious learning of many generations of athletes and their mentors."

Quest for Success is about Bill Toomey and his mentorship experiences with Dee Rowe, his very first coach. "He was a terrific mentor then, and continues to be there for young folks today," says Toomey. "Coaches are usually people with a passion. And when you combine that passion with a deep interest in an adventure and a focus on the human struggle within, you then have all the rich dimensions of a fine mentor. And when you have a mentor that follows that passion with his athletes, then you have a special situation that offers a kid a terrific role model for achievement."

Quest for Success is about life after the podium, after the winner's circle. This is a period in life when the hot media lights are dimmed, the roar of the crowd turns to a faint whisper, and athletes must face the inevitable: retirement from sport. What happens next? Do we read about these high achievers thirty years from now becoming chemically dependent, completely destitute, with no focus, no direction? In some cases, our high achievers did struggle, many stumbled and a few fell.

Mitch Gaylord, an elegant and graceful athlete in gymnastics, was not so sure-footed in life after the gold medal. He experienced what many great athletes do when they come off the podium with a medal or two. "Many jump heavily into alcohol and other drugs, to try and fill the emotional space, the empty void." Mitch knew the fear in transitioning his high achiever personality in sports and shifting it to a high achiever personality with drugs. "This combined with my competitive nature spelled absolute disaster! I knew as a competitor that I would party harder and longer than anyone else. Being stuck in a destructive world of substance abuse scared the hell out of me!"

Quest for Success is also about finding a new focus, a new direction, and making a successful transition to the world beyond sport. Mary Osborne Andrews packaged her love and passion of sport using dimensions of inner focus, mental practice, and visualization strategies, and directed it into a successful career path. She and other high achievers are now encouraging corporate America to take up the challenge and set higher standards of excellence in the workplace.

Quest for Success is about fifty-one unique individuals and their stages of growth, maturity, and paths toward personal fulfillment. Several of the steps along that path dealt with family, peer, and social influences that supported each of these high achievers. *Quest for Success* is about Marilyn King teaching her students to "dare to imagine a new day of higher expectations and reshaping goals for a healthier life." It's about Mike Eruzione and the 1980 Olympic Hockey Team, who pushed the envelope and beat a superior Soviet team because they "believed in themselves and believed in each other." It's about Willie Davenport, grounded with two career-ending knee injuries, whose determination to return to the Olympics for a record fifth time left his doctor speechless and "stumped the orthopedic world."

Quest for Success is about Bobby Douglas who instills "a faith and confidence that's necessary to be the best. That's the important thing, to be the very best all-around person and to have faith in yourself. Every day is a masterpiece; you are living a life, you are living a dream."

Quest for Success is more than just the sports pages and their images of slam dunks, home runs, quick photo finishes, and the amazing grace and agility of a high-flying athletic maneuver. In fact, there is more to the game of high achievement. It is a complete package, a matrix of physicality, psychological training, and emotional support. It is about vision, passion, and dreams. It is also about family, coaches, and the mentorship experience. As the father of two very talented teenage daughters, I see the effects of mentorship experiences already taking shape. In the words of decathlete champion Bill Toomey, "There's something special that goes on between a coach and an athlete that probably could never go on between parents and a child. When you get on a bus with a bunch of kids from your soccer, basketball, swimming or gymnastics team, and you are traveling four or five hours to the state championship and you're going up against a major competition, it's a special circumstance. That's where special people are bred. This country starts to lose that if we don't have funding, trained coaches, and our mentors. If we don't provide that whole experience for our children, we will just become another group of ordinary folks."

APPENDIX

THE OLYMPIANS

MARY OSBORNE ANDREWS was born in 1961 (Billings, Montana) and presently lives with her husband in Boulder, Colorado. She received a bachelor's degree in sociology along with a master's in education from Stanford University and now works as an organizational development and corporate training consultant. Ms. Andrews was a member of the 1980 U.S. Olympic Team in the women's javelin and nearly made the 1992 team twelve years later, finishing 13th at the U.S. trials. In addition to her Olympic success, she takes particular pride in having received the Dorothy Fontis Award while at Stanford: an award named after her college coach's mother and one given to the person who best exemplifies both academic and athletic abilities at the collegiate level. *(Page 121)*

THERESA ANDREWS was born in 1962 (Maryland) and presently lives in Virginia. She received a bachelor's degree in therapeutic recreation from the University of Florida before moving on to The Ohio State University where she obtained her master's in social work. Ms. Andrews currently works in pediatric oncology at the University of Virginia Medical Center. A double gold medalist in the 100-meter backstroke at the 1984 Olympics, she touched the hearts of millions around the world when, shortly after her first-place finish, she awarded her gold medal to her brother, Danny, who had recently become paralyzed from the waist down as the result of a tragic bicycle accident. *(Page 31)*

BOB BEAMON was born in 1946 (New York) and presently lives in Miami, Florida, with his wife and their two daughters. He attended the University of Texas at El Paso and Adelphi University earning bachelor's degrees in sociology and anthropology. For the past ten years, Mr. Beamon has worked as a counselor and role model for troubled inner-city youth through the Metro-Dade Park and

Recreation Department. In addition to his social work, he has appeared in a motion picture, numerous television commercials, and authored an autobiography, *The Perfect Jump.* In 1968 he captured a gold medal in the long jump, shattering the world record by almost two feet to achieve a distance of 29 feet, 2 1/2 inches. Beamon's was a record that would last twenty-three years and is widely considered one of the greatest moments in modern Olympic history. He is a winner of the prestigious Sullivan Award and a charter member of The United States Olympic Committee Hall of Fame. *(Pages 99, 162)*

JEFF BLATNICK was born in 1957 (Schenectady, New York) and presently lives in Half Moon, New York, with his wife. He earned a bachelor's degree in physical education from Springfield College and was later awarded an honorary doctorate in humanics from the same school. Today, Mr. Blatnick works as a television sportscaster while also maintaining a busy schedule as a much sought-after motivational speaker. A member of the 1980 and 1984 U.S. Olympic Teams, he both won a gold medal in the Greco Roman wrestling competition and served as the U.S. flagbearer in the closing ceremonies of the 1984 games in Los Angeles. What is perhaps most remarkable about Mr. Blatnick's athletic achievements was his ability to overcome Hodgkin's disease and lymphatic cancer to capture Olympic gold in 1984. Few who watched him receive his medal as tears poured down his face will ever forget such an intense moment of personal glory. *(Page 45)*

BILL BOWERMAN was born in 1911 (Portland, Oregon) and presently lives in Eugene, Oregon, with his wife, Barbara. He received bachelor's degrees in business administration, physical education, and premed from the University of Oregon where he competed in track and field and quarterbacked the Duck's football team. He then earned his master's in education from Columbia University. From 1949 through 1972 he served as the University of Oregon head track and field coach, during which time he won four NCAA team titles, coached twenty-four individual NCAA champions, and produced twenty-eight Olympians on the way to becoming a legend. He was appointed head track and field coach of the

1972 U.S. Olympic Team and after retiring from coaching in 1975 became cofounder of the Nike Corporation. Father of three children and grandfather of six, Mr. Bowerman continues to be active with his wife in university, community, and sports activities. *(Pages 61, 113, 165)*

ED BURCH was born in 1951 (Las Vegas) and presently lives with his wife and their two children in Albuquerque, New Mexico. He received both bachelor's and master's degrees in special education from the University of New Mexico and is currently owner and head coach of the Gold Cup Gymnastics Club in Albuquerque. During his twenty years of coaching, Burch has consistently led gymnasts to national and international championships. As U.S. head coach for the 1992 World Gymnastics Championships, two of his most notable students included 1992 Olympians Lance Ringnald and gold medalist Trent Dimas. *(Page 76)*

ED BURKE was born in 1940 (Napa Valley, California) and presently lives in Los Gatos, California, with his wife and their two daughters. He received bachelor's and master's degrees in political science from San Jose State University and currently serves as CEO of Aerobic Sports Corporation, a company he founded in 1978. Along with his entrepreneurial activities, Mr. Burke has worked as a university professor and served on a number of national committees to help develop world-class American hammer throwers. A three-time Olympian in the hammer throw, he competed in the 1964, 1968, and also in the 1984 Los Angeles Olympics where, at age forty-four, he was oldest competitor in the games and was chosen to represent the U.S. as flagbearer in the opening ceremonies. *(Pages 143)*

MILT CAMPBELL was born in 1933 (Plainfield, New Jersey) and still lives there after raising three children. He studied physical education at Indiana University and currently makes his living as a motivational speaker while devoting much of his time to community service in his native New Jersey. Mr. Campbell won a silver medal in the decathlon at the 1952 Olympics and followed with a gold medal performance in 1956, making him the first African-American to ever win the event and earning the title "World's

Greatest Athlete." Shortly after retiring from track and field, he went on to play professional football for the Cleveland Browns. A member of the National Track and Field Hall of Fame, he was inducted into the U.S. Olympic Committee Hall of Fame, an honor most believe has been long overdue. *(Page 6)*

BEN NIGHTHORSE CAMPBELL was born in 1933 (Auburn, California) and presently divides his time between Washington, D.C., and his home in Colorado. He received a bachelor's degree in physical education from San Jose State University and attended Meiji University in Tokyo. A former jewelry designer, rancher, and champion quarter horse trainer, he was most recently a third-term Democrat in the U.S. House of Representatives before his November 1992 election to the U.S. Senate. He was a 1964 U.S. Olympic Judo Team gold medalist and a medalist at the 1963 Pan American Games. Senator Nighthorse Campbell, himself the father of two children, is the son of a Portuguese immigrant and a Northern Cheyenne Indian and is the only Native American presently serving in either the House of Representatives or the United States Senate. *(Page 4)*

KIM CARLISLE was born in 1961 (Ft. Lauderdale, Florida) and presently lives in Menlo Park, California, with her husband and their son. She received a bachelor's degree in communications from Stanford University and currently works as the Director of Annual Giving for Stanford Athletics and as a freelance writer and sports consultant. Ms. Carlisle is a two-time NCAA swimming champion, four-year All American, and was a member of the 1980 U.S. Olympic Team. Today, she continues to compete as a master's swimmer and is a three-time national master's champion. *(Page 145)*

STEPHEN CLARK was born in 1943 (Oakland, California) and presently lives in northern California with his wife and their three daughters. He graduated cum laude from Yale University with a degree in political science, received his JD from Harvard Law School, and a master's in taxation from Golden Gate University. He is currently an attorney with the law firm of Bronson, Bronson, & McKinnon specializing in general business, real estate, and corporate practice. Mr.

Clark swam for the U.S. at the 1960 and 1964 Olympics, winning three relay gold medals at the 1964 games in Tokyo. From 1965 to 1966 he served as the Peruvian national swimming coach, and in 1966 he was inducted into the International Swimming Hall of Fame. *(Page 21)*

ANNE WARNER CRIBBS was born in 1945 (Burlingame, California) and presently lives in Palo Alto with her husband and their two youngest of nine children. She received a bachelor's degree with honors in political science from Stanford University and is currently a partner and vice president of Cavalli & Cribbs, a northern California advertising and public relations firm. A Pan American Games gold medal winner at fourteen, Ms. Cribbs won a gold medal in the 400-medley relay at the 1960 Olympics and is a two-time American record holder in both the 100- and 200-meter backstroke. She remains active in community athletic affairs today and is president of Northern California Olympians. *(Page 139)*

TIM DAGGETT was born in 1962 (West Springfield, Massachusetts) and continues to live there today. He received a bachelor's degree in psychology from UCLA and worked as a television sportscaster for NBC at the 1992 Olympics in Barcelona. He is currently the head coach of the Tim Daggett Gold Medal Gymnastics Club. Mr. Daggett won a bronze medal in the pommel horse and scored a perfect 10 on the high bar to give the United States the team gold medal at the 1984 Olympics in Los Angeles. *(Page 104)*

WILLIE DAVENPORT was born in 1943 (Troy, Alabama). A graduate of Southern University with bachelor's and master's degrees in physical education, he is now a major and communications officer for the U.S. Army National Guard. A U.S. Olympic Team member in 1964, Maj. Davenport won a gold medal in the 110-meter high hurdles at the 1968 Olympics. He competed for the U.S. once again in the 1972 Olympics and earned a bronze medal in the hurdles at his fourth Olympics in 1976 along with being chosen by his teammates to carry the country's flag in the closing ceremonies. In 1980 he became the first African-American to participate in the Winter Olympics as a member of the four-man bobsled team. A five-time Olympian, he was inducted into the

National Track and Field Hall of Fame in 1981 and into the Olympic Hall of Fame ten years later. *(Page 92)*

BOBBY DOUGLAS was born in 1942 (Bellaire, Ohio) and presently lives with his wife and their son in Ames, Iowa. He received a bachelor's degree in physical education from Oklahoma State University and a master's in physical education from Arizona State University. Recognized as an expert technician and scholar of the sport, Mr. Douglas served as head wrestling coach at Arizona State University for eighteen years before accepting the same position at Iowa State University. A two-time Olympian in 1964 and 1968, he served as a valuable member of the U.S. coaching staff for the last four Olympics before being appointed U.S. Head Coach for the 1992 games in Barcelona. Under his guidance, three American wrestlers captured gold medals, including his assistant coach at Iowa State. Winner of five national AAU titles and a runnerup in the 1966 World Championships, Mr. Douglas is a member of both the NAIA and National Wrestling Halls of Fame. *(Pages 29, 64)*

MIKE ERUZIONE was born in 1954 (Winthrop, Massachusetts) and continues to live there today with his wife and their three children. He received his bachelor's degree in education from Boston University and currently divides his time between a busy schedule as a motivational speaker and successful television sportscasting career. Captain of the 1980 U.S. Olympic hockey team, Mr. Eruzione scored the winning goal against the much-favored Soviets in the final seconds of their semifinal game and went on to lead his teammates to the gold medal two nights later in Lake Placid. The U.S. victory shocked sports fans around the world and will long be remembered as one of the greatest upsets in Olympic history. *(Page 140)*

EDWARD ETZEL was born in 1952 and presently lives with his wife Pam in Morgantown, West Virginia. He received a bachelor's degree in secondary education from Tennessee Technological University before moving on to West Virginia University where he earned a master's in physical education and an Ed.D in counseling psychology. A licensed psychologist in private practice, he currently works part-time as an assistant professor in the School of Education at West Virginia University and with the WVU Carruth Center for Counseling and Psychological Services as an outreach psychologist for the department of intercollegiate athletics. Dr. Etzel is co-editor of *Counseling College Student Athletes*, a book that deals with issues and interventions among collegiate athletes. He is a twelve-time national rifle champion and won a gold medal in shooting for the U.S. at the 1984 Olympics. As coach of the West Virginia University rifle team, he led his teams to five NCAA championships and was a three-time collegiate All-American himself. *(Page 180)*

HOLLY FLANDERS was born in 1957 (Arlington, Massachusetts) and presently lives with her husband and two children in Park City, Utah. She studied at Middlebury College while training for the U.S. Ski Team. She is a two-time Olympic skier, making the 1980 and 1984 Olympic teams. Ms. Flanders was the top American finisher in the downhill in the 1984 Olympics and between 1982 and 1984 won three World Cup championships. *(Page 82)*

DICK FOSBURY was born in 1947 (Medford, Oregon) and presently lives in Ketchum, Idaho, with his wife and their son. He is a graduate of Oregon State University with a degree in engineering and currently works as a civil engineer. Inventor of the now standard "Fosbury Flop" style of high jumping backwards over the bar, he captured a gold medal for the U.S. at the 1968 Olympics and went on to win the NCAA Championships the following year while completing his studies at Oregon State University. *(Page 75)*

HERMAN FRAZIER was born in 1954 (Philadelphia) and presently lives in Phoenix, Arizona. He received a bachelor's degree in political science from Arizona State University and is currently the school's associate athletic director. In addition to his responsibilities at Arizona State University, Mr. Frazier has long been an active member of many national athletic associations and governing bodies. A former world-record holder in the indoor 500 meters, he won a gold medal in the 4x400-meter relay and a bronze in the 400 meters at the 1976 Olympics. He also earned a spot on the U.S. Olympic Team in 1980. *(Page 131)*

LYNN VIDALI GAUTSCHI was born in 1952 (San Francisco) and presently lives in Morgan Hill, California, with her husband and their two children. She received a bachelor's degree in physical education from San Jose State University and now works as a high school teacher and head swimming coach. A former world-record holder, Ms. Gautschi won a silver medal in the 400-meter individual medley at the 1968 Olympics and captured an Olympic bronze medal in the 200-meter individual relay four years later. In 1988 she was voted Woman Coach of the Year by the California Association of Coaches and has been a member of the Northern California Olympians since 1983. *(Page 128)*

MITCH GAYLORD presently makes his home in Los Angeles where he was born (1961) and raised. Currently pursuing an acting career, Mr. Gaylord has starred in the film *American Anthem*, hosted the television show "Fan Club," and frequently inspires corporate audiences from some of America's leading companies to reach for success. Inventor of the "Gaylord Flip" and the "Gaylord II," he was the first American gymnast to ever score a perfect 10 in Olympic competition. He led the 1984 Olympic Team to its gold medal upset over the favored People's Republic of China. Along the way he captured an individual silver and two bronze medals, making him the winningest U.S. Olympic gymnast in history. *(Page 125)*

HARVEY GLANCE was born in 1957 (Phoenix, Alabama) and presently lives with his wife and their child in Alabama. He received a bachelor's degree in health and human performance from Auburn University and is currently Auburn's Men's and Women's head track and field coach, following in the footsteps of famed Olympic Coach Mel Rosen. Mr. Glance won a gold medal in the 400-meter relay at the 1976 Olympics, earned a spot on the U.S. Olympic Teams again in 1980 and 1984, and was the 1979 and 1987 Pan American Games gold medalist in the 100 meters. *(Pages 16, 102)*

STEVEN GREGG was born in 1955 (Wilmington, Delaware) and presently lives with his wife in Algonquin, Illinois. He received bachelor's, master's and doctorate degrees in exercise physiology from North Carolina State

University, the University of Arizona, and the University of California at Berkeley respectively. Dr. Gregg is currently a research scientist at the Gatorade Exercise Physiology Laboratory and the author of numerous studies on the relationship between anemia and exercise. A member of fifteen U.S. International Swim Teams, he was a silver medalist at the 1976 Olympics as well as a Pan American Games silver medalist in 1975. *(Page 184)*

SCOTT S. HAMILTON was born in 1958 (Toledo, Ohio) and presently makes his home in Denver, Colorado. Mr. Hamilton has been one of the world's most-celebrated figure skaters since 1981, when he won the first of eight consecutive national and world titles. The Olympic gold medal he won in 1984 was the first won by an American since 1960. He is known for his extraordinary speed, footwork and stunts, among them a back flip and battery of triple jumps. Coping with a mistaken and still-undiagnosed childhood disease, Scott used his commitment to exercise and skating to overcome his medical and physical disabilities. He has been inducted into both the U.S. Olympic and World Figure Skating Halls of Fame. Mr. Hamilton is active in numerous charities including Athletes Against Drugs, the Make-A-Wish Foundation, and pediatric AIDS. *(Page 169)*

TONYA HARDING was born in 1970 (Portland, Oregon) where she presently lives. She graduated from Mount Hood Community College with a GED prior to making her first Olympic figure-skating team in 1988. She went on to Albertville, France, for her second Olympics in 1992 and placed fourth in skating, and competed in the 1994 Olympics in Lillehammer, Norway. In 1988 she won the Prize of Moscow, Skate America Gold Medal in 1989, and the silver medal in the 1990 NHK of Japan. *(Page 39)*

RUSS HELLICKSON was born in 1948 (Stoughton, Wisconsin) and presently lives in Columbus, Ohio, with his wife and their three daughters. A graduate of the University of Wisconsin with a bachelor's and master's degree in physical education, he is currently in his seventh season as The Ohio State University head wrestling coach. Along with his coaching responsibilities, Mr. Hellickson is widely recognized as an authority on the sport and also works as a television sportscaster, having covered wrestling at the 1992 Barcelona Olympic Games. An eleven-time National Freestyle Champion, he won a silver medal in the 1976 Olympics and was named captain of the 1980 U.S. Olympic Team which unfortunately never had the opportunity to compete. He was inducted into the National Wrestling Hall of Fame in 1988. *(Pages 9, 68)*

NANCY HOGSHEAD was born in 1962 (Iowa City, Iowa) and presently lives in New York City. She is an honors graduate from Duke University with a bachelor's degree in political science and women's studies. Ms. Hogshead now works as a motivational speaker, addressing over one-hundred groups annually, and is associate director of The Women's Sport Foundation in New York City. Herself an asthmatic, she is author of the book *Asthma and Exercise* and a national spokesperson for the American Lung Association. At the age of fourteen, she was the number-one ranked swimmer in the world and qualified for the 1980 U.S. Olympic Team a year later. Unable to compete due to the American-led boycott of the Moscow games, she again earned a spot on the 1984 U.S. Team and went on to win three golds and a silver medal in Los Angeles. *(Page 160)*

BRUCE JENNER was born in 1949 (Ossining, New York) and presently lives in southern California with his wife, Kris, and their eight children. He received a bachelor's degree in physical education from Graceland College and is currently involved in a wide range of activities including acting, directing, working as a television sportscaster, writing books, and running a number of diverse business ventures. Having himself struggled with dyslexia, Mr. Jenner now spends a large amount of time with outreach to the LAB School for Learning Disabilities which assists children with dyslexia. An avid pilot, race car driver, and much sought-after motivational speaker, he won a gold medal in the decathlon at the 1976 Olympics earning the title of "World's Greatest Athlete." A Sullivan Award winner and Associated Press Male Athlete of the Year in 1976, he was inducted into the Olympic Hall of Fame ten years later. *(Page 49)*

BROOKS JOHNSON was born in 1934 (Pahokee, Florida) and presently lives in San Luis Obispo, California. A graduate of Tufts University with a bachelor's degree in physical education, Mr. Johnson completed his thirteenth year as director of track and field at Stanford University where he had become the first black head coach in the school's history. Named coach of the year by *Runner's World* magazine in 1982, he served as the 1976 Olympic sprint coach and the U.S. women's track coach for 1984 Olympic Games in Los Angeles. A world class sprinter in his own right, he gained international recognition for the first time in 1960 when he established the indoor world record for the 60 yards. Along with his new coaching responsibilities at Cal Poly Institute, Mr. Johnson is currently training world record holders Butch Reynolds and Andrew Valmon, and internationalists Merredith Rainey, Chryste Gaines, and Ceci Hopp. *(Pages 28, 57)*

KATHY JOHNSON was born in 1959 (Oncrioge, Tennessee) and presently lives in Los Angeles. She studied at Centenary College and now works as a television sportscaster for ABC and ESPN. Ms. Johnson is widely recognized for the length of her gymnastics career and the sense of style she brought to the sport. She captained the 1980 and 1984 U.S. Olympic Teams, winning silver and bronze medals in 1984. She also captained the U.S. World Championship Teams in 1978, 1979, 1981, and 1983 and is a two-time U.S. Gymnast of the Year, 1977 and 1985. She began her gymnastics career at twelve and continued to compete at the elite level until deciding to retire a month before her 25th birthday. *(Page 135)*

EARVIN "MAGIC" JOHNSON was born in 1959, attended Michigan State University, and presently lives in Beverly Hills, California, with his wife and their baby boy, Earvin III. Magic led his university to an NCAA championship and then left for the west coast where he joined the Los Angeles Lakers under coach Pat Riley. As a professional athlete, he contributed to five NBA world titles, and seven Western Conference championships. Retired from the NBA in 1991, he re-entered basketball when he joined the United States 1992 Olympic gold medal team in Barcelona. In October of

1992, he resigned in protest from President Bush's AIDS Commission. Today, Johnson is devoting most of his time and energy to the Magic Johnson Foundation. *(Page 173)*

MARILYN KING was born in 1949 (Boston) and presently lives in Oakland, California. She received a bachelor's degree in kinesiology from California State University at Hayward. Ms. King competed for the United States in the pentathlon at the 1972 and 1976 Olympics and placed second at the Olympic Trials for the ill-fated 1980 Olympic Games which fell victim to political boycott. She is now an internationally known consultant and educator teaching Olympian Thinking^{SM} to clients in the areas of business, education and peace. *(Page 88)*

PETER KORMANN was born in 1955 (Braintree, Massachusetts) and presently lives with his wife and their two children in Columbus, Ohio. He received a bachelor's degree in physical education from Southern Connecticut State University and is currently head men's gymnastics coach at The Ohio State University. Mr. Kormann became the first U.S. gymnast to win an Olympic medal since 1932 when he captured a bronze at the 1976 Games in Montreal. *(Page 132)*

PHIL MAHRE was born in 1957 (Yakima, Washington) and presently lives in his home town with his wife and three children. He is co-owner (with his talented twin brother) of the Mahre Training Center in Keystone, Colorado. Mr. Mahre also competed in three Olympics with his twin brother (1976, 1980, and 1984), winning the silver medal in slalom in 1980, and the gold medal in 1984. Keeping great success "all in the family," he won gold medals in 1980 as well, at the World Championships. He is co-author of a well received book, *No Hill Too Fast. (Pages 11, 87)*

STEVE MAHRE was born in 1957 (Yakima, Washington) and presently lives in his home town with his two children. He is co-owner (with his talented twin brother) of the Mahre Training Center in Keystone, Colorado. Mr. Mahre is a three-time Olympian for the U.S. Ski Team: 1976, 1980, and 1984; and topped off a distinguished athletic career in 1984 by winning the silver medal in the slalom. He is co-author of a well received book, *No Hill Too Fast. (Pages 11, 86)*

BOB MATHIAS was born in 1930 (Tulare, California) and presently lives in Fresno, California, with his wife. They have four daughters. He attended Stanford University, graduating with a bachelor's degree in education before serving two and half years in the U.S. Marine Corps. He was elected to the U.S. 91st Congress in 1966 and was reelected three more times, eventually earning key committee posts in Agriculture and Foreign Affairs. In addition to his political career, he has starred in four major motion pictures and one television series, and served as director of the Olympic Training Center at Colorado Springs and executive director of the National Fitness Foundation. Mr. Mathias won gold medals in the decathlon at the 1948 and 1952 Olympics, is a recipient of the Sullivan Award, and is a member of both the National Track and Field and U.S. Olympic Committee Halls of Fame. *(Page 19)*

KEN MATSUDA was born in 1935 (Fresno, California) and presently lives in Torrance, California. He received a bachelor's degree in physical education and a master's in special education from San Jose State University. The father of two and grandfather of five, Mr. Matsuda played college football and competed in track and field but soon discovered his real love was coaching. During his thirty-six year career (eighteen years of it at the University of Southern California) he has won seven NCAA Team Championships, coached over 130 All Americans, and worked with such world class athletes as Bob Seagren, Daley Thompson, O.J. Simpson, Charles White, Ronnie Lott, and tennis stars Tracy Austin, Michael Chang, and Jim Grabb. Mr. Matsuda is currently head coach of the Stars and Stripes track and field team. *(Page 67)*

FRANK E. McKINNEY JR. was born in 1938 in Indianapolis and made his home in Indianapolis with his wife prior to his tragic death in a plane crash. He received a bachelor's degree and MBA from Indiana University and was awarded an Honorary Doctorate of Laws from Butler University. Mr. McKinney was chairman of the board and chairman of the Executive Committee for the Bank One

Indiana Corporation and served as a board member for more than three dozen corporate, educational, and philanthropic organizations throughout his professional career. A three-time world record holder and winner of fourteen national AAU swimming titles, he won a bronze medal in the 100-meter backstroke at the 1956 Olympics and repeated with a silver medal in the same event in addition to a gold medal in the 400-meter relay at the 1960 Olympics. A nominee for the Sullivan Award in 1957, 1958, and 1959, he was inducted into the International Swimming Hall of Fame in 1975. *(Page 151)*

TOM McMILLEN was born in 1952 (Elmira, New York) and presently divides his time between Washington, D.C., and his home in Crofton, Maryland. He graduated Phi Beta Kappa with a degree in chemistry from the University of Maryland where he was the first student in the school's history to be awarded a Rhodes Scholarship. He attended Oxford University and received a master's in politics, philosophy, and economics. In 1986 he was elected to the U.S. House of Representatives where he served on the Energy and Commerce Committee, the Science, Space and Technology Committee, and chaired the Congressional Chesapeake Bay Caucus. While in college, Congressman McMillen was a three-time All American and earned a spot on the 1972 U.S. Olympic Team before going on to play for eleven years in the NBA. A strong advocate for both amateur and professional sports reform, he is the co-author of a book on sports and ethics in America titled *Out of Bounds*. *(Page 110)*

JULIANNE McNAMARA was born in 1965 (Flushing, New York) and presently lives with her husband in California. Having studied briefly at UCLA before pursuing an acting career, she has starred in two full-length feature films, appeared on numerous television programs, and continues to work as television sportscaster for CBS, NBC, and ESPN. A member of the 1980 U.S. Olympic Team and winner of one gold medal and two silvers in gymnastics at the 1984 Olympics, she became the first American to ever score five perfect 10s in Olympic competition and the only American woman to ever win an individual gold medal in Olympic competition. Ms. McNamara is also the creator of the innovative gymnastics skill, "the McNamara Mount," and received the delightful honor of having a rose named after her by the Netherlands. *(Page 146)*

KENNY MOORE was born in 1943 (Portland, Oregon) and presently lives with his wife in Kailua, Hawaii. He attended the University of Oregon where he received a bachelor's degree in philosophy and a master's in creative writing. He is currently a senior staff writer for *Sports Illustrated*, where he has worked for the past twelve years. He authored a book about sports titled *Best Efforts*, and his second manuscript chronicles the life and times of Bill Bowerman. Mr. Moore is a two-time Olympic marathoner, 1968 and 1972, (tying Frank Shorter at the U.S. Olympic Trials in 1972) as well as a former National AAU marathon and cross country champion. *(Page 147)*

MAMIE ANNETTE RALLINS was born in 1941 (Chicago) and presently lives in Columbus, Ohio. She received a bachelor's degree in office administration from Tennessee State University and has been the head women's cross country/track and field coach at The Ohio State University for the past sixteen years. A Sullivan Award nominee and four-time world record hurdler, Ms. Rallins competed for the United States in the 1968 and 1972 Olympics. *(Pages 71, 112)*

LOUISE RITTER was born in 1958 (Dallas, Texas) and continues to live there today. She received a bachelor's degree in physical education from Texas Women's University and is currently the owner of Sports Connection of Dallas, a sports fitness shop. She was a member of the 1980, 1984, and 1988 U.S. Olympic Track and Field Teams, winning a gold medal in the high jump at the 1988 Games in Seoul. *(Page 137)*

BOB SEAGREN was born in 1946 (Pomona, California) and presently lives in southern California with his wife, Peggy. He attended USC where he received a bachelor's degree in business administration. Since retiring from track and field, he has lived a dual life as both a popular actor and television personality while also capitalizing on his vast international sporting background to become a successful businessman. He is currently the director of sports marketing for Marketing & Financial Management Enterprises Inc., while also the host of the nationally syndicated "The Home Restoration and Remodeling Show." Mr. Seagren set fifteen world records as a pole vaulter and captured a gold medal in the 1968 Olympics. However, he is perhaps best remembered for his silver medal performance in the 1972 Munich Olympics where he was forced to use a borrowed pole when the judges refused to allow him to compete with his own. *(Page 129)*

PETER SNELL was born in 1938 (Opunake, New Zealand) and presently lives in Dallas, Texas, with his wife and their two daughters. He received a bachelor's degree in human performance from the University of California at Davis and then went on to earn a Ph.D. in exercise physiology from Washington State University. Dr. Snell is currently the director of the St. Paul Human Performance Laboratory at the University of Texas Southwestern Medical Center. An eight-time world record holder and track and field hero in his native New Zealand, he won a gold medal in the 800 meters in the 1960 Olympics, and became the first runner to win gold medals in both the 800 and 1500 meters at the same Olympics in 1964. Dr. Snell remains an active runner today and competed in the 1992 World Veterans Orienteering Championships. *(Page 187)*

TERRI STICKLES STRUNCK was born in 1946 (San Mateo, California) and presently lives in northern California with her husband and their son. Currently pursuing a career in criminal justice and corrections, she has worked as a police officer, youth sports counselor, and served as the Colombian 1968 Olympic Swim Coach while a United States Peace Corps volunteer. A former world record holder, Ms. Strunck won a gold and silver medal in swimming at the 1963 Pan American Games and captured a bronze medal at the 1964 Olympics in Tokyo. *(Page 141)*

ALEXANDER G. TARICS was born in 1913 (Budapest, Hungary) and presently lives in Belvedere, California. He is a graduate of Joseph Nador Technical University, Hungary, with a master's and Ph.D. in civil engineering. Today, Dr. Tarics is an award-winning structural engineer and internationally recognized for his pioneering work in the field of earthquake protection for buildings. He was a 1933, 1935, 1937, and 1939 gold medalist at the World University Games and won a gold medal at the 1936 Olympics in water polo. In 1953, Dr. Tarics became a U.S. citizen, a peak life experience he considers even more precious than his world-class athletic achievements. *(Page 182)*

BILL TOOMEY was born in 1939 (Philadelphia) and presently lives in southern California with his two daughters, Sarah and Samantha. He received a bachelor's degree in education from the University of Colorado and a master's in education from Stanford University. Mr. Toomey is presently the director of the U.S. Olympic Training Center in San Diego and is strongly committed to raising funds to assist Olympians in all sports. Famous for his "bag of tricks" (a different pair of shoes for each event), he won a gold medal in the decathlon at the 1968 Olympics, earning the coveted title "World's Greatest Athlete." *(Pages 106, 156)*

BERNY WAGNER was born in 1924 (Fresno, California) and presently lives with his wife in Salem, Oregon. He received bachelor's and master's degrees in education from Stanford University. Mr. Wagner was the head coach of track and field at Oregon State University from 1965 through 1975, coached the 1975 Saudi Arabian Team and 1976 U.S. Olympic Team, and served as National Coach/Coordinator of the U.S. Athletics Congress from 1981 through 1989. During his coaching tenure at Oregon State, he produced twenty All Americans, ten NCAA Champions, and five Olympians, including famed high jumper Dick Fosbury. *(Page 73)*

PETER WESTBROOK was born in 1952 (St. Louis) and presently lives in New York City with his wife and their child. He received a bachelor's degree in marketing from New York University and is currently director of The Peter Westbrook Foundation, a New York City outreach program aimed at helping disadvantaged youths by exposing them to the art of fencing. As America's first black fencing champion, Mr. Westbrook has gone on to win an unprecedented twelve national titles and become a legend in the sport. He is the first American fencer to make it to the finals of the World Championships since 1958, a Pan American gold medalist, and five-time Olympian, winning a bronze medal at the 1984 Los Angeles Games. *(Page 24)*

BIBLIOGRAPHY

CHAPTER 1

Barbati, C. (1991, December 31)."Impressive... after all the years." *The Courier-News*.

Eldridge, B. (1986, April 29). "Decathlon star Milt Campbell bypassed again by Olympic hall." *The Christian Science Monitor*.

Glicken, L.S. (1991, June 20). "Campbell finds sports still give him that winning motivation." *The Star-Ledger*.

Hellickson, R.. "Champion ingredients." Address to the Department of Athletics at Ohio State University; available from author.

Mahre, P., Mahre, S., & Fry, J. (1985). *No hill too fast*. New York, N.Y.: Simon & Schuster.

Massie, J. (1988, December 18). "The Wrestler." *Capitol Magazine*, pp. 8-13.

Murray, J. (1991, July 16). "Forgotten decathlete speaks out." *Los Angeles Times*. pp. C1, C12.

Romano, M. (1989). "Teacher and Olympian honored by governor." The *Courier-News*.

Werstein, L. (1989). "Olympic gold medal leads to his own stretch of road." *The Courier-News*.

CHAPTER 2

Ashe, A. (1988). *A hard road to glory*. New York, N.Y.: Amistad Books: Dodd, Mead.

Ashe, A. (1988). *A hard road to glory*. New York, N.Y.: Warner Books.

Ashe, A. (1993). *A hard road to glory* (rev. ed.). New York, N.Y.: Amistad: Penguin USA.

Ashe, A. (1967). *Advantage Ashe. New York, N.Y.: Coward-McCann.*

Ashe, A.. (1980). "Arthur Ashe's tennis clinic." Norwalk, CT: Golf Digest/Tennis; New York, N.Y.: trade book distribution by Sim#.

Clark, S. (1967). "Competitive swimming as I see it." *Swimming World Publications*.

Clark, S. (1987, March 30). "Clients should set rules, limits when dealing with attorneys." *San Francisco Business Times*.

Clark, S. (1987, April 6). "Common sense can cure phobia about the size of attorney's fees." *San Francisco Business Times*.

Clark, S. (1988, February 22). "Toxic time bomb ticking down in Proposition 65." *San Francisco Business Times*.

Clark, S. (1989, July 27). "A means to hasten end to disputes." *The Recorder*.

Clark, S., et al. (1986, May). "Gatekeeper liability for wrongful reconveyance of trust deeds." *CEA News*.

Clark, S., et al. (1988, September 12). "Cleanup liability includes everyone." *Northern California Real Estate Journal*.

Clark, S., et al. (1989, May/June). "Toxic-cleanup laws and real estate transactions." *Journal of Property Management*.

Froug, W. (1984). "The ancient and modern Olympic games" (Sound Discs). Anaheim, CA: Mark 56 Records.

Janofsky, M. (1992, June 1). "Bronze medal winner, gold medal idea: Fencing as a Method of Escape." *The New York Times*, B1.

McDonald, J. Mathias. *San Francisco Examiner:* Feature Article.

Nieves, E. (1994, March 22). "Kindness, then rage: The death of a woman." *The New York Times*. Metro section.

Thoele, M. (1992). Profile of A.C. Gilbert in *Eugene Register Guard*.

Westbrook, P. (1992). Mission Statement for the Peter Westbrook Foundation available from the foundation at GPO Box 7564, New York City, New York.

CHAPTER 3

Brown, D. (1992). "Andrews' gold still appreciating." *Baltimore Sun*.

Corwin, M. (1984). "Andrews wins medal – then gives it away." *Los Angeles Times*.

Douglas, B. (1992, August). "A long way from stop-32." *The Guideposts*, pp. 35-37.

Hogshead, N. & Couzens, G. (1989). *Asthma and Exercise*. Henry Holt and Company, Inc. New York:NY.

Laws, A. (1993). "Does a history of sexual abuse in childhood play a role in women's medical problems? *"The Journal of Women's Health*. Volume 2, No.2.

McKenzie, M. (1984). "Swimmer gets her strength from brother." *Baltimore Sun*.

Moore, K. (1992, March 9). "A man of the ash." *Sports Illustrated*, pp. 140-146.

Nevius, C.W. (1984). "Winner keeps medal in the family: paraplegic brother gets the gold." *Chronicle*.

O'Brien, D. (1984). "Happy Andrews contingent returns." *Anne Arundel County Bureau*.

Rape in America (April, 1992). "A Report to the Nation," National Victim Center. Virginia.

Sorenson, S., Stein, J., Siegal, J., Golding, J.M., & Burnam, A. (1987). "The prevalence of adult sexual assault." *American Journal of Epidemiology*. Volume 126; No. 6.

Stephenson, M. (1992, July 5). "Still ambitious: Hogshead tries to motivate others." *The Florida Times-Union*, p. C-3.

Stewart, J.W. (1984). "Theresa Andrews provided inspiration to paralyzed kin." *Baltimore Sun*.

Valanoski, M. (1992, June 28). "Asthma sufferers don't have to be its victims, ex-Olympic swimmer says." *Standard-Speakers*.

Wieberg, S. (1984, July 31). "Andrews dedicates medal to paralyzed brother." *USA Today*.

Williams, N. (1985). "Paralyzed brother proved inspiration for olympian." *The Times Dispatch*.

CHAPTER 4

Blatnick, J. (1985). "Pin down problems with a positive attitude." Inspirational corporate brochure; available from Jeff Blatnick.

Froug, W. (1984). "The ancient and modern Olympic games" (Sound Discs). Anaheim, CA: Mark 56 Records.

Jenner, B. (1979). *Bruce Jenner's Guide to the Olympics*. Kansas City, KS: Andrews & McMeel.

Jenner, B. (1984). *Bruce Jenner's The athletic body*. New York, NY: Simon & Schuster.

Jenner, B. (1980). *The Olympics and me*. (1st ed.). Garden City, NY: Doubleday.

Jenner, B., & Finch, P. (1977). *Decathlon Challenge: Bruce Jenner's Story*: Prentice-Hall, Engelwood Cliffs: NJ.

Morris, R. (1991, August 1). "Playing Bruce Jenner is his full-time job." *Tallahassee Democrat*.

Ungerleider, D.F. (1985) *Reading Writing and Rage*. Jalmar Press: California

— . "Awrright! Bruce Jenner wins big." (1976, August 9). *Sports Illustrated*.

CHAPTER 5

Bowerman, B., Harris, W.E., and Shea, J.M. (1967). *Jogging*. New York: Grosset and Dunlap.

Casaus, P. (1992). "Gymnastics guru Burch unafraid to speak mind." The Journal, pp. D1, D5.

Douglas, B. (1992, August). "A long way from stop-32." The Guideposts, pp. 35-37.

Hellickson, R. "Champion ingredients." Address to the Department of Athletics at Ohio State University; available from author.

Leutzinger, D. (1993. Summer). "Jogging into history." *Old Oregon*, pp. 21-23.

Massie, J. (1988, December 18). "The Wrestler." *Capitol Magazine*, pp. 8-13.

Matsuda, K. "Guideline for success." Unpublished manuscript.

Moore, K. (1993. Summer). "Muleskinner." *Old Oregon*, pp. 18-20.

Moore, K. (1992, March 9). "A man of the ash." *Sports Illustrated*, pp. 140-146.

O'Toole, T. (1992). "Best in the world." *The Albuquerque Tribune*, Sports Section.

— . "Olympics: Five Oregon-bred athletes courageously face challenges." (1992, July). *The Oregonian* pp. L1, L4.

CHAPTER 6

Davenport, W. (1993). "Davenport: an Olympian and an Officer." A press release from Department of the Army National Guard Office of Public Affairs. Washington, D.C.

Flanders, H.B. (1992). Press release from Action Sports Management. Park City, Utah.

King, M. (1988, Winter). "Ordinary Olympians: The secrets of superior performance." *In Context*, pp. 14-15.

King, M. (1993). "Toward An Olympian Technology in the Classroom: the King Model." Unpublished manuscript.

King, M., Whisler, J., Marzano, R. (1988). "Dare to Imagine: An Olympian Technology." Mid Continent Regional Educational Lab. Aurora, Colorado.

Mahre, P., Mahre, S., & Fry, J. (1985). *No hill too fast.* New York, NY: Simon and Schuster.

McNeill, B. (1984). Interview with Marilyn King, director of Beyond Sports. *Journal of the Institute of Noetic Sports*, pp. 14-16.

Ungerleider, S. and Golding, J.M. (1991). *Beyond Strength: Psychological Profiles of Olympic Athletes.* Wm. C. Brown: Madison, Wis.

CHAPTER 7

Fleschner, M.K., II. (1992, September). "Focus on gold: Lessons from an Olympic innovator." *Motivation*, pp. 48-49.

Toomey, B., & King, B. (1980). "The Olympic experience: Job success for the 80s." Available from Sports Directions Foundation, 26944 Camino de Estrella, Capistrano Beach, California, 92624.

Ungerleider, S. and Golding, J.M. (1991). *Beyond Strength: Psychological Profiles of Olympic Athletes.* Wm. C. Brown: Madison, Wis.

CHAPTER 8

Friedland, B. (1992). "'72 Games still have bitter taste for McMillen."

The Capital, pp. D1.

Leutzinger, D. (1993. Summer). "Jogging into history." *Old Oregon*, pp. 21-23.

McMillen, T., & Coggins, P. (Eds.). (1992). *Out of bounds*. New York, NY: Simon & Schuster.

Miller, B. (1992). "New district a challenge for McMillen." *The News Journal*, pp. A1, A6.

Moore, K. (1993 Summer). "Muleskinner." *Old Oregon*, pp. 18-20.

Moore, K. (1982). *Best Efforts: World Class Runner and races*. Doubleday; Garden City, NY.

Yardley, J. (1992, May 27). "Message from an angry athlete." *The Washington Post*, pp. C2.

CHAPTER 9

Andrews, M. (1992, October). "Olympic visions: Mary Andrews trains for Barcelona 1992." *Industrial Indemnity Magazine*, pp. 11, 14.

Ashe, A. (1993). *Days of grace. New York, N.Y.: Alfred A. Knopf.*

Ashe, A. (1993). *Days of grace (2 Sound Cassettes). New York, N.Y.:* Random House Audio Publishing.

Ashe, A. (1977). *Getting started in tennis*. New York, N.Y.: Athenaeum/ SMI.

Ashe, A. (1981). *Off the court. New York, N.Y.: New American Library.*

Ashe, A. (1992). "Kids and lead hazards" (Videorecording). Chicago, IL: Public Media Video.

Ashe, A. (1987). "Tennis our way" (Videorecording). (S.1.): Worldvision.

Ashe, A., & Deford, F. (1975). *Portrait in Motion*. Houghton Mifflin: Boston, Mass.

Ayer, L. (1984). "Problems facing a woman police officer." Unpublished manuscript.

Carlisle, K. (1983, Winter). "Kim Carlisle '83." *Stanford Magazine*, pp. 80-81.

Carlisle, K. (1991, December). "Title IX: how far have women really come?" *Stanford Magazine*, pp. 14-15.

Carlisle, K. (1991, June). "Whatever happened to track and field?" *Stanford Magazine*, pp. 10-11.

Cunliffe, G. (1991, April 30). "Ted and Terri: born to swim." *The San Francisco Times*, pp. B1, B3.

Gross, J. (1993, January 16). "Arizona hopes holiday for King mends image." *The New York Times*.

Hannah, S. (1989, May 12). "Osborne's passion focuses on career, '92 Games." *The Gazette*.

Hoffer, R. (1984). "She can't set back the clock." *The New York Times.*

Hurlbert, R. (1984, August 4). "Making the rounds." *The Peninsula Times Tribune.*

Kreutzer, R., & Black, W. (1982. November/December). "The eye of the tiger." *USGF Gymnastics*, pp. 48-54.

Merkin, M. (1991, September). "How teamwork led Mike Eruzione to Olympic victory." *Motivation*, pp. 26-29.

Moore, K. (1992, December 21). Sportsmen of the Year: The Eternal Example. *Sports Illustrated.*

Nevius, C.W. (1984). "Gymnast's Final Test? Last shot is a long shot." *The Chronicle.*

Osborne, M.T. (1984. June). "A study of the effects of the evaluation system and the caring relationship on effort: The first step in the building of a model on support versus pressure" (first draft). Unpublished manuscript.

Press, A. (1992. August). "Old too soon, wise too late?" *Newsweek*, pp. 16-18.

Sandomir, R. (February, 1992). "CBS takes a big shot and scores." *New York Times*, pp. B9.

Sandul, D. (1984, February 22). "Law enforcement award goes to woman officer." *The Times, San Mateo County.*

Staff. (1984, February 22). "Officer of the year." *The Peninsula Times Tribune.*

Strachan, A. (February, 1992). "Americans easily win the battle of television hockey coverage." Source unknown.

CHAPTER 10

Fleschner, M.K., II. (1992, September). "Focus on gold: Lessons from an Olympic innovator." *Motivation*, pp. 48-49.

Froug, W. (1984). "The ancient and modern Olympic games" (Sound Discs). Anaheim, CA: Mark 56 Records.

Hogshead, N. & Couzens, G. (1989). *Asthma and Exercise.* Henry Holt and Company Inc. New York, NY.

Leutzinger, D. (1993. Summer). "Jogging into history." *Old Oregon*, pp. 21-23.

McDonald, J. (1980). Mathias; feature story. *Los Angeles Times* F1.

Moore, K. (1993. Summer). "Muleskinner." *Old Oregon*, pp. 18-20.

Reith, K. (1992). Data from the Women's Sport Foundation: An Advocacy Report on Title IX.

Stephenson, M. (1992, July 5). "Still ambitious: Hogshead tries to motivate others." *The Florida Times-Union*, pp. C3.

Toomey, B., & King, B. (1980). "The Olympic experience: Job success for the 80s." Available from Sports Directions Foundation, 26944 Camino de Estrella, Capistrano Beach, California, 92624.

Valanoski, M. (1992, June 28). "Asthma sufferers don't have to be its victims, ex-Olympic swimmer says." *Standard-Speakers.*

CHAPTER 11

Hamilton, S. (1992). Conversations with Michael Sterling and Associates.

Johnson, E. (1992, July). Personal conversations with author in Barcelona during the Olympic Games.

Johnson, E. (1983). *Magic.* New York, NY: Viking Press.

Johnson, E. (1992). *Magic's touch.* Reading, MA: Addison-Wesley Publishing Company.

Johnson, E. (1992). "My life" (2 Sound Cassettes). New York, NY: Random House Audio Publishing.

Johnson, E. (1992). *My life* (1st ed.). New York, NY: Random House.

CHAPTER 12

Balaban, E.P., Cox, J. V., Snell, P.G., Vaughan, R.H., & Frenkel, E.P. (1989). "The frequency of anemia and iron deficiency in the runner." *Medicine and Science in Sports and Exercise*, 21, 643-648.

Brooks, D., Etzel, E., & Ostrow, A. (1987). "Job responsibilities and backgrounds of NCAA Division I athletic academic advisors and counselors." *The Sport Psychologist*, 1(4), 281-290.

Etzel, E. (1979). "Validation of a conceptual model characterizing attention among international rifle shooters." *Journal of Sport Psychology*, 1(4), 281-290.

Etzel, E. (1992). "Selecting your major or career path." *WVU Athlete's Academic Newsletter*, 3(1).

Etzel, E., Ferrante, A., & Pinkney, J. (Eds.) (1991). "Counseling college student-athletes: Issues and interventions." Morgantown, WV: Fitness Information Technology.

Flores, R. (1991, January). "Front of the pack." *Runner The Athlete News*, pp. 10.

Gregg, S.G., & Brooks, G.A. (1987). "The effects of anemia and training on the endurance capacity of rodents." *The Physiologist*, 152(3), 1150. (Abstract).

Gregg, S.G., Mazzeo, R.S., Budinger, T.F., & Brooks, G.A. (1989). "Acute anemia increases lactate production and decreases clearance." *Journal of Applied Physiology*, 67(2), 756-764.

Gregg, S.G., Willis, W.T., & Brooks, G.A. (1989). "Interactive effects of anemia and muscle oxidative capacity on endurance capacity."

Journal of Applied Physiology, 67(2), 765-770.

Gregg, S.G., & Wilmore, J.H. (1982). "Alterations in the post exercise plasma lactate response following swim training." *Medicine and Science in Sports and Exercise*, 14(2), 160. (Abstract).

Martin, W.H., Montgomery, J., Snell, P.G., Corbett, J. R., Sokolov, J.J., Buckey, J.C., Maloney, D.A., & Blomqvist, C.G. (1987). "Cardiovascular adaptations to intense swim training in middle-aged men and women." *Circulation*, 75, 323-330.

Pinkerton, R., Etzel, E., Talley, J., Rockwell, K., & Moorman, J. (1989). "Psychotherapy and career counseling: Toward an integration for use with college students." *Journal of American College Health*, 39(3), 129-136.

Pitetti, K. H., Snell, P. G., & Stray-Gundersen, J. (1987). "Maximal response of wheelchair-confined subjects to four types of arm exercise." *Archives of Physical Medicine and Rehabilitation*, 68, 10-13.

Pitetti, K.H., Snell, P. G., Stray-Gundersen, J., & Gottschalk, F.A. (1987). "Aerobic training exercises for individuals who had amputation of the lower limb." *Journal of Bone and Joint Surgery*, 69-A, 914-921.

Snell, P. G. (1984). "Exercise and risk for middle-aged adults." *Houston Heart Bulletin IV*.

Snell, P.G. (1985). "Physiological basis for athletic training." In G. Finerman (Ed.). *Sports Medicine—The Knee*. St. Louis, MO: Mosby .

Snell, P.G. (1990). "Physiology of middle-distance running." In Reilly, T., Williams, C., Secher, N., & Snell, P.G. (Ed.). *The Physiology of Sports*. London, Spon.

Snell, P. G., & Vaughan, R. H. (1990). "Longitudinal physiological testing of elite female middle- and long-distance runners." *Track Technique*.

Tarics, A.G. (1987, September-October). "Earthquake! Are we ready?" *The Military Engineer*, pp. 486-490/

Tarics, A.G. (1990, March-April). "Earthquakes and our national defense." *The Military Engineer*, pp. 31-35.

Vernon, R. (1989). "After the gold rush." *Dallas Morning News*.

Winter, F.D., Snell, P.G., & Stray-Gundersen, J. (1989). "Effects of 100% oxygen on performance of professional soccer players." *Journal of American Medical Association*, 262, 227-229.

BIOGRAPHY

Steven Ungerleider completed his undergraduate work at the University of Texas, Austin, where he also competed as a collegiate gymnast. He holds a Ph.D. from the University of Oregon and is a licensed psychologist and director of Integrated Research Services Inc. in Eugene. In addition to his clinical responsibilities, Ungerleider has been the recipient of several Alcohol Drug Abuse Mental Health Administration (ADAMHA) and U.S. Department of Education grant awards and has published many journal articles on substance abuse prevention. Since 1984 he has served on the United States Olympic Committee Sport Psychology Registry and has consulted with several sports organizations, including a recent alcohol and drug prevention evaluation for the NBA Los Angeles Lakers. In November 1991, Ungerleider was presented with the Distinguished Alumni Award from the University of Texas, Austin. In July of 1992, Ungerleider's work was the feature article in *Psychology Today* and he subsequently was made a special correspondent for the magazine. His first major assignment for the magazine included covering the 1994 Summer Goodwill Games in Russia. Ungerleider's first book, *Beyond Strength*, (with co-author Jackie Golding) received favorable reviews in *Elle*, *Longevity*, *Outside*, *Runners World*, *Allure*, *New York Daily News*, *Boston Herald*, *Dallas Morning News*, and the *International Herald Tribune*. When not in his office, he may be found running whitewater rivers with his wife, shooting hoops with his oldest daughter, or attending gymnastics competitions with his youngest daughter.

A MESSAGE FROM THE PUBLISHER

A funny thing happened to this book on the way to the printer. The life of Tonya Harding, one of 51 Olympic athletes whose inner psyches were explored in search of the driving element to their high achievement, took a strange pre-Olympic twist. But the author, a nationally renowned sports psychologist, got a last-minute chance to alter his manuscript to include a discussion of her dysfunctional acting out. In spite of Tonya's fall from grace, this book inspires all of us to tap our inner drive for higher achievement in our own quest for success.

W. R. Spence, M.D.
Publisher

*A*t WRS Publishing, we are only interested in producing books that we can be proud of—books that focus on people and/or issues that enlighten and inspire, books that change lives for the better. **Call us toll-free at 1-800-299-3366 for suggestions or for a free book catalog.**

WATCH FOR THESE OTHER WRS TITLES:

DID I WIN? A revealing, insightful farewell to George Sheehan, America's beloved champion of runners, as written by his closest friend and colleague, Joe Henderson.

DAMN THE DISABILITIES: FULL SPEED AHEAD Profiles in courage of 14 young athletes who refused to let physical limitations deter them from playing—and excelling—at their favorite sport. An inspiration to other young athletes that demonstrates that competing, not winning, is everything.

RUDY'S RULES—GAME PLANS FOR LIFE After years of naysayers and overcoming obstacles, Rudy Ruettiger, the underqualified kid from Joliet, Illinois, realized his dream of going to Notre Dame and playing football for the Fighting Irish. Now Rudy inspires others to rise above their own limitations in pursuit of their dreams.

WRS
PUBLISHING
A Division of WRS Group, Inc.
Waco, Texas